Statutory Interpretation

by the late

Sir Rupert Cross, DCL, FBA
Solicitor, Vinerian Professor of English Law
in the University of Oxford

Third edition by

John Bell
Professor of Public and Comparative Law,
University of Leeds

Sir George Engle, KCB, MA, QC
Formerly First Parliamentary Counsel

Learning Resources
Centre

Butterworths
London, Dublin, Edinburgh
1995

United Kingdom	Butterworths, a Division of Reed Elsevier (UK) Ltd, Halsbury House, 35 Chancery Lane, LONDON WC2A 1EL and 4 Hill Street, EDINBURGH EH2 3JZ
Australia	Butterworths, SYDNEY, MELBOURNE, BRISBANE, ADELAIDE, PERTH, CANBERRA and HOBART
Canada	Butterworths Canada Ltd, TORONTO and VANCOUVER
Ireland	Butterworth (Ireland) Ltd, DUBLIN
Malaysia	Malayan Law Journal Sdn Bhd, KUALA LUMPUR
New Zealand	Butterworths of New Zealand Ltd, WELLINGTON and AUCKLAND
Puerto Rico	Butterworths of Puerto Rico Inc, SAN JUAN
Singapore	Butterworths Asia, SINGAPORE
South Africa	Butterworth Publishers (Pty) Ltd, DURBAN
USA	Butterworth Legal Publishers, CARLSBAD, California, and SALEM, New Hampshire

A CIP Catalogue record for this book is available from the British Library.

First edition 1976
Second edition 1987
Reprinted 1989, 1991, 1994

ISBN 0 406 04971 8

Typeset by Doyle & Co, Colchester
Printed and bound in Great Britain by Clays Ltd, St Ives plc

Preface to the third edition

'The subject of statutory interpretation does not lend itself to legislation, and the extraction from the cases of reasonable general principles of interpretation was a task for the academic lawyer, even though they [sic] had long neglected it. Cross's book is a major contribution, temperate, constructive, and scholarly, to the repair of that neglect.' [1]

This comment of Herbert Hart explains the special quality of Rupert Cross's *Statutory Interpretation* which justifies the appearance of a third edition. Although, since its first appearance in 1976, there have been published many articles and some books which have done much to repair the academic neglect of the subject, Cross's book remains unrivalled as a short, systematic introduction to the general principles of statutory interpretation, intended primarily for law students.

The aim of this new edition is to make available Cross's insights to a new generation of students by further updating some of the examples and by applying Cross's approach to recent developments both in the case law and in academic writings. The text shows significant changes from the first and second editions, but we have attempted to retain the basic ideas which Cross brought to the subject. Even after nearly 20 years, we as editors have only a very few points on which we have departed from the views expressed in the first edition. Indeed, many of Cross's opinions have been amply justified by subsequent events: notably the dominance of a single rule of interpretation, the inappropriateness of legislation as a means of reforming the rules of statutory interpretation, the need for a short and simple form of presenting the purpose of an enactment, and the justifiability of 'rectifying' statutory provisions in some circumstances.

Since the second edition, the House of Lords in *Pepper v Hart* has brought about a major change by allowing reference to *Hansard* as an aid to

---

1. H L A Hart, 'A R N Cross', LXX Proceedings of the British Academy at 432 (1984).

interpretation, with consequences also for the use of pre-parliamentary materials. This has led to extensive changes throughout the text. The increasing importance of European law, both Community law and the European Convention on Human Rights and Fundamental Freedoms, is also reflected both in the basic rules set out and illustrated in chapters 3 and 4 and in the treatment of presumptions in chapter 7. The contrast between the drafting of Community law and of domestic law is examined as part of the review of statutory drafting in chapter 8. Chapter 2 has been altered to reflect continuing advances in jurisprudential analysis in this area.

As in the second edition, John Bell has been primarily responsible for selecting new cases, for the discussions of academic writings and for the European dimension of the subject. George Engle (who was a member of the Hansard Society Commission on the Legislative Process which reported in 1992) has brought to bear his experience as Parliamentary Counsel both in revising the discussions of legislative drafting, notably in chapter 8, and in ensuring precision and uniformity in the text. We hope that our efforts may give a further lease of life to Cross on *Statutory Interpretation*.

May 1995   John Bell
                                                                         George Engle

Preface to the first edition

When reading for a law degree at Oxford in the early 1930s, I studied jurisprudence, a subject which, then as now, was commonly assumed to include statutory interpretation. I was told to write an essay criticising the English rules and I dutifully said my piece about the literalism of the Courts, their failure to implement the purpose of the statutes with which they dealt and, worst of all, their intransigent refusal to consult *travaux préparatoires*. All the time I was experiencing a malaise which, I am bound to confess, was not wholly set at rest by my tutor, with regard to the nature of the English rules of interpretation. What were they? Where were they stated? I then practised the law for a decade and it was as much as I could do to make sense of the day-to-day operation of the legislation that came my way. The mystery of the precise nature of the general rules of statutory interpretation remained unsolved. When teaching law at Oxford in the 1950s and 1960s I treated my pupils as I had been treated and told them to write essays criticising the English rules governing the subject. By that time Willis's landmark article mentioned on p 198 of this book had appeared in the Canadian Bar Review. Each and every pupil told me that there were three rules—the literal rule, the golden rule and the mischief rule, and that the Courts invoke whichever of them is believed to do justice in the particular case. I had, and still have, my doubts, but what was most disconcerting was the fact that whatever question I put to pupils or examinees elicited the same reply. Even if the question was What is meant by 'the intention of parliament'? or What are the principal extrinsic aids to interpretation? back came the answers as of yore: 'There are three rules of interpretation—the literal rule, the golden rule and the mischief rule.' I was as much in the dark as I had been in my student days about the way in which the English rules should be formulated.

This book, an enlargement on lectures given from time to time at Oxford, has been composed in order to clarify my own mind as much as anyone else's. It is intended for law students, but I hope that it may be found to be sufficiently brief to constitute spare time reading for any practitioner who likes to devote part of his spare time to the contemplation of the law.

May 1976   Rupert Cross

Contents

List of cases

Decisions of the European Court of Justice are listed both alphabetically and numerically. The numerical Table follows the alphabetical.

Introduction

Statutes (and subordinate legislation made under them) are the most abundant source of legal rules in the United Kingdom. To be a lawyer, you have to be able to read and interpret statutes correctly and effectively. This book attempts to set out the major features of the contemporary approach to statutory interpretation in the United Kingdom. That approach is best studied in the light of history and jurisprudence, which are dealt with in Chapters 1 and 2.

The basic rules are set out and illustrated in Chapters 3 and 4. The essential rule is that words should generally be given the meaning which the normal speaker of the English language would understand them to bear in the context in which they are used. It would be difficult to over-estimate the importance of this rule because the vast majority of statutes never come before the courts for interpretation. If it were not a known fact that, in the ordinary case in which the normal user of the English language would have no doubt about the meaning of the statutory words, the courts will give those words their ordinary meaning, it would be impossible for lawyers and other experts to act and advise on the statute in question with confidence. The reference to lawyers and other experts is made advisedly because we would be deceiving ourselves if we were to imagine that some form of expertise is not necessary for the comprehension of most statutes; indeed, the ordinary meaning rule is qualified so as to allow for the application of a technical meaning when the words in question are used in a statute dealing with a particular trade or business. The regulation of most of the affairs with which they deal is such a complex matter that it is unlikely that it will ever be possible to draft Acts of Parliament in such a way that a significant number of them will be comprehensible to the ordinary layman; but this unfortunate fact should not be allowed to depreciate the importance of the ordinary meaning rule. Some criticisms of the canons of statutory interpretation are couched in terms which suggest that their authors do not realise that it is only a very small proportion of the statute book that ever comes before the courts. The process of reading a statute and applying it is 'interpretation' in the broad sense, though it might better be described as 'understanding followed by application'.

In a more specific sense, 'interpretation' is required when a doubt or dispute arises about the meaning of a statutory provision. Questions of interpretation can be divided into two broad categories, namely those which arise from the terms of the statute alone, before any set of facts has been presented for its application, and those which arise in the application of the words of a statute to a particular set of facts.[1] The first category is exemplified by cases where the ordinary meaning of the words used is uncertain, whether because of faulty grammar, ambiguous wording or some other failure to express clearly what is meant. To the second category belong cases where it is unclear whether or how the words in question apply to a particular set of facts. Acts often use broad terms, such as 'fair', 'reasonable' or 'dishonest', whose ordinary meaning is clear enough, but whose application in particular circumstances is left to the discretion of the interpreter.

Even when more precise terms are used, social or material conditions may change, with the result that a statutory provision falls to be applied in new circumstances, unforeseeable by the drafter — for example, is a hovercraft at sea a 'ship' or an 'aircraft',[2] and is a 'source code' for a computer program protected by copyright law drafted with only 'literary works' in mind?[3] Often the best efforts of the drafter risk defeat by the inventiveness of citizens and their advisers in seeking to avoid the application of statutory rules which do not suit them, most notably in the area of taxation. The question for the interpreter is then whether the citizen has succeeded or not in finding a way round the statute.

Other doubts arise because of faults in the legislation. Sometimes potential problems arise which were noticed but not resolved during the passage of the Bill through Parliament. A classic illustration is s 2 of the European Communities Act 1972, which failed to resolve explicitly the question whether an Act of Parliament passed after the United Kingdom entered the European Economic Community would be valid if it contradicted a previously made rule of European Community law.[4] In other cases, the text of the Act may be expressed badly so as apparently to cover more, or less, than was really intended.

In these cases, answers can often be found by reading more widely than the provision itself and making use of what are described in Chapters 5 and 6 as aids to interpretation. At the end of this process, the interpreter may still

---

1. W A Wilson 'Questions of Interpretation' [1987] Stat LR 142; and see p 34 below.
2. Hovercraft Act 1968.
3. *IBM Corpn v Computer Imports Ltd* [1989] 2 NZLR 395.
4. The matter had to be resolved by judicial interpretation: see *Factortame Ltd v Secretary of State for Transport (No 2)* [1991] 1 All ER 70; see p 107 below.

be left in doubt and will have to produce an answer by making sense of the provision in the light of the purpose, structure, and antecedents of the legislation in which it occurs. Over the years, the courts have developed certain presumptions which sometimes help in doubtful cases. For example, when it is unclear whether the conduct of the accused comes within a criminal statute, there is a presumption in favour of a narrow construction which would result in an acquittal; or, where one interpretation would produce an unjust or inconvenient result and another would not have these effects, there is a presumption in favour of the latter. These presumptions are only guides, and two of them may point in different directions in the same case, but they certainly have their uses; the more important of them are discussed in Chapter 7.

The emphasis which has been placed upon the merits of the plain meaning rule must not be taken to suggest that anything in the nature of an attitude of complacency with regard to the contemporary canons of statutory interpretation is justified. They have been the subject of much scrutiny and criticism in recent years, notably in the Law Commission's report of 1969, which was debated ultimately in the House of Lords.[5]

Legislative drafting is, and almost always has been, under attack (much of it unjustified). It was the principal subject of a report entitled *The Preparation of Legislation*, produced in 1975 by a committee chaired by Sir David (now Lord) Renton.[6] It has been reviewed more recently by a Hansard Society Commission chaired by Lord Rippon of Hexham, whose report, *Making the Law*, was published in 1992. There have also been studies, notably by Sir William Dale.[7] This topic is reviewed in Chapter 8, together with a number of more general questions. Do the courts interpret statutes too narrowly, without adequate regard to the social purpose of the legislation? Are they unduly timorous when confronted with an obvious mistake or omission in a particular statute? Is their approach to interpretation of statutes designed to effect social change too conservative?

Although this book is only seriously concerned with the major contemporary canons of statutory interpretation, it is important to bear in mind the context in which they are situated. There are three contexts to which the judicial canons studied here should be related. First, a statute is above all part of the political process. Most of government policy is established and implemented by means of ministerial decisions or directions,

---

5. *The Interpretation of Statutes* (Law Com no 21; Scottish Law Com no 11; 1969). For Parliamentary debates see 405 HL Official Report (5th series) cols 276-306 (13 February 1980), 418 HL Official Report (5th series) cols 64-83 (9 March 1981) and cols 1341-1347 (26 March 1981); 503 HL Deb, cols 278-307 (18 January 1989).
6. Cmnd 6053.
7. See especially *Legislative Drafting: A New Approach* (1977).

or by subordinate legislation. It has been calculated that, in a typical session, an average of only 42 programme Bills are presented to Parliament by the government.[8] Most of them, however, are likely to be of considerable importance, both because of their political content and because of the authority they provide for subsequent ministerial actions or for subordinate legislation. Judicial interpretations can affect the success of such political programmes. Second, the statute has to be implemented, most frequently by officials who will need guidance on the objectives to be pursued and workable procedures by which to achieve them. Statutory provisions rarely provide complete solutions, and an official will rely on guidance from his superiors. Judicial interpretation will define the scope for discretion exercised by officials in completing the details of a policy, and will affect their flexibility in responding to new situations. Third, the ultimate subjects of the law are human or legal persons who seek to organise their lives and activities in the light of their legal powers and duties. For this, they will often need the help of legal and other advisers. All the same, the freedom of the subject to choose what to do is enhanced by the predictability of judicial interpretation.

Viewed as a whole, the canons of interpretation represent a position taken by the judiciary on their constitutional role in relation to those who establish the political programme, those who have to carry it out, and those affected by it. The interests of these groups may well conflict, so that the canons adopted by the judges will effect a balance between them. As we shall see, the canons of statutory interpretation are frequently statements not so much of hard-and-fast rules of law, as of a general judicial approach to the task of interpreting statutes in particular contexts.[9]

It is also useful to say a few introductory words about the duration and varieties of statutes, although for more detailed discussion the reader is referred to Bennion's *Statutory Interpretation.*[10] Provided that an Act appears on the Parliament Roll, the courts will treat it as an Act of Parliament and will not accept any challenge to its validity, except in relation to its compatibility with European Community law.[11] Statutes come into force on the day on which they receive the royal assent in the absence of a provision

---

8. G Engle ' "Bills are made to pass as razors are made to sell": practical constraints in the preparation of legislation' [1983] Stat LR 7 at 11; also Report of the Hansard Society Commission on the Legislative Process, *Making the Law* (1992) pp 11-12. See generally D R Miers and A C Page *Legislation* (1990) Chs 4-7, and M Zander *The Law-Making Process* (4th edn, 1994) pp 1-25.
9. See pp 39-43 below.
10. 2nd edn, 1992, ss 28, 47, 62-66, 71-95, 102-107 (hereafter '*Bennion*').
11. *British Railways Board v Pickin* [1974] 1 All ER 609; *Bennion* p 142; *Factortame Ltd v Secretary of State for Transport (No 2)* [1991] 1 All ER 70.

to the contrary.[12] The endorsement by the Clerk of the Parliaments on the Act, immediately after its title, of the date of the royal assent forms part of the Act. Express provisions in the Act with regard to the date of coming into force of the whole or any part of it are very common. Where the two differ, references to 'the passing of this Act' are references to the first moment of the day of royal assent and not to the date on which the Act comes into force.[13] There is no doctrine of desuetude in English law, so a statute never ceases to be in force merely because it is obsolete. Normally there must be an express repeal, but the whole or part of an enactment may be impliedly repealed by a later statute.

> 'The test of whether there has been a repeal by implication by subsequent legislation is this: are the provisions of a later Act so inconsistent with, or repugnant to, the provisions of an earlier Act that the two cannot stand together.'[14]

The fact that two provisions overlap is therefore not enough, and general words in a later enactment do not repeal earlier statutes dealing with a special subject. Accordingly, it was held in *R v Horsham Justices, ex p Farquarson*[15] that s 4(2) of the Contempt of Court Act 1981, which empowered a court 'in any legal proceedings' to postpone the publication of a report of those proceedings, did not prevail over the special provision about the reporting of committal proceedings contained in s 8 of the Magistrates' Court Act 1980. Contrary to what was the common law rule, where an Act passed after 1850 repeals a repealing enactment, 'the repeal does not revive any enactment previously repealed, unless words are added reviving it'.[16]

The general rule with regard to territorial extent is that 'every parliamentary draftsman writes on paper which bears the legend, albeit in invisible ink, "this Act shall not have an extra-territorial effect, save to the extent that it expressly so provides" '.[17] Notable instances of statutes with an extra-territorial effect are the Royal Marriages Act 1772,[18] the Hijacking Act 1971, the Suppression of Terrorism Act 1978, and the War Crimes Act 1991. In general, the jurisdiction of the English criminal courts is confined to

---

12. Acts of Parliament (Commencement) Act 1793.
13. *Coleridge-Taylor v Novello & Co Ltd* [1938] 2 All ER 318.
14. *West Ham Church Wardens and Overseers v Fourth City Mutual Building Society* [1892] 1 QB 654 at 658, per A L Smith J.
15. [1982] 2 All ER 269.
16. Interpretation Act 1978, s 15 and Sch 2, para 2.
17. *R v West Yorkshire Coroner, ex p Smith* [1983] QB 335 at 358, per Donaldson LJ; see also *Clark (Inspector of Taxes) v Oceanic Contractors Inc* [1983] 2 AC 130 at 152.
18. *Sussex Peerage Case* (1844) 11 Cl & Fin 85.

crimes committed in this country, but there are exceptions applicable to British subjects, for example, murder and bigamy.[19] It is now usual for statutes to provide expressly that they do not extend to Scotland or Northern Ireland, where this is the intention.

A distinction is drawn between public general Acts and private Acts. A public general Act relates to some matter of public policy, while a private Act relates to the affairs of some individual or body in a matter which is not of public concern. The only clear practical importance of the distinction relates to the law of evidence, and even that is minimal nowadays. Someone who wishes to rely on the provisions of a public general Act does not have to produce any special kind of copy, whereas private Acts must be proved by production of a Queen's Printer's copy or, if they have not been printed, by an examination or certified copy of the original. Section 3 of the Interpretation Act 1978 provides that every Act passed after 1850 shall be a public general Act and judicially noticed as such unless the contrary is expressly provided by the Act. Some of the older cases show a tendency to construe private Acts more strictly than public general Acts,[20] but the distinction is of no importance in relation to the general law of interpretation.

Another distinction of limited importance in this field is that between consolidating and codifying statutes. A consolidating statute is one which collects the statutory provisions relating to a particular topic, and embodies them in a single Act of Parliament, making as a rule only minor amendments and improvements, if any. A codifying statute is one which purports to state exhaustively the whole of the law on a particular subject (the common law as well as previous statutory provisions).[1] An example of a consolidating statute is the Companies Act 1985, while the Bills of Exchange Act 1882 is one of the comparatively few instances of a codifying statute. The importance of the distinction is now confined to the existence of a special procedure with regard to consolidating statutes.

The Consolidation of Enactments (Procedure) Act 1949 lays down a special procedure, allowing for minor amendments in the consolidated provisions of the relevant statutes. Since 1965 there has existed a procedure whereby consolidation effected by the Law Commissions, which may contain amendments that are not merely minor, can be placed before the relevant joint committee of both Houses of Parliament with a view to prompt enactment. Changes in wording under these procedures may produce a different result from the earlier legislation,[2] and the presumption against a

---

19. Offences Against the Person Act 1861, ss 9 and 57.
20. *Bennion* p 631.
1.   For a full discussion, see *Bennion* ss 211-212.
2.   Eg *Champion v Maughan* [1984] 1 All ER 680; *Pocock v Steel* [1985] 1 All ER 434.

change of law on consolidation does not extend to provisions amended in the course of consolidation.[3]

Consolidating and codifying statutes are interpreted fundamentally like any other statute, namely by giving primacy to the ordinary meaning of their provisions read in context. Superseded statutes or the previous common law can be consulted only where the consolidating or codifying statute is ambiguous or, exceptionally, where a word or phrase can be understood only by examining its original social context. As Lord Wilberforce said:[4]

> 'I would agree and endorse the principle that it is quite wrong that, in every case where a consolidation Act is under consideration, one should automatically look back through the history of its various provisions, and the cases decided upon them, and minutely trace the language from Act to Act . . . Self-contained statutes, whether consolidating the previous law, or doing so with amendments, should be interpreted, if reasonably possible, without recourse to antecedents, and . . . the recourse should only be had when there is a real and substantial difficulty or ambiguity which classical methods of construction cannot resolve.'

Where a consolidated statute may be consulted, so may judicial decisions interpreting it; and where the new Act is identical with the previous Act, those decisions will retain their value as precedents.[5]

From these developments it follows that the presumption that consolidating statutes do not change the law has lost much of its force. Where it is clear from the Lord Chancellor's Memorandum which accompanies a consolidation Bill under the 1949 procedure, that no amendment of the previous law was intended, then the presumption retains its force.[6] And the same applies in the case of a consolidation with amendments proposed in a report made by the Law Commission,[7] though in this case it may be necessary to ascertain how far the recommendations were implemented by Parliament.[8]

---

3. See *Farrell v Alexander* [1976] 2 All ER 721 at 734.

4. *Farrell v Alexander* [1976] 2 All ER 721 at 725-726. See also Lord Simon of Glaisdale at 735-736 and *Maunsell v Olins* [1975] 1 All ER 16 at 28; *R v West Yorkshire Coroner, ex p Smith* [1983] QB 335, p 169 below.

5. The re-enactment of a statutory provision does not imply Parliamentary approval of judicial interpretations made of it: see pp 169-170 below.

6. Lord Upjohn, *Atkinson v United States* [1971] AC 197 at 249.

7. Lord Scarman, *R v Heron* [1982] 1 WLR 451 at 460-461; cf Lord Simon of Glaisdale, *Maunsell v Olins* [1975] 1 All ER 16 at 27.

8. In the case of a Bill to consolidate with amendments to give effect to the recommendations of the Law Commission, the only amendments permissible (apart from ones designed to make the Bill reproduce the existing law better) are ones 'relating directly' to the recommendations: see Erskine May *Parliamentary Practice* (21st edn, 1993) pp 494-495.

In a sense, the distinction between remedial and other statutes is of greater importance from the point of view of the law of interpretation than either of the distinctions previously mentioned; but it is not one which it is possible to draw with precision. The essence of a remedial statute is that it was passed to remedy some defect in the common law or, more usually today, in statute law. The cases suggest that such a statute should be broadly construed. A good example is the Water Charges Act 1976 which enabled water charges to be levied on the occupier of a 'hereditament' if he had the 'use' of facilities draining to a sewer or drain provided by a water authority. The House of Lords held that this applied to the rateable occupier of a ground-floor shop which had no water supply or drainage into the sewer, but which formed part of a structure whose roof drained into the sewer. Lord Scarman said that the English language was flexible and that the words used should not be narrowly construed:[9]

> 'I have no doubt that it would be contrary to the legislative purpose of the enactment to restrict or refine their breadth and flexibility in the context of this legislation, which has to cover a wide range of circumstances and situations present and future. A restrictive interpretation of the legislature's language would defeat the broad purpose of this innovative and reforming statute.'

Finally, it is necessary to mention Interpretation Acts. Many statutes contain interpretation sections relating to some of their key words, but an Interpretation Act provides that, unless the contrary intention appears, all statutes shall be construed as indicated; for example, so that the singular includes the plural, the masculine the feminine, and vice versa. The current English Interpretation Act is that of 1978. There were earlier ones in 1850 and 1889. Some countries have more ambitious Interpretation Acts. For instance, s 5(j) of the Acts Interpretation Act 1924 of New Zealand reads as follows:

> 'Every Act, and every provision or enactment thereof, shall be deemed remedial, whether its immediate purport is to direct the doing of anything Parliament deems to be for the public good, or to prevent or punish the doing of anything it deems contrary to the public good, and shall accordingly receive such fair, large and liberal construction and interpretation as will best ensure the attainment of the object of the Act and of such provision or enactment according to its true intent, meaning and spirit.'

---

9. *South West Water Authority v Rumble's* [1985] 1 All ER 513 at 517.

The New Zealand Law Commission has had occasion to review the operation of this provision.[10] It concluded that such a guide or direction was helpful in setting the background against which judges and lawyers interpret statutes, even if it is rarely referred to directly.[11] By contrast, Lord Wilberforce doubted whether legislation could really grapple with statutory interpretation. Rather, he said, 'it is a matter of educating the judges and practitioners and hoping that the work is better done'.[12] The editors must at once disclaim any intention of attempting to do any such thing in this little book which is intended more for the student than for the practitioner.

---

10. *A New Interpretation Act. To Avoid "Prolixity and Tautology"* (Report no 17, 1990) paras 33-74.
11. Paras 61-65.
12. 277 HL Official Report (5th series) col 1294 (16 November 1966); also 418 HL Official Report (5th series) col 73 (9 March 1981).

Chapter 1
Historical[1]

'The days have long passed when the courts adopted a strict-constructionist view of interpretation which required them to adopt the literal meaning of the language. The courts now adopt a purposive approach which seeks to give effect to the true purpose of legislation and are prepared to look at much extraneous material that bears upon the background against which the legislation was enacted.'

This statement was made in 1992 by Lord Griffiths in *Pepper v Hart*,[2] a case in which the House of Lords accepted for the first time that judges could refer to the Parliamentary debates reported in *Hansard* in order to ascertain the meaning of an Act of Parliament. That decision demonstrates how far judges are now prepared to go in order to ascertain the purpose of an Act of Parliament and apply it accordingly. But this approach has not always been adopted, and many of the criticisms of British statutory interpretation relate to an earlier period when an excessively literal approach was favoured. Whether statutes are still construed in a way which unduly impedes the achievement of their purposes is discussed in Chapter 8, but it is important to realise from the outset that the approach of the courts varies according to the judges' perception of their constitutional role at any given period.

In the 16th century, Plowden reports *Stradling v Morgan*,[3] a case in which a statute of Edward VI's reign referring to receivers and treasurers without any qualifying words was held to be confined to such officials appointed by

---

1. This chapter owes a great deal to the article by J A Corry entitled 'Administrative Law and the Interpretation of Statutes' 1 Toronto LJ 286 (1936) – reprinted with new introductory paragraphs in Appendix 1 of E A Driedger *The Construction of Statutes* (2nd edn, 1983 Toronto), a work to which this whole book owes a very great deal. On the history of statutory interpretation, see also S E Thorne's introduction to T Egerton *A Discourse upon the Esposicion and Understandinge of Statutes* (1570, 1942, San Marino).
2. [1993] 1 All ER 42 at 50.
3. (1560) 1 Plowd 199 at 205.

the King and not to extend to receivers and treasurers acting on behalf of private persons. Various authorities were cited—

> 'from which cases it appears that the sages of the law heretofore have construed statutes quite contrary to the letter in some appearance, and those statutes which comprehend all things in the letter they have expounded to extend but to some things, and those which generally prohibit all people from doing such an act they have interpreted to permit some people to do it, and those which include every person in the letter they have adjudged reach some persons only, which expositions have always been founded on the intent of the legislature which they have collected sometimes by considering the cause and necessity of making the Act, sometimes by comparing one part of the Act with another, and sometimes by foreign circumstances. So that they have ever been guided by the intent of the legislature, which they have always taken according to the necessity of the matter, and according to that which is consonant to reason and good discretion.'

In modern terms *Stradling v Morgan* was an example of restrictive interpretation; the broad effect of general words was held to be limited by the context, which was mainly concerned with royal revenue. *Heydon's* case,[4] on the other hand, could be said to be an instance of extensive interpretation because a grant of copyholds for life at the will of the lord was held to create 'an estate and interest for lives' within the meaning of the statute of Henry VIII in spite of decisions to the effect that the words in question were, when used in other statutes, confined to freeholds; but its real importance lies in the resolutions of the Barons of the Exchequer which contain the classic statement of the 'mischief rule':

> 'And it was resolved by them that for the sure and true interpretation of all statutes in general (be they penal or beneficial, restrictive or enlarging of the common law), four things are to be discerned and considered:
> 1st. What was the common law before the making of the Act,
> 2nd. What was the mischief and defect for which the common law did not provide,
> 3rd. What remedy the Parliament hath resolved and appointed to cure the disease of the Commonwealth, and
> 4th. The true reason of the remedy;
> and then the office of all the judges is always to make such construction as shall suppress the mischief, and advance the remedy, and to

---

4.   (1584) 3 Co Rep 7a at 7b; cf Egerton, note 1 above, pp 146–147.

suppress subtle inventions and evasions for continuance of the mischief, and *pro privato commodo*, and to add force and life to the cure and remedy, according to the true intent of the makers of the Act, *pro bono publico.'*

Heydon's case was decided in 1584 and the spirit which animated the Barons of the Exchequer tended in the main to animate the judges of the 17th century. The resolutions of 1584 were, like Plowden's observations in *Stradling v Morgan*, the typical product of the period preceding the complete establishment of the sovereignty of Parliament. Indeed, meetings of Parliament were very infrequent at that time, so judicial rectification of statutes was a practical necessity.

A more literal approach is to be discerned in the decisions of the 18th and 19th centuries. This was the outcome of the attitude towards government engendered by Locke and the revolution of 1688. The judges were willing to apply the enactments of Parliament, but, if it was to be enforced by the courts, any change in the existing state of affairs had to be framed by Parliament in the clearest possible terms. Examples of this approach are provided by decisions placing a strikingly strict interpretation on criminal statutes, and by the courts' complacent attitude towards the *casus omissus*— the inexplicable and probably inadvertent failure of the draftsman to use words entirely apt to cover the instant case.

It is open to question whether the Barons of the Exchequer had criminal statutes in mind when, in *Heydon*'s case, they declared their resolutions to be applicable to all statutes in general 'be they penal or beneficial'.[5] Other legal writing of that period suggests that, whereas statutes remedying the common law would receive a wide interpretation, those encroaching on the liberty of the subject or on common law rights would not.[6] It is certain, however, that the 18th century witnessed the growth of a presumption in favour of a strict construction of criminal statutes which persists to this day. In *R v Harris*[7] it was held that an accused who bit off the end of his victim's nose was not guilty of wounding within the meaning of a statute of George IV which punished anyone who 'shall unlawfully and maliciously stab, cut, or wound any person'. The court took the view that the intention of Parliament was, according to the words of the statute, that an instrument should have been used, a conclusion strengthened by an earlier reference to shooting.[8]

---

5. See *A-G v Sillem* (1864) 2 H & C 431 at 509.
6. See Egerton Ch 9.
7. (1836) 7 C & P 446.
8. The decision is rendered nugatory so far as the construction of the contemporary statutory equivalent is concerned by the inclusion in s 20 of the Offences Against the Person Act 1861 (prohibition of wounding or inflicting grievous bodily harm) of the words 'either with or without any weapon or instrument'.

Jones v Smart[9] may be taken as an illustration of the attitude of 18th-century courts to the *casus omissus*. The question was whether a doctor of physic was qualified to kill game under a statute of Charles II which disqualified those who lacked various property qualifications 'other than the son and heir apparent of an esquire, or other person of higher degree'. It was not disputed that he was of higher degree than an esquire or the son and heir apparent of an esquire, but the majority of the court held that the words 'son and heir apparent' governed 'other persons of higher degree', although the *casus omissus* could easily have been provided for by confining them to esquires.

As we shall see, strict construction of penal statutes and timidity in the face of a *casus omissus* are not simply things of the past. Indeed there is something to be said on both sides with regard to the merits of such an approach. The important point for present purposes is that they are apt to produce a Parliamentary reaction. This has been the baneful effect of the literal approach to statutory interpretation as contrasted with the approaches canvassed in *Stradling v Morgan* and *Heydon*'s case.[10] At times a state of war has appeared to exist between the courts and the Parliamentary drafter. The courts declined to come to the rescue when a *casus omissus* was revealed, so words appropriate to cover the *casus omissus* were added to the statute. More frequently the drafter got in first and, anticipating a strict construction by the courts coupled with a total lack of sympathy if there should happen to be a *casus omissus*, produced a statute which was nothing less than horrific in its detail. One of the most notorious examples was, until 1983, provided by s 1 of the Wills Act Amendment Act 1852.[11] It was passed in order to resolve doubts concerning the requirement of the Wills Act 1837 that the will must be signed 'at the foot or end thereof' and it reads:

> 'Where by an Act passed in the First Year of the Reign of Her Majesty Queen Victoria, intituled An Act for the Amendment of the Laws with respect to Wills, it is enacted, that no Will shall be valid unless it shall be signed at the Foot or End thereof by the Testator, or by some other Person in his Presence, and by his Direction: Every Will shall, so far only as regards the Position of the Signature of the Testator, or of the Person signing for him as aforesaid, be deemed to be valid within the said Enactment, as explained by this Act, if the Signature shall be so placed at or after, or following, or under, or beside, or opposite to the End of the Will, that it shall be apparent on the Face of the Will that

---

9. (1784) 1 Term Rep 44.
10. Pp 10-12 above.
11. The Act was repealed by the Administration of Justice Act 1982 (s 17 of which simplified the formal requirements for making wills).

the Testator intended to give Effect by such his Signature to the Writing signed as his Will, and that no such Will shall be affected by the Circumstance that the Signature shall not follow or be immediately after the Foot or End of the Will, or by the Circumstance that a blank Space shall intervene between the concluding Word of the Will and the Signature, or by the Circumstance that the Signature shall be placed among the Words of the Testimonium Clause or of the Clause of Attestation, or shall follow or be after or under the Clause of Attestation, either with or without a blank Space intervening, or shall follow or be after, or under, or beside the Names or One of the Names of the subscribing Witnesses, or by the Circumstance that the Signature shall be on a Side or Page or other Portion of the Paper or Papers containing the Will whereon no Clause or Paragraph or disposing Part of the Will shall be written above the Signature, or by the Circumstance that there shall appear to be sufficient Space on or at the Bottom of the preceding Side or Page or other Portion of the same Paper on which the Will is written to contain the Signature; and the Enumeration of the above Circumstances shall not restrict the Generality of the above Enactment; but no Signature under the said Act or this Act shall be operative to give Effect to any Disposition or Direction which is underneath or which follows it, nor shall it give Effect to any Disposition or Direction inserted after the Signature shall be made.'

This is not a book on legislative drafting, an insufficiently appreciated art,[12] but it is important to appreciate the mutual dependence of the drafter and the courts when the latter are engaged in statutory interpretation. It is the courts' duty to give effect to the intention of Parliament[13] but their main source of information on this matter is the wording of the statute; if this is not clear there is obviously a risk that the courts will be unable to do their work properly. On the other hand the drafter will find it difficult to convey the Parliamentary intent to the courts unless he knows that they will attach the same meaning to his words as that in which he employs them. Hence the need for a common standard of interpretation, and there can hardly be a better standard than the ordinary, or, in appropriate cases, the technical, meaning of English words.

As legislation increased in quantity and as it came to deal more with matters unknown to the common law, the resolutions of *Heydon*'s case became less and less satisfactory as the sole guide to interpretation. Primacy,

---

12. Useful books are E A Driedger *The Composition of Legislation* (2nd edn, 1976, Ottawa), Reed Dickerson *The Fundamentals of Legal Drafting* (1965, Boston), and G C Thornton, *Legislative Drafting* (3rd edn, 1987).
13. See pp 23-31.

though not total supremacy, had to be given to the words of the statute. The mischief rule came to be largely, though not entirely, superseded by the 'literal' or, as it came to be called in America, the 'plain meaning' rule. One of the most frequently quoted of the numerous statements of this latter rule is that of Tindal CJ when advising the House of Lords on the *Sussex Peerage Case*:[14]

> 'The only rule for the construction of Acts of Parliament is that they should be construed according to the intent of the Parliament which passed the Act. If the words of the statute are in themselves precise and unambiguous, then no more can be necessary than to expound those words in that natural and ordinary sense. The words themselves alone do, in such case, best declare the intention of the lawgiver. But if any doubt arises from the terms employed by the legislature, it has always been held a safe means of collecting the intention, to call in aid the ground and cause of making the statute, and to have recourse to the preamble, which, according to Chief Justice Dyer,[15] is "a key to open the minds of the makers of the Act, and the mischiefs which they intend to redress".'

This passage is of especial interest because it states the then commonly accepted view concerning the appropriate relationship of the literal and mischief rules—the latter only applying when the court found that the statutory words were manifestly obscure or ambiguous. (In Chapter 3, we discuss whether, under the purposive approach, the purpose may be taken into account to suggest that an otherwise clear and unambiguous meaning is not the right one.)

Although focusing on the words of the enactment, the proper application of the literal rule did not mean that the effect of a particular word, phrase or section was to be determined in isolation from the rest of the statute in which it was contained. Tindal CJ recognised in the *Sussex Peerage Case* that, before deciding whether the words are 'in themselves precise and unambiguous', the court must have regard to the whole of the enacting part of the statute. The proper application of the literal rules does not mean that the effect of a particular word, phrase or section is to be determined in isolation from the rest of the statute in which it is contained.

This had been recognised by Parker CB in the middle of the 18th century; but his words may be thought to have contained the germs of a third rule which, in order that it may be distinguished from the mischief and literal

---

14. (1844) 11 Cl & Fin 85 at 143.
15. *Stowe v Lord Zouch* (1569) 1 Plowd 353 at 369.

rules, is commonly called the 'golden' rule.[16] It allows for a departure from the literal rule when the application of the statutory words in the ordinary sense would be repugnant to or inconsistent with some other provision in the statute or even when it would lead to what the court considers to be an absurdity. The usual consequence of applying the golden rule is that words which are in the statute are ignored or words which are not there are read in. The scope of the golden rule is debatable, particularly so far as the meaning of an 'absurdity' is concerned. This word was not used by Parker CB who said:[17]

> 'In expounding Acts of Parliament, where words are express, plain and clear, the words ought to be understood according to their genuine and natural signification and import, unless by such exposition a contradiction or inconsistency would arise in the Act by reason of some subsequent clause, from whence it might be inferred that the intent of the Parliament was otherwise.'

In *Becke v Smith*[18] Parke B (as he then was) said:

> 'It is a very useful rule, in the construction of a statute, to adhere to the ordinary meaning of the words used, and to the grammatical construction, unless that is at variance with the intention of the legislature, to be collected from the statute itself, or leads to any manifest absurdity or repugnance, in which case the language may be varied or modified, so as to avoid such inconvenience, but no further.'

Neither Parker CB nor Parke B found it necessary to modify the application of the literal rule in the judgments from which the above passages are taken. In *Becke v Smith*, Parke B may have used the word 'absurdity' to mean no more than repugnant to other provisions in the statute;[19] but the same judge's statement of the golden rule in *Grey v Pearson*,[20] a case concerned with the construction of a will, is less easily susceptible of that interpretation, and this statement of the rule (made after Parke B had become Lord Wensleydale) is probably the one which is most commonly cited today:

---

16. The 'literal' rule, with or without the qualification mentioned in the text, is also often spoken of as the 'golden' rule.
17. *Mitchell v Torup* (1766) Park 227 at 233.
18. (1836) 2 M & W 191 at 195.
19. 'I subscribe to every word of that [the statement of Parke B in *Becke v Smith*], assuming the word "absurdity" to mean no more than "repugnance".' (Willes J, *Christopherson v Lotinga* (1864) 15 CBNS 809 at 813).
20. (1857) 6 HL Cas 61 at 106.

'I have been long and deeply impressed with the wisdom of the rule now, I believe, universally adopted, at least in the courts of law in Westminster Hall, that in construing wills and indeed statutes, and all written instruments, the grammatical and ordinary sense of the words is to be adhered to, unless that would lead to some absurdity, or some repugnance or inconsistency with the rest of the instrument, in which case the grammatical and ordinary sense of the words may be modified, so as to avoid the absurdity and inconsistency, but no farther.'

On occasions the golden rule simply serves as a guide to the court where there is doubt as to the true import of the statutory words in their ordinary sense. When there is a choice of meanings there is presumption that one which produces an absurd, unjust or inconvenient result was not intended; but it should be emphasised that when the rule is used as a justification for ignoring or reading in words, resort may only be made to it in the most unusual cases. This is borne out by two dicta in the same volume of Appeal Cases which also reveal the difference of opinion about the scope of the rule discernible in a number of judgments.

'It is a strong thing to read into an Act of Parliament words which are not there, and in the absence of clear necessity it is a wrong thing to do.'[1]

'We are not entitled to read words into an Act of Parliament unless clear reason for it is to be found *within the four corners of the Act* itself.'[2]

In their review of statutory interpretation in 1969, the Law Commissions concluded that there was a tendency among some judges to over-emphasise a narrow version of the literal rule and to refuse to go beyond the meaning of a statutory provision in the light of its immediate and obvious context.[3] They proposed that judges should adopt a 'purposive' approach to the construction of statutes, namely 'that a construction which would promote the general legislative purpose underlying the provision in question is to be preferred to a construction which would not'.[4] Although this has much in common with the 'mischief' rule, the Law Commissions disapproved of that term. First, the rule in *Heydon*'s case[5] related to a different constitutional context and stressed the curing of a defect in the law without adequate

---

1. Lord Mersey in *Thompson v Good & Co* [1910] AC 409 at 420.
2. Lord Loreburn in *Vickers, Sons and Maxim Ltd v Evans* [1910] AC 444 at 445.
3. *The Interpretation of Statutes* (Law Com no 21; Scottish Law Com no 11) para 80(c). See also p 192 below.
4. Appendix A, Draft Bill, clause 2(a).
5. See pp 11-12 above.

emphasis on the extent to which the judge should adhere to the actual wording of the statute. Second, the rule is archaic and misleading:[6]

> 'It tends to suggest that legislation is only designed to deal with an evil and not to further a positive social purpose. Furthermore, it seems too narrow to speak of the "mischief of the statute". The general legislative purpose underlying a provision may emerge from a series of statutes dealing with the same subject matter . . . or from other indications of that purpose [afforded by information relating to legal, social, economic and other aspects of society of which a judge is able to take judicial notice].'

Since the Law Commissions' report, the judges have embraced a 'purposive' approach to the construction of statutes. They have rejected the narrow literalism which the Law Commissions criticised, but this does not mark a radical departure from the approach suggested in *Grey v Pearson*.[7]

Pepper v Hart[8] illustrates the extent to which 'purposive construction' differs from previous approaches. Schoolmasters at Malvern College, a public school, were offered a concessionary rate (one-fifth of the normal fee) to send their children to the school, if there were spare places. They were taxed by the Revenue under s 61(1) of the Finance Act 1976 on the 'cash equivalent' of this benefit provided by their employer. Under s 63(1) of the Act the 'cash equivalent' was equal to the cost of the benefit (less 'so much, if any, of it as is made good by the employee'); and s 63(2) provided that 'the cost of a benefit is the amount of expense incurred in or in connection with its provision [by the employer]'. The Revenue and the Court of Appeal construed this as meaning that the cost was to be measured as the cost of providing the service to the general public, so that the benefit given to the schoolmasters was the difference between the full fee which other parents paid and the concessionary fee which the schoolmasters paid. After counsel had argued the case in the House of Lords before five Law Lords, a majority were in favour of dismissing the appeal against liability to tax brought by the schoolmasters. But their Lordships' attention was then drawn to passages in *Hansard* which showed that the Minister in charge of the Bill did not intend schoolmasters to be taxed in this way. During the Committee Stage of the Bill's passage through the House of Commons, a subsection was removed which, had it remained in the Bill, would have produced the result contended

---

6. *The Interpretation of Statutes* note 177; see also para 33.
7. (1857) 6 HL Cas 61:pp 16-17, above. For an example of a recent judgment expressing essentially the 'golden' rule with modified wording see Donaldson MR in *Re British Concrete Pipe Association* [1983] 1 All ER 203 at 205.
8. [1993] 1 All ER 42 and see also pp 156-157, below.

for by the Revenue. Asked to confirm that, as a result of its removal, teachers would not be taxed by reference to the full fees, the Minister replied:

> 'The removal of [that subsection] will affect the position of a child of one of the teachers at the child's school, because now the benefit will be assessed on the cost to the employer, which would be very small indeed in this case.'[9]

The case was re-heard before seven Law Lords, who decided unanimously that the schoolmasters did not have to pay any tax on the concessionary fees for their children, since the reduced fees paid by them covered the small cost to the school of admitting their children as pupils. In coming to this decision, the House of Lords departed from its previous rule that *Hansard* could not be used in determining the meaning of a statute, and this departure was justified by Lord Griffiths, in the passage quoted at the beginning of this chapter, by the need to give effect to the purpose of a statute.

Unlike the approach under the golden rule, there was no reliance on an absurdity manifest from the statute read as a whole. It sufficed that there was an ambiguity in the meaning of the provision and that the purpose of the provision as revealed by the legislative history could resolve that ambiguity. Under the purposive approach, the judge may look beyond the four corners of the statute to find a reason for giving a particular interpretation to its words, and his role is one of active co-operation with the policy of the statute.

All the same, this purposive approach is more limited than the appeal to the 'equity of the statute' found among 16th-century mischievists. This can be illustrated by *Jones v Wrotham Park Settled Estates*.[10]

The Leasehold Reform Act 1967 gave the tenant of a long lease the right to purchase the freehold from his landlord at the equivalent of the going market rate when occupied by the tenant. Two days before Jones gave notice of his intention to exercise this right, his landlord entered into a 300-year lease of the reversion with an associated property company at a highly favourable rent. The effect of this transaction was to raise the value of the freehold from £300 to £4,000 at the going market rate. The House of Lords thought that, had such a device been considered by Parliament, it would have been proscribed, since it made the purchase of the freehold by tenants more difficult. However, their Lordships applied the clear wording of the statute in favour of the landlord, requiring the tenant to pay the £4,000 if he wished to purchase the reversion and holding the lease of the reversion valid. Lord Diplock noted that there were limits to the purposive approach:[11]

---

9. Mr R Sheldon, Financial Secretary to the Treasury, Standing Committee E, col 1098 (17 May 1976).
10. [1980] AC 74.
11. At 105–106.

'First, it [must be] possible to determine from a consideration of the provisions of the Act read as a whole what the mischief was that it was the purpose of the Act to remedy; secondly, it [must be] apparent that the draftsman and Parliament had by inadvertence overlooked, and so omitted to deal with, an eventuality that required to be dealt with if the purpose of the Act was to be achieved; and thirdly, it [must be] possible to state with certainty what were the additional words that would have been inserted by the draftsman and approved by Parliament had their attention been drawn to the omission before the Bill passed into law. Unless this third condition is fulfilled any attempt by a court of justice to repair the omission in the Act cannot be justified as an exercise of its jurisdiction to determine what is the meaning of a written law which Parliament has passed. Such an attempt crosses the boundary between construction and legislation. It becomes a usurpation of the function which under the constitution of this country is vested in the legislature to the exclusion of the courts.'

Thus the purposive approach is more limited than one which tries to 'suppress the mischief, and advance the remedy, and to suppress subtle inventions and evasions for continuance of the mischief'.[12]

Though the precise contours of the purposive approach will be considered later, it is clear that it retains a focus on fidelity to the text as well as fidelity to the objectives aimed at by Parliament. If there has been a change in recent years, then it lies in a greater emphasis on the latter aspect of statutory interpretation.

---

12. Pp 11-12 above.

Chapter 2
Jurisprudential

There is a great deal of juristic writing on the subject of statutory interpretation, and no attempt will be made here to summarise it all. This chapter will focus on a number of key jurisprudential issues raised in connection with the subject. The issues involve an analysis both of the basic approach of the judges in the interpretation of statutes and of the character of the canons and methods adopted in their performance of this task. The focus on judges is deliberate, even though, as was mentioned in the Introduction, it is fully recognised that most instances of statutory interpretation do not come to court. The written judgments of the higher courts in most systems of law offer the best examples of responsible agencies justifying legal interpretations in a methodologically self-conscious way.[1] Furthermore, in common law systems, the attitudes and practices of the judges provide a model of authoritative interpretation, which constitutes a standard to be followed.[2] In relation to judicial approaches, it is necessary to ask what the judges are seeking to interpret, and especially what is the relationship they conceive between a statute and the intention of Parliament. It is also necessary to analyse what concepts such as 'interpretation', 'ordinary meaning' and 'purpose' involve in this context. With regard to the canons and methods, it is necessary to analyse the character and status of the various 'rules' and 'principles' which are often invoked by the judges in explaining their decisions. Although the presentation will be essentially analytical, the constitutional questions which the subject necessarily raises will require some consideration of its political aspects.

---

1. See D N MacCormick and R S Summers *Interpreting Statutes. A Comparative Study* (1991) p 14.
2. D R Miers and A C Page *Legislation* (2nd edn, 1990) p 157.

A. THE SUBJECT-MATTER OF STATUTORY INTERPRETATION

As Bennion points out, the 'unit of enquiry' in statutory interpretation is 'an enactment whose legal meaning in relation to a particular factual situation falls to be determined'.[3] The text of the relevant enactment may be determined by looking at a single Act of Parliament, or even a single provision within it, or by combining elements from several Acts. Having thus established the wording of the statutory text, the lawyer can then proceed to determine its meaning in the light of the principles of interpretation or construction.[4]

Seen in this light, statutory interpretation involves determining the meaning of a text contained in one or more documents. Yet judges and writers frequently talk about interpreting 'the will of the legislator' or giving effect to 'the intention of Parliament'. Indeed, judges are often criticised for being tied too closely to the statutory words and for failing to give effect to the intentions of Parliament. Such language may appear to suggest that there are two units of enquiry in statutory interpretation—the statutory text and the intention of Parliament—and that the judge must seek to harmonise the two. However, this appearance is deceptive. English law takes the view that the two are closely connected, but that primacy is to be given to the text in which the intention of Parliament has been expressed. Blackstone tells us that:[5]

> 'The fairest and most rational method to interpret the will of the legislator is by exploring his intentions at the time when the law was made, by *signs* the most natural and probable. And these signs are either the words, the context, the subject matter, the effects and consequence, or the spirit and reason of the law.'

For him, words are generally to be understood 'in their usual and most known signification', although terms of art 'must be taken according to the acceptation of the learned in each art, trade and science'. 'If words happen still to be dubious', we may establish their meaning from the context, which includes the preamble to the statute and laws made by the same legislator on the same subject.

Words are always to be understood as having regard to the subject-matter of the legislation:

---

3. *Bennion* s 137.
4. A distinction is drawn in some works between interpretation and construction, but it is not employed in this book because it lacks an agreed basis.
5. *Commentaries on the Laws of England* (facsimile of 1st edn of 1765, University of Chicago Press, 1979) vol 1, p 59.

'But lastly, the most universal and effectual way of discovering the true meaning of a law, when the words are dubious, is by considering the reason and spirit of it; or the cause which moved the legislator to enact it.'

This brief account of the rules of statutory interpretation approximates closely to the present law. All these precepts are typical rules of language applicable to understanding any text, whether legal or other.[6] As with literature, the role of the judge is to seek the intention of the legislative author from what is written in the text, and not to seek to construct a text on the basis of the subjective intentions of the author (assuming that they could be discovered).

Blackstone's approach would be adopted today with few modifications. As Lord Scarman stated:[7]

'If Parliament . . . says one thing but means another, it is not, under the historic principles of the common law, for the courts to correct it. That general principle must surely be acceptable in our society. We are to be governed not by Parliament's intentions but by Parliament's enactments.'

The criticism that judges are too tied to the wording of the statutory text is thus not a suggestion that the judges are looking at the wrong subject-matter when interpreting statutes. Rather, the criticism merely suggests that the judges are adopting too narrow a view of the context in which the statutory text is to be read.

B.   THE INTENTION OF PARLIAMENT

In the light of what has been said, it is necessary to ask what sense can be given to the notion of 'the intention of Parliament'.[8] The phrase is frequently

---

6. See, for example: K S Abraham 'Statutory Interpretation and Literary Theory: Some Common Concerns of an Unlikely Pair' 32 Rutgers L Rev 676 (1979); the 'Interpretation Symposium' 58 Southern California L Rev, issue No 1 (1985), especially articles by R R Garet, D C Hoy and M J Perry; and S Fish *Doing What Comes Naturally* (1989) Ch 4.
7.   418 HL Official Report (5th Series) col 65 (9 March 1981).
8.   There is an abundant literature on this subject which cannot be listed here. But, for example, see R Dickerson *The Interpretation and Application of Statutes* (1975, Boston) Ch 7; G C MacCallum 'Legislative Intent' 75 Yale LJ 754 (1966) (reprinted in R S Summers (ed) *Essays in Legal Philosophy* (1970) p 237), which contain references to many of the principal articles on the subject.

used by the judges although it is meaningless unless it is recognised for what it is, an expression used by analogy, but in no way synonymously, with the intention of an individual concerning the general and particular effects of a document he prepares and signs. A testator may, with perfect propriety, be said to have intended to dispose of all of his property, to have intended to do so in accordance with a particular scheme (equality among his children, or with a preference for sons, for example) and to have intended that his will should have a certain effect in the situation before the court (eg that X should or should not benefit under one of its provisions); but the word 'intention' is used in a very different sense when it is said that, in passing the Equal Pay Act 1970, Parliament did or did not intend the Act to apply to discrimination between the sexes in relation to all conditions of employment, or did or did not intend to cover discrimination between those doing different jobs, or did or did not intend to cover discrimination in relation to successors in a job. Each of these statements can be used meaningfully although it is quite impossible to point to specific individuals, like the testator in the previous example, who did or did not entertain the intention in question.

The 'intention of Parliament' with regard to a particular statute cannot mean the intention of all those who were members of either House when the royal assent was given, for many of them might have been out of the country at all material times and never have heard of the statute. Equally plainly the phrase cannot mean the intention of the majority who voted for the statute as this will almost certainly have been constituted by different persons at the different stages of the passage of the Bill and, in any event, it would be rash to assume that all those who vote for it have the same intentions with regard to a particular piece of legislation. For example, it has been pointed out that, in a debate on what became the Statute of Westminster 1931, Winston Churchill and the Solicitor-General agreed that there was no obscurity in the provisions concerning the Irish Free State, although they took diametrically opposite views concerning their effect.[9]

Someone bent on identifying the intention of specific human beings as that to which reference is made when people speak of the intention of Parliament might resort to the notion of agency. It could be said that the promoters of a Bill must have some consequences in mind as its general and particular effects, but promoters, whoever they may be, are initiators who place proposals before Parliament rather than act as its agents; and many Bills contain amendments which are not the work of the promoters. Nonetheless, when judges are consulting Parliamentary debates in order to discover the intended meaning or effect of an Act, *Pepper v Hart*[10] requires

---

9.   G Marshall *Constitutional Theory* (1971) p 76.
10. See pp 18-19 above and pp 156-157 below.

them to pay attention to the statements made by the promoters of the Bill for that Act. But if such statements are thus considered as evidence for what Parliament meant by a particular provision, this is not to say that the intention of the promoter is to be treated in all cases as that of Parliament.

In modern times, promoters give instructions to the drafter who can be regarded as their agent. As a result, when trying to give effect to the intention of Parliament, Lord Simon of Glaisdale has suggested that:[11]

> 'The court sometimes asks itself what the draftsman must have intended. This is reasonable enough: the draftsman knows what is the intention of the legislative initiator (nowadays almost always an organ of the executive); he knows what canons of construction the courts will apply; and he will express himself in such a way as accordingly to give effect to the legislative intention.'

But the drafter is not the agent of Parliament itself.

An analogy could be drawn with cases in which the intention of its officers is imputed to a corporation, but it would be a false analogy. Parliament is not a corporation and those who speak of the intention of Parliament do so in spite of the fact that they know that proof that members of Parliament, even those who were the legislative initiators, believed that a statute would produce certain results is not a condition precedent to the proper use of the phrase.

The court may justify the meaning it ultimately attaches to statutory words by suggesting that this is the meaning which, it believes, members of the legislature would have attached to them had the situation before the court been present to their minds. But, although the purpose of the statute may be treated as part of its context and judges may look to other sources outside the statute (even to Parliamentary debates) in the limited circumstances discussed in Chapter 6, the courts are confined to the meaning which may be legitimately attributed to the statutory text. The following words of a South African judge surely hold good for English law:[12]

> 'Evidence that every member who voted for a measure put a certain construction upon it cannot affect the meaning which the court must place upon the statute, for it is the product, not of a number of individuals, but of an impersonal Parliament.'

---

11. *Ealing London Borough Council v Race Relations Board* [1972] AC 342 at 360.
12. *Swart & Nicol v De Kock* 1951 3 SA 589 at 621, per Van den Heever JA, AD.

This last quotation helps to make clear, as R M Dworkin pointed out,[13] that the question of legislative intention is not about the historical or hypothetical views of legislators, but rather concerns the meaning of words used in a particular context. The objective is not to reconstruct a psychological model of Parliament or the promoters of a Bill, or even of the drafter, and then to use it to determine what was meant by them when they used certain words, or what would have been provided had a particular eventuality been envisaged at the time of drafting or enactment. Although judicial language, like that of Lord Simon of Glaisdale, may sometimes give this impression, it is clear that judges do not act in this way and that they make little effort to discover what the legislator or drafter thought that the words meant. Judges are concerned instead with using the conventions of ordinary language and of statutory interpretation to determine the meaning of words in their context.

In *Black-Clawson International Ltd v Papierwerke Waldhof-Aschaffenburg AG* Lord Reid said:[14]

> 'We often say that we are looking for the intention of Parliament, but that is not quite accurate. We are seeking the meaning of the words which Parliament used. We are seeking not what Parliament meant but the true meaning of what they said.'

The remark is somewhat cryptic, but it does point to the fact that the intention to be attributed to the legislator is to be determined from the objective words used, rather than from any subjective intentions which were not expressed in the text. All the same, the remark suggests a distinction which is in reality less clear cut, because in ordinary language, when in doubt, we must do our best to make sense of what the author said in the context appropriate to his speaking, which requires some knowledge of the author and what he was trying to say.

The above discussion makes it clear that one needs to distinguish between the subjective intentions of individual legislators or the drafter and the objective intention which can be attributed to the words used, read in the context of the purpose of the statute and various admissible materials (including, possibly, reports of Parliamentary debates). Though these sometimes coincide, this is not always the case. As MacCormick and Summers point out, there is no single factor which exclusively identifies the

---

13. 'Political Judges and the Rule of Law' (1978) 64 *Proceedings of the British Academy* 259, 270-274 (reprinted in R M Dworkin *A Matter of Principle* (1985, Cambridge, Mass) pp 9, 18-23), and *Law's Empire* (1986) pp 317-327, 337-341.
14. [1975] AC 591 at 613.

intention of the legislature.[15] Arguments based on 'ordinary meaning' or 'purpose' typically focus on the objective meaning which can be attributed to a provision in the context of the usages of ordinary language, how the provision fits into the rest of the law, or how the words relate to a declared purpose. But the courts may arrive at their interpretation on appropriate occasions in the light of evidence as to what was subjectively intended, even if this is not a conclusive or overriding factor. Even where *Hansard* is consulted, it is clear that its content can only be used to resolve ambiguities in the enacted words, not to justify disregarding those words altogether.[16]

In the context of the interpretation of statutes there are three principal situations in which people in general and judges in particular speak of the intention of Parliament. In the first place, whenever the meaning of specific words is under consideration, the idea that a particular meaning is that which would or would not have been attached to a word or phrase by the average member of Parliament, sitting at the time when the statute was passed, may be expressed or refuted by some such statement as 'that is (or is not) what Parliament intended by those words'. Second, when the consequences of a particular construction are under consideration, the idea that a particular consequence might well have been in the mind of the average member of Parliament is often expressed by some such statement as 'that was likely (or unlikely) to have been the intention of Parliament'. Finally, although it is impossible to identify the individual members whose purpose it was, it is common to speak of the purpose, aim or object of a statute as the intention of Parliament. The third situation is the most important if only because reflection upon it shows that those who feel uncomfortable about the use of the expression 'the intention of Parliament' ought not to feel any more at ease if they abandon the phrase for some other one such as 'the intention of the statute', 'legislative purpose' or 'the object of the statute'. Only human beings can really have intentions, purposes or objects, but, in the situation under consideration, the intentions, purposes or objects are not those of identifiable human beings. The words are used by close analogy to the intentions of a single legislator. The analogy is more remote when the 'intention of Parliament' is used as a synonym for what the average member of Parliament of a particular epoch would have meant by certain words or expected as the consequences of a statutory provision. All the same, the

---

15. *Interpreting Statutes*, pp 522-525; J Evans *Statutory Interpretation. Problems of Communication* (1988, Auckland) pp 67-70. See also Lord Watson: ' "Intention of the Legislature" is a common but very slippery phrase, which, popularly understood, may signify anything from intention embodied in positive enactment to speculative opinion as to what the legislature probably would have meant, although there has been an omission to enact it' (*Saloman v Saloman & Co Ltd* [1897] AC 22 at 38).

16. *Pepper v Hart*. See p 19 above and pp 156-157 below.

notion of 'the intention of Parliament' has an advantage over the phrase 'legislative purpose' in that a single statute, like the Companies Act 1985, may have several purposes which may have to be reconciled. The analogy with the human mind emphasises a certain coherence and consistency, both within an enactment and between enactments, which judges expect to find. Consistency and coherence are values which guide judicial interpretation of the law,[17] and the metaphor of a single legislative will or intention gives expression to this ideal. The expression is thus not so much a description as a linguistic convenience.

The major judicial statements with regard to the intention of Parliament have been made in cases in which the issue has been whether statutory wording could be ignored or the meaning of statutory language strained in order to prevent an injustice, or supposed injustice, which, it was thought, could not have been contemplated by Parliament. The answer has almost always been in the negative, and the preponderant view seems to be that, when the question is whether Parliament did or did not intend a particular result, the 'intention of Parliament' is what the statutory words mean to the normal speaker of English. The fact that a judge feels confident that, had the situation before him been put to them, the members of the Parliament in which the statute was passed would have voted for a different meaning or for additional words is immaterial.

Such an approach reflects a conception of the judicial role which is fundamentally linked to the constitutional principle of the rule of law. As Lord Simon of Glaisdale expressed the connection,[18]

> 'in a society living under the rule of law citizens are entitled to regulate their conduct according to what a statute has said, rather than by what it was meant to say or by what it would otherwise have said if a newly considered situation had been envisaged.'

Similarly, Lord Oliver has argued that those who claim to be able to divine the actual mind of Parliament,[19]

> 'misunderstand the nature of the task upon which the judge has been compelled to engage himself, which is to discover, using the tools which the law has furnished him—the accepted presumptions and canons of construction—not some speculative but unexpressed

---

17. See D N MacCormick *Legal Reasoning and Legal Theory* (1978) pp 203-213; R M Dworkin *A Matter of Principle* pp 327-328.
18. *Stock v Frank Jones (Tipton) Ltd* [1978] ICR 347 at 354; see also 418 HL Official Report (5th series) col 76 (9 March 1981).
19. 'A Judicial View of Modern Legislation' [1993] Stat LR 1 at 2.

"intention of Parliament" but the ambit of the written rules that Parliament has imposed for the regulation of the subject's conduct and his rights and duties under the law. For every legislative enactment constitutes a *Diktat* by the state to the citizen which he is not only expected but obliged to observe in the regulation of his daily life and it is the judge and the judge alone who stands between the citizen and the state's own interpretation of its own rules. That is why it is so vitally important that legislation should be expressed in language that can be clearly understood and why it should be in a form that makes it readily accessible.'

By giving effect to the meaning which the normal speaker of English would attribute to the words in their context, the judges are giving effect to the normal expectations of citizens and are upholding this conception of the rule of law.

Despite its difficulty, there are three constitutional reasons for retaining the notion of 'the intention of Parliament'. The first is that it expresses the subordination of the judiciary to Parliament. As J W Hurst put it:[20]

'Of course we use a fiction if we speak of the legislature as if it were a being of one mind. But so durable a fiction endures because it has a use validated by experience. This formula reminds all who deal with a statute that they are operating in a field of law in which they are not free to define public policy simply according to their own judgment.'

The courts try to give effect to the instructions they have received from Parliament and do not simply decide as they think best. All the same, this dichotomy can be overstated. Subordinates do receive instructions, but they are usually left with a degree of latitude about how to execute them. At best, the notion of 'the intention of Parliament' identifies a perspective or orientation within which judicial decision-making takes place, rather than a rigid set of instructions whose execution requires little originality or discretion.

The second reason for appealing to 'the intention of Parliament' is the desire of the judiciary to disavow a large creative role in the interpretation of statutes. Denning LJ may have said in *Magor and St Mellons RDC v Newport Corpn*:[1]

---

20. *Dealing with Statutes* (1982, New York) p 33.
1. [1950] 2 All ER 1226 at 1236; also *Nothman v Barnet London Borough Council* [1978] ICR 336 at 344; *R v Sheffield Crown Court, ex p Brownlow* [1980] QB 530 at 538-539. At one point Lord Denning accepted that judges cannot fill in gaps: see *London Transport Executive v Betts* [1959] AC 231 at 247.

'We do not sit here to pull the language of Parliament and of Ministers to pieces and make nonsense of it. That is an easy thing to do, and it is a thing to which lawyers are too often prone. We sit here to find out the intention of Parliament and of Ministers and carry it out, and we do this better by filling in the gaps and making sense of the enactment than by opening it up to destructive analysis.'

But this approach was rejected by the House of Lords at the time,[2] and in later cases Lord Denning MR's approach to statutes came under similar criticism for being unduly creative. For example, in *Duport Steels Ltd v Sirs*,[3] s 13(1) of the Trade Union and Labour Relations Act 1974 (as amended) gave an immunity from suit for 'an act done by a person in contemplation or furtherance of a trade dispute'. There was no specific provision which prevented this immunity extending to actions directed against employers other than the one with whom the employees were in dispute. Nevertheless, the Court of Appeal, presided over by Lord Denning MR, granted an injunction against union officials who were seeking to induce their members working for private steel companies to come out on strike in order to make more effective their strike action against the nationalised British Steel Corporation. It restricted the wording of the Act by requiring that the actions protected by the immunity should not be too remote from the dispute, and Lord Denning MR justified this by pointing to the serious and deleterious consequences for the country of such secondary action. The House of Lords unanimously reversed the decision, and categorically denounced the approach of the Court of Appeal. While having sympathy with the view that secondary action ought not to be lawful, their Lordships were of the opinion that it was not the role of the courts to outlaw such action by means of statutory interpretation. As Lord Diplock put it:

'My Lords, at a time when more and more cases involve the application of legislation which gives effect to policies that are the subject of bitter public and parliamentary controversy, it cannot be too strongly emphasised that the British Constitution, though largely unwritten, is firmly based upon the separation of powers: Parliament makes the laws, the judiciary interprets them. When Parliament legislates to remedy what the majority of its members at the time perceive to be a defect or lacuna in the existing law . . . the role of the judiciary is confined to ascertaining from the words that Parliament has approved as expressing its intention what that intention was, and giving effect to it. Where the meaning of the statutory words is plain and unambiguous

---

2. See *Magor and St Mellons RDC v Newport Corpn* [1952] AC 189.
3. [1980] 1 All ER 529; also *Nothman v Barnet London Borough Council* [1979] ICR 111.

it is not for the judges to invent fancied ambiguities as an excuse for failing to give effect to its plain meaning because they themselves consider that the consequences of doing so would be inexpedient, or even unjust or immoral. In controversial matters such as are involved in industrial relations there is room for differences of opinion as to what is expedient, what is just and what is morally justifiable. Under our Constitution it is Parliament's opinion on these matters that is paramount.'[4]

The third reason is that of legal certainty, which was invoked by Lord Diplock and other members of the House of Lords in *Duport Steels*, as well as in other cases.[5] The certain injustice of a legislative text may be preferable for the citizen in the long run than the uncertainty caused by judicial interventions to correct perceived 'injustices'.

Even if an appeal to 'the intention of Parliament' is justified, the use made of it differs from judge to judge. It is used as a statement of attitude or approach, not an element of social fact to be researched. Such statements are expressions of a constitutional role adopted by judges, and the quotations given here and elsewhere in this book illustrate that the judges are not unanimous in their perception of what is the correct constitutional role for them to adopt.

C. 'ORDINARY MEANING' AND 'PURPOSE'

Since interpretation focuses on the objective meaning of statutory provisions, it is important to analyse what is meant by the key phrases which are used to describe that meaning. Judges talk about the 'ordinary meaning' or the 'grammatical meaning' of words and about the 'purpose' of an enactment, and this book adopts that usage. Each of those terms is the subject of jurisprudential debate, some elements of which may appropriately be discussed at this point. In essence, the central question is how far the phrases denote real constraints on the freedom of the judge to decide a case as he thinks fair and just.

In their interesting comparison of the practices of nine countries in interpreting statutes, MacCormick and Summers conclude that 'linguistic arguments', based on the ordinary meaning of words, are very important in

---

4. [1980] 1 All ER 529 at 541.
5. See especially Lord Scarman at 551; also Lord Simon of Glaisdale, *Stock v Frank Jones (Tipton) Ltd* [1978] ICR 347 at 354.

all legal systems.[6] Such arguments cover both the meaning of the words in everyday language and technical meanings appropriate to the context. 'The governing idea here is that if a statutory provision is intelligible in the context of ordinary language, it ought, without more, to be interpreted in accordance with the meaning an ordinary speaker of the language would ascribe to it as its obvious meaning, unless there is sufficient reason for a different interpretation.'[7] But 'the context of ordinary language' already involves a certain number of assumptions. Even in ordinary language, words have more than one meaning, eg a 'chair' can be something to sit on, the president of a meeting, or a job as a professor. The ordinary user of language selects the appropriate 'ordinary meaning' according to the context in which a communication takes place.[8] Certain assumptions are made about the most likely use of the words in this context. Those assumptions relate, in part, to the purpose of the speaker or writer— if the word 'chair' is used by a university in an advertisement on the jobs page of a newspaper, it is unlikely to intend to refer to furniture. We still refer to this as an interpretation by reference to 'ordinary meaning' because the reader is able to rely on an immediate understanding of the purpose behind the use of the words without engaging in any further research. If this interpretation of the writer's words proves to be wrong, the reader can rightly complain that a warning should have been given that it was necessary to read the words in a different, less immediate context. Thus, an 'ordinary meaning' or 'grammatical meaning' does not imply that the judge attributes a meaning to the words of a statute independently of their context or of the purpose of the statute, but rather that he adopts a meaning which is appropriate in relation to the immediately obvious and unresearched context and purpose in and for which they are used.[9] By enabling citizens (and their advisers) to rely on ordinary meanings unless notice is given to the contrary, the legislature contributes to legal certainty and predictability for citizens and to greater transparency in its own decisions, both of which are important values in a democratic society.[10]

---

6. *Interpreting Statutes* p 466. See also R S Summers and G Marshall 'The Argument from Ordinary Meaning in Statutory Interpretation' (1992) 43 NILQ 213.
7. *Interpreting Statutes* pp 512-513.
8. See J Evans *Statutory Interpretation* Ch 2.
9. When judges criticise a suggested interpretation as 'literal', they are in fact often disagreeing about the purpose to be attributed to the legislature: compare, for example, Lord Griffith and Lord Bridge in *Francis and Francis (A Firm) v Central Criminal Court* [1988] 3 All ER 775 at 782-783, 790.
10. See D N MacCormick 'Argumentation and Interpretation in Law' (1993) 6 Ratio Juris 16 at 22.

This explanation suggests that there are several meanings which can be attributed to the notion of the 'purpose' of an enactment.[11] The reader may immediately think of one purpose as the reason for a given statutory provision, but may be led to a different conclusion if encouraged to examine the issue more thoroughly. From the perspective of the legislator, there are a number of different levels at which reasons can be given for enacting a provision. There may be a very general aim behind legislation—eg in the case of the Equal Pay Act 1970, to improve the social position of women. Such an aim merely states a broad political objective of which the Act is a manifestation. More immediately, the objective of the 1970 Act was to remove unjustified discrimination against women in relation to pay and conditions of employment. But the actual provisions of the Act are directed to outlawing certain specific forms of discrimination, such as paying women less than men doing an equivalent kind of work; so the purpose, as exhibited by the words of the statute, has a more limited scope. Judges use the concept of 'purpose' in all three senses, but they are usually concerned to relate the third or narrowest sense to situations in which the means provided by the Act for achieving that purpose produce undesirable consequences. In some cases, the provisions of the Act will fail to cover a particular form of discrimination between men and women, and the question will be whether the purpose of the Act can be used to justify a departure from the obvious meaning of the words in order to outlaw this discrimination.[12]

In other cases, conflicts will arise either with other purposes of the Act or with other objectives which the law regards as legitimate.[13] The judge will then have to articulate more fully the purpose of the Act (often in a way that Parliament did not) in order to strike a balance between the various values involved. In some cases, general knowledge or preparatory materials for the legislation, or simply a careful reading of the text, will provide the judge with an immediate understanding of the purpose of the Act. But the more the issue becomes specific—why these particular means were adopted, whether these particular consequences are acceptable in order to achieve the purpose of the Act—the more the judge is left to make a critical judgment of his own about how to develop that immediate understanding into a statement of the purpose of the Act capable of resolving the case in hand. Resort to 'purpose' does not provide a simple solution to cases involving the interpretation of statutory words; it merely sets a context in which judges have to exercise critical judgment.

---

11. J Evans *Statutory Interpretation* pp 54-59 identifies six different senses of the idea of 'purpose', and D R Miers and A C Page *Legislation* pp 188-191 identify five.
12. Eg *Macarthys Ltd v Smith (No 1)* [1979] ICR 785 and *(No 2)* [1980] IRLR 209: discrimination by comparison with the previous holder of a post was not made unlawful by the Act, but was made unlawful by EC law.
13. Eg *Rainey v Greater Glasgow Health Board* [1987] AC 224: the relationship between ensuring equal pay and the employer's need to attract recruits from the higher-paid private sector.

D.   THE MEANING OF INTERPRETATION

In the light of what has been said, one may say that interpretation is the process by which the courts determine the meaning of a statutory provision for the purpose of applying it to the situation before them.

It is hardly necessary to state that the meaning which persons other than a judge trying a case would attach to a statutory provision for the purpose of applying it to a given situation is dependent on their views of what the courts have done in similar situations, or would do in the situation were it to come before them. Throughout the rest of this book it is assumed that the word 'interpretation' is only apt in its application to statutes when there is a dispute about the meaning of words. This excludes the discussion of two procedures which certainly have claims to be described as 'interpretation', the process of determining how words of undisputed meaning apply to an undisputed situation of fact and the process of applying words of undisputed meaning after a conclusion has been reached with regard to disputed facts. These processes are best referred to as 'application' of the statute.

The first of these processes takes place out of court. It is the process followed by legal advisers and any number of other kinds of adviser. Someone consults a solicitor about his rights under the intestacy of a parent or brother. The solicitor gives his advice with confidence on the assumption that the facts are as stated by his client. There is a sense in which the solicitor is interpreting the relevant statutory provisions for his client who may even have read the provisions without understanding them. If it be thought that, in the case of intestacy, these provisions are simple enough for anyone to understand, let the case be one in which a solicitor or accountant is consulted on a simple question of tax liability, when the relevant statutory provisions are almost certain to baffle the layman even though they are clear beyond the possibility of dispute to the expert adviser. Equally, state officials, such as tax inspectors making a tax assessment or civil servants at a local benefits office processing a claim for income support, are most typically involved in the application of rules to the facts of individual situations. Whether it be right or wrong to call this process 'interpretation', it is the process to which statutes are most commonly subjected and one which renders it essential that the first rule of statutory interpretation should be that the courts must give effect to the ordinary, or, where appropriate, the technical meaning of statutory words. The fact that most statutes are 'interpreted' in the sense mentioned in this paragraph out of court is one of the justifications of the restrictions mentioned in Chapter 6 concerning the admission of evidence of the purpose of a statute.

Courts spend more of their time applying words of undisputed meaning to facts which have been disputed than in interpreting statutory words of disputed meaning. To appreciate the truth of this assertion it is only necessary to think of the imposition of prison sentences within the maxima allowed by the various statutes, or the apportionment of damages in the ordinary case of contributory negligence. Likewise the decisions of officials may involve disputed questions of fact, such as whether a person is 'living with' another person in a permanent and stable relationship so as to affect eligibility for income support. The point does not call for comment.

The process of interpretation has also to be contrasted with that of alteration. At first sight, the process of making sense of the wording of a statutory text would appear clearly distinct from that of amending its wording. In *Of Laws in General*, Bentham distinguished the two processes under the headings of 'strict' and 'liberal' interpretation:[14]

> 'It may be styled strict where you attribute to the legislator the will which at the time of making the law, as you suppose, he really entertained. It may be styled liberal where the will you attribute to him is not that which you suppose he really entertained, but a will which as you suppose he failed of entertaining only through inadvertency: insomuch that had the individual case which calls for interpretation been present to his view, he would have entertained that will, which by the interpretation put upon his law you act up to, as though it had been his in reality.'[15]

Liberal interpretation is subdivided into extensive and restrictive. An extensive interpretation applies a statutory provision to a case which does not fall within its words when literally construed; restrictive interpretation fails to apply a statutory provision to a case which does fall within its words when literally construed.

> 'In either case thus to interpret a law is to alter it: *interpretation* being put by a sort of euphemism for *alteration*. Now to extend an old law is in fact to establish a new law: as on the other hand to qualify the old law is *pro tanto* to destroy it. The only circumstance that can serve to distinguish the alteration itself, when made in this way, from alteration at large is, that the alteration goes no farther from what it appears was the legislator's will to what, it is supposed, would have been his will had the case in question been present to his view: from his actual to his hypothetical will. If then there is a new law made, it is made however upon the pattern, and with some of the materials of the old: if there is part of the old law destroyed, it is such part only as he himself it is

---

14. *Of Laws in General* (ed H L A Hart, 1970) p 162. This book was substantially completed in 1782 but was not published in Bentham's lifetime.
15. Words such as 'strict', 'liberal', 'restrictive' and 'extensive' are frequently used with less precision, roughly as synonyms for narrow and broad.

supposed would have destroyed, had the particular case in question come before him.'[16]

Bentham was not opposed to liberal interpretation. He spoke of it as 'that delicate and important branch of judiciary power, the concession of which is dangerous, the denial ruinous'.[17] He suggested that, whenever a statute was interpreted liberally, the judge should draw up a statement to be placed before the legislature indicating how the statute should be amended, the proposed amendment to have the force of law if not vetoed within a specified time.[18] No doubt the implementation of such a proposal would give rise to many difficulties.

In reality, it is not easy to distinguish between cases in which an interpretation is 'liberal' in Bentham's sense of attributing to the legislator an intention with regard to a particular situation which he plainly did not entertain, and cases where an interpretation attributes to the legislator's words a restricted or extended meaning on account of an intention which he was believed to entertain. It is said that the courts have no power to amend the statute, although they may read in words which it can be inferred that the legislature meant to insert.

> 'It is one thing to put in or take out words to express more clearly what the legislature did say, or must from its own words be presumed to have said by implication, it is quite another matter to amend a statute to make it say something it does not say, or to make it say what it is conjectured that the legislature could have said or would have said if a particular situation had been before it.'[19]

But do the courts really confine their activities to putting in words which were already in the statute by implication? Section 3 of the Official Secrets Act 1920 provides that 'no person shall *in the vicinity of* any prohibited place obstruct any member of Her Majesty's Forces . . .' In *Adler v George*[20] the defendant, a member of the Committee of 100, was actually *on* a Norfolk airfield (a prohibited place) when he obstructed a member of the Forces; nonetheless he was convicted because 'in the vicinity of' could be taken to mean 'in' as well as 'near'. Lord Parker CJ said:[1]

---

16. *Of Laws in General* pp 163-164.
17. P 239.
18. P 241.
19. E A Driedger *Construction of Statutes* (2nd edn, 1983, Toronto) p 101.
20. [1964] 2 QB 7.
1. At 9-10.

'I am quite satisfied that this is a case where no violence is done to the language by reading the words "in the vicinity of" as meaning "in or in the vicinity of". Here is a section in an Act of Parliament designed to prevent interference with members of Her Majesty's Forces, among others, who are engaged on guard, sentry, patrol or other similar duty in relation to a prohibited place such as this station. It would be extraordinary, I venture to think it would be absurd, if an indictable offence was thereby created when the obstruction took place outside the precincts of the station, albeit in the vicinity, and no offence at all was created if the obstruction occurred on the station itself . . . There may, of course, be many contexts in which "vicinity" must be confined to its literal meaning of "being near in space", but under this section, I am quite clear that the context demands that the words should be construed in the way I have said.'

Was this a case in which the ordinary meaning of the words was rejected in favour of an implied extended meaning which they were just capable of bearing, or was it a case of rectification by the insertion of the intended, though inadvertently omitted, words 'in or'? The point is a nice one and Lord Parker evidently took the former view.

A clear case of rectification is *Deria v General Council of British Shipping*.[2] Section 4(1) of the Race Relations Act 1976 made it unlawful to discriminate, among other things, by refusing a person employment 'in relation to employment by him at an establishment in Great Britain', and s 8(1) provided further that, for this purpose, 'employment is to be regarded as being at an establishment in Great Britain unless the employee does his work wholly outside Great Britain'. An employment agency refused to recruit three Somali sailors in Cardiff for service on a requisitioned ship due to sail from Gibraltar to the Falkland Islands and back during a military campaign. The alleged ground of refusal was the policy of the agency to recruit crews on the basis that cabins would not be shared by seamen of mixed races. The agency contended that the alleged discrimination fell outside the scope of s 4(1) (and of s 14 which related specifically to employment agencies) because the voyage for which the sailors had sought employment was to be performed wholly outside Great Britain. Now, contrary to the original plans, the ship had docked at Southampton on its return voyage some four months after setting sail, and the crew had been paid off there. The sailors argued that, since the crew had actually done work in British territorial waters, the work which they had sought was not work that 'the employee does . . . wholly outside Great Britain', and that the discrimination thus fell within s 4(1). The Court of Appeal rejected this

---

2. [1986] 1 WLR 1207.

argument, considering that the words 'the employee does his work wholly outside Great Britain' in s 8(1) must refer to the intention of the employer at the time when the crew was to be engaged, and not to what actually happened. Accordingly, s 8(1) had to be read as providing that 'employment is to be regarded as being at an establishment in Great Britain unless the employee does *or is to do* his work wholly outside Great Britain'. The italicised words added to the subsection would make sense in the case of a person refused employment, who would necessarily never 'do' any work for the prospective employer. Furthermore, they would enable the employer to be certain of his position at the time of the act in question, rather than permit this position to be altered by subsequent events.

Rectification may equally cover the exclusion of words. For example, in *McMonagle v Westminster City Council,*[3] s 12(4) of the Greater London Council (General Powers) Act 1986 provided that, in certain areas, licences were required for 'sex encounter establishments', which were defined as including 'premises at which entertainments *which are not unlawful* are provided by one or more persons who are without clothes or who expose their breasts or genital, urinatory or excretory organs during the entertainment' (emphasis added). An unlicensed establishment claimed that it had not breached this provision because its entertainment amounted to the criminal offence of public indecency and was thus 'unlawful'. Lord Bridge held that —

> 'in order to avoid the substantial frustration of the main object of [the paragraph containing the definition] it is both necessary and legitimate that the words "which are not unlawful" should be treated as surplusage and as having been introduced by incompetent draftsmanship for no other reason than to emphasise (quite unnecessarily . . .) that a licence confers no immunity from the ordinary criminal law.'[4]

The foregoing points demonstrate clearly that, if the word is construed broadly, 'interpretation' is a many-sided process.

E. THE CANONS OF INTERPRETATION

It has become common in recent years to adopt Dworkin's categories of *rules* and *principles* to describe the different kinds of legal precepts. These categories may usefully be used to analyse the character of the canons of

---

3. [1990] 1 All ER 993.
4. At 998.

interpretation adopted by the judges. Are they best conceived as legally binding precepts of one or other of Dworkin's categories, or merely as traditions of good practice among judges?

Dworkin characterises 'rules' as being applicable in an 'all-or-nothing fashion', eg the speed limit on a particular road is either 60 miles per hour or it is not.[5] By contrast, 'principles' are values which, if relevant, incline a decision in a particular direction without being conclusive.[6] For instance, English law applies the principle 'no one may profit from their own wrong' but sometimes permits a person so to profit, as when it protects the adverse possessor of property against its owner.

Principles, unlike rules, may conflict without detriment to the operation of the legal system as a whole, and, again unlike rules, they may vary in the degree of their persuasiveness. Of course rules can and do have exceptions, but if two rules are contradictory of each other there is something seriously wrong with the law. No one has suggested that there is something seriously wrong with the canons of statutory interpretation because of the frequent conflict between the principles that statutes should be construed so as to alter the common law as little as possible, and that they should be construed so as to conform to international law.

If we apply Dworkin's terminology to the canons of statutory interpretation, there are two rules, one so general as to approximate to a principle, and the other subject to an ill-defined limitation. For the rest there is a congeries of principles capable of pointing in different directions and incapable of arrangement in any kind of systematic hierarchy according to their differing degrees of persuasiveness. This paucity of rules and confusion of principles amply justifies Lord Wilberforce's description of statutory interpretation as 'what is nowadays popularly called a non-subject'.[7] He has since amplified this remark by stating:

> 'I still think that the interpretation of legislation is just part of the process of being a good lawyer; a multi-faceted thing, calling for many varied talents; not a subject which can be confined in rules.'[8]

Lord Wilberforce was expressing doubts about the subject's suitability for law reform, but the matters which have just been mentioned might seem to call into question whether the canons of interpretation are legally binding

---

5. R M Dworkin *Taking Rights Seriously* (revised edn, 1978) p 24. See also D N MacCormick *Legal Reasoning and Legal Theory* pp 152-153.
6. *Taking Rights Seriously* p 26.
7. 274 HL Official Report (5th series) col 1294 (16 November 1966).
8. 418 HL Official Report (5th series) col 73 (9 March 1981).

precepts or, as Lord Wilberforce seems to imply, simply traditions of good practice.

The following three quotations from speeches of Lord Reid in House of Lords cases may be cited in support of the remarks made at the beginning of the last paragraph:

(i) 'In determining the meaning of any word or phrase in a statute the first question to ask always is what is the natural or ordinary meaning of that word or phrase in its context in the statute? It is only when that meaning leads to some result which cannot reasonably be supposed to have been the intention of the legislature that it is proper to look for some other possible meaning of the word or phrase.'[9]

(ii) 'Then [in case of doubt] rules of construction are relied on. They are not rules in the ordinary sense of having some binding force. They are our servants, not our masters. They are aids to construction, presumptions or pointers. Not infrequently one "rule" points in one direction, another in a different direction. In each case we must look at all relevant circumstances and decide as a matter of judgment what weight to attach to any particular "rule".'[10]

(iii) 'It is a cardinal principle applicable to all kinds of statutes that you may not for any reason attach to a statutory provision a meaning which the words of that provision cannot reasonably bear. If they are capable of more than one meaning, then you can choose between those meanings, but beyond that you must not go.'[11]

The inverted commas round the word *rule* in the second quotation show that Lord Reid was fully aware of the distinction between rules and principles made by Dworkin; but consistency with Dworkin's terminology requires the substitution of 'principle' for 'rule' in that quotation.

The first quotation sets out a rule in Dworkin's sense of the word—the judge *must* ask himself what is the natural or ordinary meaning of the word or phrase in question and apply it to the facts of the case unless the result is something which cannot reasonably be supposed to have been intended by the legislature; but the rule is one which leaves a lot to the discretion of the particular judge. In a great many cases it can plausibly be contended that

9. *Pinner v Everett* [1969] 3 All ER 257 at 258-259. Although formulated in a manner similar to the 'golden rule' described in Ch 1 above, Lord Reid's statement represents a change in emphasis involving a clear focus on the context and purpose of the legislation.
10. *Maunsell v Olins* [1975] AC 373 at 382.
11. *Jones v Director of Public Prosecutions* [1962] AC 635 at 662.

there is more than one ordinary meaning in the context. In that event the judge may consider that there is sufficient doubt to bring the principles mentioned in the second quotation into play; or he may conclude that there is no doubt that one of the meanings is the ordinary one. In cases which come before appellate tribunals it is by no means uncommon for different judges to express diametrically opposite views with regard to the ordinary meaning of a word or phrase,[12] and the same is true when the question is whether the result of applying the ordinary meaning to the facts can or cannot reasonably be supposed to have been intended by the legislature. A decision on the interpretation of one statute generally cannot constitute a binding precedent with regard to the interpretation of another statute. The consequence is that a rule of interpretation, unlike most other common law rules, can never be rendered more specific by decisions on points of detail; it can only lead to the creation of particular rules of construction applicable to particular statutes. All the same, the rule in the first of the three quotations from Lord Reid set out on p 40 does set out a general obligation of the judge in relation to all statutes.

The second of those quotations comes from a case in which Lord Reid entertained doubts about the meaning of the word 'premises' in s 18(5) of the Rent Act 1968. Was the word in the particular context limited to premises which were dwelling houses? There was a wide choice of meanings and no question of avoiding an absurdity produced by the application of the literal meaning. Accordingly, when answering the question raised in the affirmative, Lord Reid considered it was right to review the legislative history of the provision and to lean in favour of the construction involving the least interference with the common law. Although there is no fixed hierarchy of the rules of construction (or presumptions) to which Lord Reid was referring, we shall see in Chapter 7 that some are, in general, less compelling than others.

The third of those quotations from Lord Reid's speeches refers to a rule rather than a principle in the sense in which those terms are used by Dworkin. It is an absolute prohibition on going beyond certain limits; words must not be given a meaning they cannot, by any stretch of imagination, bear. This point was neatly put by Eyre CB in a case concerned with the construction of private documents.

> 'All latitude of construction must submit to this restriction: namely that the words may bear the sense which, by construction, is put upon

---

12. *Newbury District Council v Secretary of State for the Environment* [1980] 1 All ER 731 (where the House of Lords adopted an interpretation of the word 'repository' which Lawton LJ in the Court of Appeal had described as one which 'no literate person' would adopt: see [1979] 1 All ER 243 at 252).

them. If we step beyond this line, we no longer construe men's deeds, but make deeds for them.'[13]

The restriction marks the boundary between interpretation and alteration which has already been discussed.

It is not simply the paucity and generality of the legal rules which distinguish statutory interpretation from other legal subjects such as criminal law, evidence or contract. The rules are of a different kind from those requiring that property must belong to another before there can be theft, or that there must be consideration or a seal to create a valid contract. The rules of statutory interpretation provide criteria for identifying legal rules, and belong to the category of 'secondary rules' of the legal system, to which H L A Hart assigns what he terms 'rules of recognition'.[14] A rule of this kind has a double aspect in that it is both a legal rule and a social practice. Seen from the perspective of the ordinary judge, the rules and principles of statutory interpretation are legally binding statements of the approach he should adopt, even if their content is more general and vaguer than other rules and principles of the legal system. They are more than mere counsels of good practice. The rules and principles for identifying the rules contained in a statutory enactment also form a social practice as to how lawyers should set about this task. The judiciary (and sometimes the legislator) establishes them according to the needs of the particular epoch and its view of the judiciary's proper constitutional role. They thus establish the respective competences of the courts and Parliament in the overall context of developing and changing the law. But, as in other constitutional contexts, the rules are not always stated with great precision and are often susceptible of diverging interpretations. It is the social practice aspect which explains the vagueness and the changing content of the rules and principles of statutory interpretation.

Judicial statements on statutory interpretation are thus not authoritative in quite the same way as those made in ordinary branches of substantive law. They may well be more like statements of attitude or approach, at best expressing principles rather than legal rules. The currently accepted practice is likely to change to a greater or lesser extent from epoch to epoch as the judges adapt to different constitutional environments. Even within a particular epoch there are, as has been seen, conflicts of opinion about the proper judicial role, and consequently about the rules and principles of statutory interpretation to be adopted. These features inevitably weaken the authority of particular statements about the rules and principles of statutory interpretation and indicate that they are frequently to be considered more as

---

13. *Gibson and Johnson v Minet and Fector* (1791) H Bl 569 at 615.
14. *The Concept of Law* (2nd edn, 1994) pp 92, 94-95, 97-107; D N MacCormick *H L A Hart* (1981) pp 111-115.

illustrations of current practice than as binding rules and principles of law. Thus the canons presented in this book should be viewed as expressing the current approach of the English judiciary to the interpretation of statutes. To this extent, Lord Wilberforce was right about the difference between statutory interpretation and other legal subjects.

F. COMMON LAW METHODS IN STATUTORY INTERPRETATION

Since statute and case law are distinct sources of English law, it might be asked whether the ordinary common law methods of reasoning and of elaborating rules can be applied to statutes in the same way as to common law rules and principles. While statute and case-law are thus distinct, they interact in significant ways. Writing in 1908, Roscoe Pound suggested that there were four different ways in which the courts might deal with legislative innovation.[15] First, they might incorporate it fully into the body of the law and treat it as a source of principle higher than the common law. This approach would justify reasoning by analogy from statutes. Second, they might receive it fully into the law to be reasoned from by analogy as of equal status to common law rules and principles. Third, they might both refuse to accept it fully into the body of the law and refuse to reason by analogy, but might give it a liberal interpretation. Fourth, they might give statutes a strict construction and refuse to reason by analogy from them. Pound thought that the fourth hypothesis represented the common law of his day. Cross in *Precedent in English Law*[16] suggested that the second hypothesis applied to English law in 1977 in that 'a legislative innovation is received fully into the body of the law to be reasoned from by analogy in the same way as any other rule of law'.[17] However, this view has recently been doubted by P S Atiyah and T R S Allan.[18] The question is whether statute law and the common law are to be conceived as separate divisions of English law to be handled distinctly. There is a significant amount of support in recent judicial statements for this view, at least in relation to some specific areas of the law. In *Shiloh Spinners Ltd v Harding*[19] Lord Wilberforce said:

---

15. 'Common Law and Legislation' 21 Harv L Rev 383 at 385 (1908).
16. (3rd edn, 1977) pp 166-171; now 4th edn, 1991 by J W Harris pp 173-177.
17. 3rd edn p 170.
18. P S Atiyah 'Common Law and Statute Law' (1985) 48 MLR 1; T R S Allan *Law, Liberty, and Justice* (1993) Ch 4.
19. [1973] AC 691 at 725.

'In my opinion where the courts have established a general principle of law or equity, and the legislature steps in with particular legislation in a particular area, it must, unless showing a contrary intention, be taken to have left the cases outside that area where they were under the influence of the general law.'

The presumption is for a minimum change to be effected by legislation in a common law area, in this case mortgages.

By contrast, where an area is substantially one of creation, the judges are reluctant to admit the use of common law principles to interpret or to supplement the legislative 'code'. In *Pioneer Aggregates (UK) Ltd v Secretary of State for the Environment*, Lord Scarman remarked:[20]

'Planning control is a creature of statute. It is an imposition in the public interest of restrictions on private rights of ownership of land . . . It is a field of law in which the courts should not introduce principles or rules derived from private law unless it be expressly authorised by Parliament or necessary in order to give effect to the purpose of the legislation. Planning law, though a comprehensive code imposed in the public interest, is, of course, based on land law. Where the code is silent or ambiguous, resort to the principles of private law (especially property and contract law) may be necessary so that the courts may resolve difficulties by application of common law or equitable principles. But such cases will be exceptional.'

Similarly, the care of children is governed by a large body of statute law and the courts have treated this as a 'code', so that it limits the scope of the equitable jurisdiction of wardship which can now be invoked only in rare cases not covered by the 'code'.[1] In such rare cases a common law power may be admitted to supplement the legislation, such as the power to exclude members of the public from a meeting where they were causing disorder, even though the statute required that the meeting be open to the public and had not provided for disruption caused by the public.[2] In a statutory area, reasoning by analogy within the statutory 'code' is perfectly acceptable by application of the general rule permitting the use of other statutes on the same subject as a guide to interpretation.[3]

---

20. [1984] 2 All ER 358 at 363.
1. *A v Liverpool City Council* [1982] AC 363 at 373, per Lord Wilberforce; *Re W (A Minor) (Wardship: Jurisdiction)* [1985] AC 791 at 796-797, per Lord Scarman and 807, per Lord Brightman. The use of wardship is now further restricted by s 100 of the Children Act 1989.
2. *R v Brent Health Authority, ex p Francis* [1985] 1 All ER 74, p 123 below.
3. See *Pioneer Aggregates (UK) Ltd v Secretary of State for the Environment* [1984] 2 All ER 358 and the discussion on the use of statutes on the same subject pp 150-152 below.

While the approach expressed by Lord Wilberforce seems to suggest that a statute creates only rules and not principles in a common law area, the approach of Lord Scarman suggests that a statute may give rise to principles capable of justifying reasoning by analogy within a statutory 'code', but that the application of these principles is confined to statutes dealing with the same subject. Furthermore, legislative innovations can certainly be seen to give rise to rules which are liberally interpreted if their purpose so requires and their wording permits it. As will be seen in Chapter 4, the courts do not necessarily permit the extension of a statute by interpretation to cover a case not provided for. As the *Jones v Wrotham Park Estates Ltd* case showed,[4] even where a case is clearly within the mischief of the legislation, the courts may refuse to interpret the statute by analogy to cover it. All the same, they may be willing to bring new developments within the ambit of a provision, provided this does not do too much violence to the statutory words used.[5] But there are clearly limits to the possibilities of an expansive interpretation of a statutory rule.

Reasoning by analogy goes further than expansive interpretation by treating the statutory provision as an illustration of a principle which can be applied generally to other areas outside the scope of the statutory rule. It is clear that this does happen in some areas of the law. A statute which imposes a duty or prohibits certain actions may, in some cases, be treated as giving rise to civil liability on the part of the wrongdoer for breach of a statutory duty or to the unenforceability of a contract by reason of illegality, even where the statute contains no provisions to this effect and merely specifies a criminal penalty or no sanction at all. In other areas, as Atiyah has shown, such reasoning by analogy from a statute is harder to find, and not all judges use this method. All the same, Atiyah and Allan do note,[6] although with disapproval, that statutes have been held to undermine or alter the reasons justifying common law principles, thus creating a new balance of principles within the common law which may lead to further changes in common law rules beyond those already introduced by the statute. Thus the Law Reform (Contributory Negligence) Act 1945 did not merely abolish the common law rule that the defendant needed to be solely to blame for a tortious loss, but also encouraged some judges to treat as abrogated the rule that a person was solely to blame if he had the last opportunity for avoiding the loss, since this latter rule had merely been a device for circumventing the harshness of the old common law rule.[7] Judges

---

4. Pp 19-20 above.
5. See pp 50-51, below.
6. Atiyah 'Common Law and Statute Law' (1985) 48 MLR 1 at pp 22-23; Allan *Law, Liberty, and Justice* (1993) pp 94-98.
7. *Davies v Swan Motor Co* [1949] 2 KB 291. See also G N Gunesekara, 'Judicial Reasoning by Analogy with Statutes: the Case of Contributory Negligence and the Law of Contract in New Zealand' [1993] Stat LR 84.

may see a trend in legislation which encourages them to perceive a change in common law principles and hence to develop common law rules in a new direction. Thus in *Erven Warnink BV v John Townsend & Sons (Hull) Ltd,*[8] Lord Diplock saw in recent legislation a trend towards demands for a higher standard of commercial probity which justified an expansion of the common law rules on the tort of passing off to include the use of misleading brand names. Similarly, in *Universe Tankships Inc of Monrovia v International Transport Workers Federation,*[9] the provisions of the Trade Union and Labour Relations Act 1974 (as amended) conferred an immunity *in tort* for actions during a trade dispute. In a *restitution* action for money obtained by duress, the House of Lords accepted that those provisions, though not directly applicable, could provide guidance as to what constituted legitimate pressure by a union on an employer.[10]

Legislative innovation frequently acts, however, as a disincentive to judicial development of the law. Recent decisions have shown that the courts treat legislative activity in the field of consumer protection as a reason for not expanding the common law on exclusion clauses or unconscionability.[11]

Overall, judges are wary of treating statutes as generating principles which can be applied generally within the law. In some circumstances, this process is undoubtedly accepted as legitimate. But the mere fact that a rule is expressed in a statute does not, of itself, make reasoning by analogy appropriate. Appropriateness depends on the character of the statutory provision and of the common law which it is claimed to affect, as well as of the proper judicial role in the branch of law in question. All the same, it is hard to see how a radical distinction in legal reasoning can be maintained when common law and statute law interact. Where common law principles, such as those of natural justice, are used to help interpret a statute, it is difficult to imagine how one could have one method for treating statutory rules and another for the common law rules used to supplement them. The proper approach for both is simply that analogies are drawn where, in all the circumstances, they are appropriate.

---

8.   [1979] 2 All ER 927 at 933.
9.   [1983] 1 AC 366.
10.   See Lord Diplock, [1983] 1 AC at 385, Lord Cross at 391 and Lord Scarman at 401.
11.   See especially *Photo Production Ltd v Securicor Transport Ltd* [1980] 1 All ER 556; *National Westminster Bank plc v Morgan* [1985] 1 All ER 821; cf *Levison v Patent Steam Co Ltd* [1978] QB 69 at 79, per Lord Denning MR. Legislative inaction may equally tell against judicial action: eg *President of India v La Pintada Cia Navigacion SA* [1984] 2 All ER 773.

G. CONCLUSION

The last section merely serves to emphasise the point that the rules and principles of interpretation and reasoning from statutes represent positions adopted by the judiciary concerning its constitutional role vis-à-vis Parliament in the development of the law. Reasoning by analogy, even more than liberal interpretation, envisages the roles of the judge and the legislator as partners in the cooperative venture of reforming the law, much in the spirit of what Denning LJ advocated in *Magor and St Mellons RDC v Newport Corpn.*[12] A more restrictive approach to analogy and to interpretation reflects the concern for the rule of law and the separation of powers mentioned by other judges.[13] In this view, the rule of law requires Parliament to state clearly what it intends, and the separation of powers requires the judge not to presume that he knows how best to complete the legislative scheme. In between these positions, a whole range of different views is possible. Nevertheless, the current tendencies among English judges would appear to incline away from the role proposed by Denning LJ and more towards the rule of law approach.

---

12. See pp 29-30 above.
13. Notably Lord Simon of Glaisdale, p 28 above, and Lord Diplock, pp 30-31 above.

Chapter 3
The basic rules stated

This chapter begins with a statement of the basic rules of English law concerning statutory interpretation. The statement is made with all the diffidence, hesitancy and reservation that the subject demands. No guidance is to be derived from a statute, for the Interpretation Act 1978, like its predecessor, contains no general principles, and various attempts to enact such principles have come to nothing. There are no binding judicial decisions on the subject of statutory interpretation generally as opposed to the interpretation of particular statutes; all that there is is a welter of judicial dicta which vary considerably in weight, age and uniformity. Naturally, it is the last of these variables which confronts anyone attempting a coherent account of the subject with most difficulty. To quote from the first paragraph of the preface to the 12th edition of Maxwell *On the Interpretation of Statutes*:

> '*Maxwell* might well be sub-titled "The practitioners' armoury": it is, I trust, not taking too cynical a view of statutory interpretation in general, and this work in particular, to express the hope that counsel putting forward diverse interpretations of some statutory provision will each be able to find in *Maxwell* dicta and illustrations in support of his case.'

The practitioner's boon is the academic's bugbear. It shows no disrespect to the author and editor of that admirable work to say that *Maxwell* is useless for anyone hoping for a general view of the subject which has the remotest claim to coherence.[1] Invaluable as those dicta and illustrations must be to a protagonist in search of authority, they cannot all be right for the simple reason that a large proportion of them are mutually contradictory. The

---

1. A more systematic treatment is now to be found in Bennion *Statutory Interpretation* (2nd edn, 1992).

academic must chance his arm at least to the extent of preferring some dicta to their opposites; but he owes it to his readers to make it clear when this has been done. He must also be on his guard against reading too much into the comparatively few dicta and illustrations which he selects.

It is submitted that the following is a reasonably brief and accurate statement of the rules of English statutory interpretation:

1. The judge must give effect to the grammatical and ordinary or, where appropriate, the technical meaning of words in the general context of the statute; he must also determine the extent of general words with reference to that context.
2. If the judge considers that the application of the words in their grammatical and ordinary sense would produce a result which is contrary to the purpose of the statute, he may apply them in any secondary meaning which they are capable of bearing.
3. The judge may read in words which he considers to be necessarily implied by words which are already in the statute; and he has a limited power to add to, alter or ignore statutory words in order to prevent a provision from being unintelligible, absurd or totally unreasonable, unworkable, or totally irreconcilable with the rest of the statute.
4. In applying the above rules the judge may resort to the aids to construction and presumptions mentioned in Chapters 5-7 of this book.
5. The judge must interpret a statute so as to give effect to directly applicable European Community law, and, in so far as this is not possible, must refrain from applying the statutory provisions which conflict with that law.

A very full statement of rules 1 and 2 is that of Lord Simon of Glaisdale in *Maunsell v Olins*:[2]

> '... in statutes dealing with ordinary people in their everyday lives, the language is presumed to be used in its primary ordinary sense, unless this stultifies the purpose of the statute, or otherwise produces some injustice, absurdity, anomaly or contradiction, in which case some secondary ordinary sense may be preferred, so as to obviate the injustice, absurdity, anomaly or contradiction or fulfil the purpose of the statute: while, in statutes dealing with technical matters, words which are capable of both bearing an ordinary meaning and being terms of art in the technical matter of the legislation will presumptively bear their primary meaning as such terms of art (or, if they must necessarily be modified, some secondary meaning as terms of art).'

---

2. [1975] AC 373 at 391. The fact that it occurs in a dissenting speech in no way detracts from the authoritative nature of this statement, which was made with the concurrence of Lord Diplock, the other dissentient in the case.

Rules 1-3 and 5 are fully illustrated in the next chapter. In this chapter something will be said about the context of a statute, the admissibility of evidence concerning the meaning of statutory words, and different kinds of meaning between which the courts must choose in interpreting those words.

A. CONTEXT

As we saw in discussing the intention of the legislature, the meaning of statutory words is determined not by reference to any subjective intentions of the legislators, but by reference to the sense which an informed legal interpreter would give to them in the context in which they are used. The context of statutory words is both internal and external. The internal context requires the interpreter to situate the disputed words within the section of which they are part and in relation to the rest of the Act. The external context involves determining the meaning from ordinary linguistic usage (including any special technical meanings), from the purpose for which the provision was passed, and from the place of the provision within the general scheme of statutory and common law rules and principles.

For some time the law relating to statutory interpretation was bedevilled by the notion that it was wrong for a court to look beyond the words with which it was immediately concerned if their meaning was clear when they were considered in isolation. Blackstone had said that recourse should only be had to the context if the words 'happen to be still dubious',[3] and the notion derived support from Tindal CJ's advice to the House of Lords in the *Sussex Peerage Case*:

> 'if the words of the statute are in themselves precise and unambiguous, then no more can be necessary than to expound those words in that natural and ordinary sense. . . . But if any doubt arises from the terms employed by the legislature, it has always been held a safe means of collecting that intention to call in aid the ground and cause of the making of the statute. . . .'[4]

It is difficult to believe that the notion of construction in complete isolation was ever taken wholly seriously. Nevertheless, even in the 20th century it has proved necessary for appellate courts to administer mild rebukes to judges for their isolationist approach to statutory construction.[5]

---

3. *Commentaries on the Laws of England* (1765) p 60: see p 22 above.
4. See p 15 above.
5. See, eg *Re Bidie* [1948] 2 All ER 995.

However, today it is clear that the internal context includes all elements of the Act—other subsections, sections and schedules, as well as the long title and the preamble (if any).[6]

In determining the external context, it has never been doubted that the date of a statute may be very relevant to its construction simply because the meaning of a word may change with the passage of time and the material time is often that at which the word was used. One of the stock examples is *The Longford*,[7] a case concerned with a private Act of William IV's reign which provided that 'no *action* in any of His Majesty's courts of law' should be brought against certain shipowners without a month's notice. The question was whether the word 'action' was apt to cover an Admiralty action *in rem* and Lord Esher gave the answer of the Court of Appeal in the following telling words:[8]

> 'The first point to be borne in mind is that the Act must be construed as if one were interpreting it the day after it was passed.... The word "action" mentioned in the section was not applicable, when the Act was passed, to the procedure of the Admiralty Court. Admiralty actions were then called "suits" or "causes"; moreover, the Admiralty Court was not called and was not one of His Majesty's Courts of Law.'

It is open to doubt whether this constitutes a rule of general application, or whether it is confined to the interpretation of Acts intended to apply only to a particular grievance current at the time of enactment. In the first edition of this book Cross took the former view,[9] whereas the present editors share the views of Bennion, Burrows, and Hurst that there is a general rule in favour of an 'updating' or 'ambulatory' approach, rather than an 'historical' one.[10]

The somewhat quaint statement that a statute is 'always speaking' appears to have originated in Lord Thring's exhortations to drafters concerning the use of the word 'shall': 'An Act of Parliament should deemed to be always speaking and therefore the present or past tense should be adopted, and "shall" should be used as an imperative only, not as a future'.[11] But the proposition that an Act is always speaking is often taken to mean that a

---

6. See below, pp 123-34.
7. (1889) 14 PD 34.
8. (1889) 14 PD 34 at 36-37.
9. Page 45. Both *The Longford* and the *Hanover* cases (pp 54-55 below) fall into this category.
10. *Bennion* s 288; J F Burrows, 'The Problem of Time in Statutory Interpretation' [1978] NZLJ 253; D J Hurst, 'The Problem of the Elderly Statute' (1983) 3 LS 21; id, 'Palm Trees in the House of Lords—Some Further Thoughts on *Boland*'s case' [1983] Stat LR 142.
11. *Practical Legislation* p 82. See also *Ex p Pratt* (1884) 12 QBD 334 at 340.

statutory provision has to be considered first and foremost as a norm of the current legal system, whence it takes its force, rather than just as a product of an historically defined Parliamentary assembly. It has a legal existence independently of the historical contingencies of its promulgation, and accordingly should be interpreted in the light of its place within the system of legal norms currently in force. Such an approach takes account of the viewpoint of the ordinary legal interpreter of today, who expects to apply ordinary current meanings to legal texts, rather than to embark on research into linguistic, cultural and political history, unless he is specifically put on notice that the latter approach is required.

At the very least, Lord Esher's words require serious qualification. First, the courts regularly apply a statutory provision to new developments in technology or society which come within its original purpose and wording. The former situation can be illustrated by *Royal College of Nursing of the United Kingdom v Department of Health and Social Security*.[12] The Abortion Act 1967 permitted the termination of a pregnancy 'by a registered medical practitioner' in certain circumstances. At the time, only surgical and intra-amniotic methods existed for terminating a pregnancy, and both required the continuous presence of a doctor. However, since 1971 a new, extra-amniotic method had become current, which involved inducing the abortion over a long period of up to 30 hours by the administration of a drug, prostaglandin. The Department of Health and Social Security advised that, as long as a doctor approved and initiated the process, a nurse could lawfully continue it, starting and regulating the actual supply of the drug. The Royal College of Nursing sought a declaration that this advice was incorrect, and that the Act did not protect the nurse in the application of extra-amniotic methods. The House of Lords upheld the view of the department, the majority reasoning that the new method came within the purpose of the Act, designed to liberalise legal abortions. The inclusion of a telephone within the notion of 'telegraph' in the Telegraph Act 1869,[13] or a microfilm within that of 'bankers books' in the Bankers Books Evidence Act 1879[14] are further examples of this process.

No one would suggest that a written constitution should be construed for all time as if the court were sitting the day after it was enacted and, when considering the question whether the British North America Act 1869 empowered the Canadian legislature to abolish the right of appeal from Canadian courts to the Privy Council, Lord Jowett said:[15]

---

12. [1981] 1 All ER 545.
13. *A-G v Edison Telephone Co* (1880) 6 QBD 244.
14. *Barker v Wilson* [1980] 2 All ER 81.
15. *A-G for Ontario v A-G for Canada* [1947] AC 127 at 154.

'It is, as their Lordships think, irrelevant that the question is one which might have seemed unreal at the date of the British North America Act. To such an organic statute the flexible interpretation must be given that changing circumstances require.'

Again, the use of general words such as 'reasonably practicable', as in Part I of the Health and Safety at Work etc Act 1974, necessarily implies that the courts have a power to adjust the application of an expression according to contemporary standards.

In the case of changes in society, the courts may go further. For example, s 12(1)(g) of the Rent and Mortgage Interest Restriction Act 1920[16] provided that:

'The expression "tenant" includes the widow of a tenant . . . who was residing with him at the time of his death, or where a tenant . . . leaves no widow, or is a woman, such member *of the tenant's family* so residing as aforesaid as may be decided in default of agreement by the county court.'

In 1950 the Court of Appeal decided, in *Gammans v Ekins*,[17] that the tenant's 'common law husband' who had had no children by her was not a member of her family within the meaning of the subsection in spite of a prolonged residence with her. In *Dyson Holdings Ltd v Fox*,[18] the same court held 25 years later that a tenant's childless 'common law wife' who had been residing with him for a long time when he died in 1961 was a member of his family. Bridge LJ said:

'If the language can change its meaning to accord with changing social attitudes, then a decision on the meaning of a word in a statute before such a change should not continue to bind thereafter, at all events in a case where the courts have constantly affirmed that the word is to be understood in its ordinary accepted meaning.'[19]

A further example is *Williams & Glyn's Bank v Boland*[20] where it was held that a wife was a person 'in actual occupation' of a house where she lived with her husband, within s 70(1)(g) of the Land Registration Act 1925, even if she would not have been so considered in 1925. According to Lord Wilberforce, the interpretation had to be made 'in the light of current social conditions'.

---

16. Now Rent Act 1977, Sch 1, para 3.
17. [1950] 2 All ER 140.
18. [1976] QB 503.
19. At 513.
20. [1980] 2 All ER 408, on which see D J Hurst, note 10 above.

An updating of more doubtful validity occurs when the purpose of the Act is reformulated in the light of the current state of the law. *R v Brittain*[1] concerned the Forcible Entry Act 1381 (now repealed), which provided that 'none may henceforth make entry into any lands or tenements, but in case where entry is given by the law; and in such case not with strong hand nor with multitude of people'. It was part of a series of measures in the 14th and 15th centuries designed to ensure that people did not settle land disputes by force, and to punish those who took the law into their own hands. For 590 years, the statute had never been applied to a situation where there was no intention to occupy the premises or to assert a legal right to the land. Yet in 1971 the Court of Appeal treated the statute as a measure designed to prevent public disorder and applied it to convict a number of people who had gatecrashed a party without any intention of occupying the premises or claiming title to them. Other attempts to redefine the purpose of a statutory provision in the light of current legal policies have been less well received,[2] and this approach must be considered as still controversial.

The adoption of either an historical or an updating approach not only affects the meaning given to statutory words, but may also have an important bearing on the question whether the court should depart from their ordinary meaning on the ground that adherence to it would lead to results contrary to the purpose of the enactment. This was made very clear by the decision of the House of Lords (affirming the decision of the Court of Appeal) in *A-G v Prince Ernest Augustus of Hanover*.[3] In 1955 the Prince sought a declaration that he was a British subject by virtue of his lineal descent from the Electoress Sophia of Hanover. The validity of his claim depended on the construction of a statute of Queen Anne's reign which provided that the Electoress and the issue of her body 'and all persons lineally descended from her *born or hereafter to be born* be, and shall be deemed to be, natural born subjects of this kingdom'. The preamble stated that:

> 'to the end that the said princess and the heirs of her body and all persons lineally descended from her may be encouraged to become acquainted with the laws and constitutions of this realm it is just and highly reasonable that they *in your Majesty's lifetime* should be naturalised.'

---

1.   [1972] 1 QB 357.
2.   See especially *Ahmad v ILEA* [1978] QB 36, where Scarman LJ proposed to interpret s 30 of the Education Act 1944 in the light of current race relations legislation and of the European Convention on Human Rights of 1950, whereas Orr LJ kept to the original meaning of the section in 1944. See also *R v Barnet London Borough Council, ex p Nilish Shah*, pp 90-91, below.
3.   [1957] AC 436.

The preamble could be invoked in support of an argument that the words 'in your Majesty's lifetime' should be read into the enacting part of the statute after the words 'hereafter to be born.' This argument was accepted by the trial judge, Vaisey J, who refused to make the declaration sought by the Prince. Vaisey J took the view that it is not permissible to take account of the preamble when the enacting words are clear but, in this instance, he thought them unclear because they led to absurd results:[4]

> 'To suppose that Parliament thought that every descendant, however remote in time or distant in kinship of the Electoress, ought to study English law is really rather absurd, however salutary the topic would have been to the immediate successors of Queen Anne.'

But the Court of Appeal held that Prince Ernest was a British subject because the question whether the enacting words led to an absurdity was to be determined by the conditions prevailing when the statute was passed. The House of Lords affirmed the decision of the Court of Appeal in favour of the Prince:[5]

> 'The question is one of interpretation, and it is not in doubt that the Act must be construed as it would have been construed immediately after it became law.'

Like *The Longford*,[6] this case was concerned with a statute remedying a problem specific to a particular time, and this affirmation of the historical approach cannot be taken as applying to the interpretation of all statutes.

The *Hanover* case is of special importance on account of the views expressed in the House of Lords concerning the use that may be made of a preamble when there is one, and further reference is made to this aspect of the decision in Chapter 5. The case is also important because of the broad views taken in the House of Lords, notably by Viscount Simonds and Lord Somervell concerning the context of a statute. They suggest that account may be taken of the general context, including the purpose of the statute and its long title, in determining the meaning of the statutory provision before the court in the first instance, and not merely at a later stage, should it become necessary to do so on account of the ambiguity of the provision. Viscount Simonds said:[7]

> '... words, and particularly general words, cannot be read in isolation, their colour and content are derived from their context. So it is that I

---

4. [1955] Ch 440 at 449.
5. *A-G v Prince Ernest Augustus of Hanover* [1957] AC 436 at 465, per Lord Normand.
6. P 51 above.
7. [1957] AC 436 at 461.

conceive it to be my right and duty to examine every word of a statute
in its context, and I use "context" in its widest sense, which I have
already indicated as including not only other enacting provisions of
the same statute, but its preamble, the existing state of the law, other
statutes *in pari materia*, and the mischief which I can, by those and
other legitimate means, discern the statute was intended to remedy.'

Viscount Simonds's words were cited by Lord Upjohn in his speech in
favour of the majority decision of the House of Lords in *DPP v Schildkamp*,[8]
a case which shows that the place in a statute occupied by a particular
provision may be decisive with regard to its construction. Section 332 of the
Companies' Act 1948 appeared among a group of sections under the cross-
heading 'Offences antecedent to or in course of Winding-Up'. Section
332(1) provided that:

'If *in the course of the winding-up* of a company it appears that any
business has been carried on with intent to defraud creditors . . . or for
a fraudulent purpose'

the court might declare that some of its officers were personally responsible
for its debts. Section 332(3) read:

'Where any business of a company is carried on with such intent or for
such purpose as is mentioned in subsection (1) of this section, every
person who is knowingly a party to the carrying on of the business in
manner aforesaid, shall be liable on conviction on indictment to
imprisonment . . .'

Was it an essential prerequisite of a conviction under subsection (3) that a
winding-up order should have been made? The answer of the majority was
in the affirmative.

The above discussion justifies us in regarding the context of a statutory
provision as including the whole of the statute in which it is contained, title
and preamble, if any, as well as the enacting parts; the place occupied by the
provision within the statute; other statutes on the same subject; the
circumstances in which the statute was passed, and its purpose. A few words
may be added about this last.

The significance of the purpose of the statute in the sense of the mischief
to be remedied and the remedy provided has of course been appreciated
since the days of *Stradling v Morgan* and *Heydon*'s case.[9] It will have been

---

8.   [1971] AC 1 at 23.
9.   Pp 10-12 above

observed, however, that Viscount Simonds spoke of ascertaining the mischief which the statute was intended to remedy from the whole enactment (including the preamble), the existing state of the law, other statutes and 'other legitimate means'. This was a reference to the restrictions to be discussed in Chapter 6 on the use which the courts may make of such extrinsic materials as reports of committees and Parliamentary debates. These restrictions, coupled with the almost total absence of preambles in modern statutes, mean that the courts' opportunities of appreciating to the full the purpose of complicated legislation is limited. At the other extreme, there is a danger that references to the purpose of a statute will become trivial simply because they are so obvious. There is not much point in exhorting a judge to keep in mind the purpose of the generality of the provisions in such statutes as the Offences Against the Person Act 1861, the Theft Acts 1968 and 1978, and the Criminal Damage Act 1971. They are all aimed at the suppression of various types of crime. A further difficulty arises from the multifarious nature of many statutes. One Act often deals with a multitude of subjects and, even when it is confined to a single subject, it may deal with many aspects of it. It is inept to speak of 'the purpose' of Acts such as the Companies Act 1985 or most Local Government or Finance Acts. It is only possible to seek out the purpose of particular provisions and, even when this has been done, it may be necessary to recognise that a single provision has more than one purpose.

Subject to reservations such as those which have just been expressed, it would be difficult to exaggerate the importance of the bearing which the purpose of statutes or statutory provisions has upon their interpretation. The significance of the speeches in the *Hanover*[10] case lies in their recognition of the fact that the purpose is something to be taken into account in arriving at the ordinary meaning of a provision and not, as the words of Tindal CJ in the *Sussex Peerage Case* suggest, merely something to be considered 'if any doubt arises from the terms employed by the legislature'.[11] The notion that the ordinary meaning of statutory words is something to be arrived at by a purely semantic process or, at most, with the aid of the other enacting parts of the statute in which they occur, has been finally exorcised.

The purpose of the statute is also very relevant in the resolution of doubt where the courts are confronted with a choice between ordinary meanings, or a choice between the primary and secondary meanings of a word. Thus, the purpose is material at two stages of the judge's deliberations—first when he enquires whether the words are 'in themselves precise and unambiguous', and second when, having answered that question in the negative, he seeks

---

10. *A-G v Prince Ernest Augustus of Hanover* [1957] AC 43.
11. See p 50 above.

to resolve the doubts arising from the terms employed by the legislature.[12] Certainly in relation to the first case, and quite often in relation to the second, the judge will rely on an obvious or unresearched understanding of the purpose of the statute.[13]

This distinction is subtle but not, it is believed, over-subtle. It is also difficult to illustrate from the *ipsissima verba* of judges for, on the whole, judges are not accustomed to give details of every stage of their reasoning when deciding a point of interpretation, and the attempt to subdivide their reasoning into stages would often be unreal. It is frequently perfectly right and proper for a judge to begin by saying that he has had doubts concerning which of two meanings is the correct one for the purpose in hand, and then to express a preference for one of them on a variety of grounds including, in some cases, the purpose of the particular provision. This can be illustrated by *Bank of Scotland v Grimes*,[14] where the defendant and her husband took out a loan for 25 years secured by an endowment mortgage. They failed to keep up the interest payments and the bank sought possession of the house. Section 8(1) of the Administration of Justice Act 1973 empowered the court to grant relief to a mortgagor who 'is entitled or is to be permitted to pay the principal sum secured by instalments or otherwise to defer payment of it in whole or in part'. Since, under an endowment mortgage, there is no obligation to repay the principal until the end of the loan period, the county court judge held that the mortgage agreement could not be said to contain an entitlement to defer payment of the whole or part of the principal within the meaning of s 8(1).

In the Court of Appeal, Sir John Arnold P confessed that he was unable to make sense of that part of the subsection. Nevertheless, the purpose of the legislation was clearly to provide a measure of relief to those persons who found themselves in temporary financial difficulties and thus unable to meet their commitments under a mortgage. This purpose applied as much to an endowment mortgage as to an instalment mortgage. Accordingly both he and Griffiths LJ concluded that, however obscure its wording, s 8(1) applied to enable the court to grant relief in the case of an endowment mortgage.

On other occasions, it will be equally right and proper simply to say that such and such a meaning is the natural one in the context and to refer to the purpose as one of the reasons for the conclusion. For example, *Mandla v Dowell Lee*[15] concerned the interpretation of the word 'ethnic' in the definition of a racial group against whom discrimination was not lawful under s 1(1)(b) of the Race Relations Act 1976. The headmaster of a private

---

12. See per Lord Simon of Glaisdale in *Maunsell v Olins* [1975] AC 373 at 385.
13. See above p 33.
14. [1985] 2 All ER 254.
15. [1983] 1 All ER 1062.

school had refused to admit a boy who was an orthodox Sikh and so wore long hair under a turban, unless he removed the turban and had short hair like the rest of the boys in the school. Since the Sikhs were not a race separate from other Punjabis, the Court of Appeal held that there was no discrimination by reference to 'colour, race, nationality or ethnic or national origins', but only by reference to religion (which the Act did not prohibit). Lord Fraser, giving the judgment of the House of Lords held 'ethnic' was not limited to strictly racial or biological characteristics in current ordinary language. It had a racial flavour, but was used to include other characteristics commonly thought of as being associated with a common racial origin and making a group distinct. The Sikh community had such a distinctive identity. He then went on to show how this interpretation fitted the purpose of the Act and the International Convention on the Elimination of All Forms of Racial Discrimination to which the United Kingdom was a signatory.

When the purpose of the statute is called in aid to resolve an ambiguity, it has the force of a mere presumption that a construction which tends to suppress the mischief and advance the remedy is to be preferred to one that does not have these effects. This is a presumption which is liable to be defeated by other presumptions, and, in criminal cases, it frequently is defeated by the presumption in favour of a strict construction of penal statutes.[16]

B. EVIDENCE

Except as regards the meaning of non-legal technical terms, the courts do not admit evidence as to the meaning of words. Judges are deemed to have common knowledge of ordinary language derived from 'the ordinary experience of those who read newspapers at the present day'.[17] They are also aware of the legal meaning of words. All the same, in practice, they do rely on dictionaries and previous cases or statutes to support their interpretations. The meaning of a word within a statute is a question of law which it is for the judge to determine, but how that word applies to a particular situation may simply be a matter of common sense or ordinary usage which the courts will treat as a question of fact. For example, in *Mallinson v Secretary of State for Social Security*,[18] the House of Lords was concerned with the question whether the assistance required by a blind person to bathe and feed himself and to walk in unfamiliar surroundings amounted to 'frequent attention . . . in

---

16. See Ch 7, below.
17. Lord Fraser, *Mandla v Dowell Lee* [1983] 1 All ER 1062 at 1066.
18. [1994] 2 All ER 295.

connection with his bodily functions' within s 35(1)(a) of the Social Security Act 1975, thereby entitling him to an attendance allowance. The delegated medical practitioner, acting on behalf of the Attendance Allowance Board, and the Social Security Commissioner both rejected the claim. It was argued for the Secretary of State and stated by Ralph Gibson LJ in the Court of Appeal that, since a blind person no longer had the bodily function of sight, the attention required by him was not *in connection with* that bodily function, but arose from a physical need resulting from the loss of that function. Speaking for the majority of their Lordships, Lord Woolf held that the meaning of 'in connection with' was a question of law and potentially covered the situation of the applicant in this case. Attention is 'in connection with [a lost] bodily function' if it 'provides a substitute method of providing what the bodily function would provide if it were not totally or partially impaired'.[19] By contrast, the issue of whether '*frequent* attention' was required was a question of fact to be decided by the tribunal in each case, and so Mr Mallison's application was remitted for reconsideration by an adjudication officer.

That case illustrates the way in which the characterisation of a question of interpretation as one of fact rather than law is in many cases used to limit the reviewing powers of a superior court or to define the roles of judge and jury in criminal cases.[20]

Even though the meaning of ordinary words may thus sometimes be treated as a question of fact, it is far from being an ordinary question of fact for legal purposes. In the first place, it is usual to think of questions of fact as something upon which evidence can be called on each side. But this is not so in the case of statutory interpretation. Only where a technical term is used or where technical background information is needed to form a judgment will evidence be admissible.[21]

Lord Esher stated the theoretical position with regard to the admissibility of evidence concerning the meaning of words on questions of interpretation when he said:[1]

---

19. [1994] 2 All ER 295 at 306.
20. See generally, I Yeats, in G Richardson and H Genn *Administrative Law and Government Action* (1994) Ch 6; *R v Hillingdon London Borough Council, ex p Puhlhofer* [1986] AC 484, p 80 below; A Briggs, 'Judges, juries and the meaning of words' (1985) 5 LS 314. In *Brutus v Cozens* [1973] AC 854, Lord Reid stated that the word 'insulting' in s 5 of the Public Order Act 1936 was an ordinary English word, not used in an unusual sense, and it was therefore for the magistrates as triers of fact to consider, as a question of fact, whether the word did or did not apply to the facts proved. It was not for the higher court to offer a legal definition. But that approach has not been followed generally in subsequent criminal cases: see D W Elliott 'Brutus v. Cozens; Decline and Fall' [1989] Crim LR 323; cf the 2nd edition of this work, p 58.
21. On the latter see *R v Skirving* [1985] QB 819 where scientific evidence as to the effects of cocaine was admissible to assist the jury to decide whether a manual on its use was an 'obscene' article within s 2 (1) of the Obscene Publications Act 1959.
1. *Unwin v Hanson* [1891] 2 QB 115 at 119.

'If the Act is directed to dealing with matters affecting everybody generally, the words used have the meaning attached to them in the common and ordinary use of language. If the Act is one passed with reference to a particular trade, business, or transaction, and words are used which everybody conversant with that trade, business or transaction knows and understands to have a particular meaning in it, then the words are to be construed as having that particular meaning, though it may differ from the common or ordinary meaning of the words.'

These remarks come from a case in which the question was whether the power conferred upon justices by s 65 of the Highway Act 1835 to direct trees near the highway to be 'pruned or lopped' was confined to directions to cut off lateral branches or whether it extended to 'topping'. It was held that the justices' powers did not extend that far. Evidence had been called on the difference between lopping and topping, but was said to be unnecessary because every countryman is familiar with the distinction. It may therefore be assumed that evidence of the ordinary meaning of statutory words is theoretically inadmissible,[2] although it may be received in practice comparatively frequently. When it is agreed or contended that statutory words have a technical meaning, evidence with regard to that meaning is unquestionably admissible, and it should generally be preferred to information gleaned from other sources such as dictionaries.[3] Expert evidence may well be admissible to determine the meaning of a statute giving the force of law to the provisions of a treaty originally written in another language.[4] Where words have changed their meaning, their original sense will be determined principally from dictionaries based on historical principles.

The second reason why the meaning of ordinary words is no ordinary question of fact is that it is the subject of judicial notice. This has at least two highly significant consequences. The first is that, although the direct evidence of witnesses concerning the ordinary meaning of statutory words is inadmissible, recourse may be had to all the other sources of information which a judge may tap when considering whether a fact is one of which judicial notice should be taken. These include dictionaries. To return to *Mandla v Dowell Lee*,[5] the Court of Appeal had held that 'ethnic' required a common racial characteristic, and both Lord Denning MR and Kerr LJ

---

2. Eg *R v Staniforth, R v Jordan* [1977] AC 699. The difficulty is that the distinction between an ordinary and a technical meaning is not all that easy to draw.

3. *Prophet v Platt Brothers & Co Ltd* [1961] 2 All ER 644; *Central Press Photos Ltd v Department of Employment and Productivity* [1970] 3 All ER 775.

4. See eg *Fothergill v Monarch Airlines Ltd* [1981] AC 251, pp 162-163 below.

5. Pp 58-59 above. For the Court of Appeal decision see [1983] QB 1.

6. [1983] QB 1 at 15.

referred to numerous dictionaries to justify their interpretation. In the House of Lords, Lord Fraser of Tullybelton also referred to a wide range of dictionaries, particularly the 1972 Supplement to the Oxford English Dictionary, in support of a wider meaning. However, the dictionaries were not treated as authoritative, and Lord Fraser found the definition in the 1972 Supplement, which defined 'ethnic' as pertaining 'to common racial, cultural, religious or linguistic characteristics', as too loose. Oliver LJ remarked in the Court of Appeal that, 'I doubt whether one can obtain anything but the most general assistance from dictionaries'.[6]

Textbooks and the practice of the business community or conveyancers may be called in aid on similar principles. Where they are relevant, assistance may also be gained from historical works and purely literary sources. In *London and North Eastern Rail Co v Berriman*,[7] for instance, a will of 1587 and Milton's *Paradise Lost* were cited to the House of Lords to help them decide the question whether a railway worker was engaged in 'repairing' within the meaning of rules made under the Railway Employment Prevention of Accidents Act 1900 when engaged on the routine oiling and maintenance of the apparatus in a signal box.

The other highly significant consequence of the ordinary meaning of statutory words being the subject of judicial notice is that decisions with regard to particular words, unlike other decisions on questions of fact, become binding precedents so far as the construction of the statute in question is concerned. As Kerr LJ remarked in *R v London Transport Executive, ex p Greater London Council*,[8]

'The interpretation of the intention of Parliament as expressed in our statutes is a matter for the courts. Once the meaning of an Act of Parliament has been authoritatively interpreted, at any rate by the Judicial Committee of the House of Lords as our highest tribunal, that interpretation is the law, unless and until it is thereafter changed by Parliament.'

In that case, the Divisional Court simply applied to a different package of measures designed to secure a similar object, namely lower fares on public transport in London, the interpretation given to the Transport (London) Act 1969 by the House of Lords in the previous year.[9] But a judicial decision may

---

7. [1946] 1 All ER 255.
8. [1983] QB 484 at 490. Even if the House of Lords has laid down an authoritative interpretation, it may sometimes overrule its previous decision: see eg *R v Shivpuri* [1986] 2 All ER 334, p 175 below. It should also be noted that, while a judicial decision may count as a precedent on the interpretation of the statute in question, it may not be authoritative for the interpretation of a consolidating statute which re-enacts the provision, unless the wording is unaltered: see p 7 above.
9. *Bromley London Borough Council v Greater London Council* [1982] 1 All ER 129; pp 70-71 below.

limit itself to providing 'helpful pointers'[10]—guidance which is indicative, but not exhaustive, about how general words in an Act should be applied. In such a case, the decision is of limited binding force in later cases.

C. THE DIFFERENT KINDS OF MEANING

In the last chapter interpretation was spoken of as the process by which the courts determine the meaning of a statutory provision for the purpose of applying it to the situation before them.[11] Something must now be said about the different kinds of meaning with which this process is concerned.[12] Distinctions are often drawn between ordinary and fringe meanings, and between primary and secondary meanings; meanings are sometimes described as 'literal'. It is useful to clarify these terms.

It is assumed that when judges speak, as they frequently do, about the 'ordinary' or 'natural' meaning of words and phrases, they have in mind the meaning which would be attached to those words and phrases by the normal speaker of English. This is taken to have been the meaning intended by the drafter or, after due allowance has been made for the metaphor, by Parliament. It is not uncommon for a judge to address directly the question what the ordinary person would understand by the words; but there are limits to the utility of this process in cases of disputed interpretation because everything depends on the context and there is often a choice of ordinary meanings. For example, as Butler-Sloss LJ has pointed out, even a simple word like 'parent' has different ordinary meanings:

> 'The term "parent" must be given its natural and ordinary meaning. It does not follow, however, that that meaning will always include the natural parents. The natural and ordinary meaning of a word is not fixed but changes according to the context in which a word is used. Thus the meaning of "parent" in a school prospectus will include a person with de facto parental responsibility even if not a natural parent, but exclude a natural parent who has no contact with the child. On the other hand, the meaning of "parent" in a work on genetics will be the biological parents, including a father who has no more connection than the initial act of fertilisation. The question is therefore whether

---

10. Lord Bridge, *In Re Smalley* [1985] AC 622 at 644: see p 81 below.
11. See p 34 above.
12. A short introduction to this subject for lawyers is G Williams 'The Meaning of Literal Interpretation' (1981) 131 NLJ 1128, 1149. A good discussion is to be found in J Evans, *Statutory Interpretation* Chs 7 and 8.

the natural and ordinary meaning of a "parent" in the Children Act 1989 can include a natural parent whose child has been freed for adoption.'[13]

Her conclusion, and that of the Court of Appeal, was that a natural father did not qualify as a 'parent' under s 10(4)(a) of the Act so as to be entitled to apply to the court for a residence order in respect of his child after a court had ordered that the child be freed for adoption.

That case shows that the choice of ordinary meanings in a particular context is a matter of statutory construction, which is a question of law for the judge. She took judicial notice of the ordinary meanings and chose the one which she considered to be most appropriate in the context. The normal speaker of English is not often of much assistance with regard to the choice, although he may have rendered yeoman service in indicating what were possible and impossible ordinary meanings just as he renders yeoman service as the yardstick of statutory interpretation, if that be the right word, where there is no problem simply because there is no possibility of a choice of meanings.[14]

Nothing need be said at this stage about the distinction between ordinary and technical meanings, but something must be said about the problem of 'fringe meaning' and the cognate problem of the restrictions to be placed on the interpretation of general words. Both are problems in defining the scope of any ordinary or specialised meaning. Problems of fringe meaning are sometimes spoken of as 'problems of the penumbra', the point being that, in the case of a great many words, there is no doubt about the hard core of their meanings, but different views may well be taken on the question whether the word is applicable to things or situations outside that hard core. No one doubts that a bar of chocolate is food, but how about chewing gum? A fully equipped motor-car is certainly a vehicle, but what if the engine and wheels are removed? Is a bicycle a carriage? Different minds may take different views concerning the answer to these and countless similar questions. In a great many cases the answer will of course vary according to the context in which the problem arises and the courts will be guided by the object of the legislation they are considering; but very frequently the judge can do little more than say that a line has to be drawn somewhere and that he has decided to draw it beyond or short of the facts of the case before him.

---

13. *Re C and anor (minors) (parent: residence order)* [1993] 3 All ER 313 at 317-318.
14. In 'The Theory of Legal Interpretation' 12 Harv LR 417 at 418 (1899), Holmes says: 'But the normal speaker of English is merely a special variety, a literary form, so to speak, of our old friend the prudent man.' In the case of statutory interpretation, the existence of a legal context which can sometimes be very complicated makes the analogy somewhat questionable.

Fringe meaning raises the question how far words extend in ordinary language as well as in law. There is the converse question, usually, though by no means always, an exclusively legal one, of whether any limit should be placed upon the generality of statutory words. We have already had an example of this kind of question in *R v Horsham Justices, ex p Farquarson*,[15] where the general power to postpone the publication of a report of proceedings in court under the Contempt of Court Act 1981 had to be restricted. The problem is, however, frequently solved by recourse to very strong presumptions, such as the presumption that statutes do not, in the absence of express provision, deprive an accused of the general defences to a criminal charge, or to less strong presumptions such as the presumption that *mens rea* is required as part of the definition of every crime. No statutory crime is defined in such a way as to admit in ordinary language of such defences as insanity, duress and necessity, but it has never been contended that these defences are not available. Quite a lot of statutory crimes are defined in absolute terms, but it is by no means uncommon for the courts to imply a requirement of guilty knowledge. The problem of the limitations, if any, to be placed upon general words is not exclusively a legal one, for we shall see in Chapter 5 that there is an important rule of language, the *ejusdem generis* rule (or *of the same kind* rule), which restricts the apparently general effect of words such as 'or other' where these follow words of limited meaning.

The distinction between primary and secondary meanings turns on that between usual and less usual meanings. Many words and phrases have more than one usual meaning since allowance has to be made for a lot of different contexts. But a time comes when it is permissible to say that, though a word is capable of bearing such and such meaning, that meaning is unusual, ie secondary. As Glanville Williams has put it, whereas the primary meaning is the most obvious or central meaning of the words, a secondary meaning is 'a meaning that can be coaxed out of the words by argument'.[16] For example, the statement 'it happened by accident' has a number of usual meanings. In criminal law it may mean either that the accused did not intend the harm or else that he neither intended nor was guilty of negligence with regard to it. In industrial law an employee's injury may be said to have been an 'accident arising out of and in the course of his employment' even though it was deliberately inflicted, as when thugs murder a cashier while robbing him,[17] or pupils murder their schoolmaster.[18] But, if someone says 'X

---

15. P 5 above.
16. 'The Meaning of Literal Interpretation' 131 NLJ 1128 at 1129.
17. *Nisbet v Rayne and Burn* [1910] 2 KB 689; cf *West Bromwich Building Society Ltd v Townsend* [1983] ICR 257 for a similar approach to the Health and Safety at Work etc Act 1974.
18. *Trim Joint District School Board of Management v Kelly* [1914] AC 667.

inherited a fortune by accident', meaning 'so many contingencies in the way of sudden deaths of relations had to occur that the settlor cannot be said to have intended X to inherit anything', the reply might well be, 'I see what you mean, but your use of the word "accident" is rather odd.' 'He acquired a fortune by the accident of his birth' is a statement involving the use of the word accident in what must now be regarded as its secondary meaning of 'chance', although etymologically the word means 'anything that happens'; but, if someone were to say 'X's winning the race was more of an accident than Y's coming second', the reply would have to be 'you are giving the word accident a meaning it will not bear. You should say "the odds against X coming first were higher than those against Y coming second".'

The distinction between the different usual meanings of words and phrases is important for interpreters of statutes because they have to decide which sense is most appropriate in the particular context. The distinction between usual or ordinary meaning on the one hand, and secondary meaning on the other hand, is important for interpreters of statutes because, from time to time, they have to opt for a secondary meaning on account of the inconvenience, injustice or absurdity of applying any of the primary meanings to the situation before them. The question whether a particular 'interpretation' gives the words a meaning they will not bear is crucial, because to do that is not interpretation; but there is a no-man's land between interpretation and making statutory provisions not made by the legislature where words are 'read in' to a section of a statute.

'Ordinary' and 'primary' meaning are often used as synonyms for the 'literal' or 'grammatical' meaning of words, as in the phrase 'literal rule' which figured in Chapter 1. But, when applied to the construction of statutes, 'literal' is often used pejoratively.[19] Then it is the meaning which results from giving to each word an ordinary meaning without much reference to the context and applying the provision to a particular situation without any regard to its purpose. Take, for example, s 8 of the Road Traffic Act 1972. It read in part as follows:

> 'A constable in uniform may require any person *driving or attempting to drive* a motor vehicle on a road or other public place to provide a specimen of breath for a breath test there or nearby if the constable has reasonable cause (*a*) to suspect him of having alcohol in his body. . . (emphasis added).'

The literal meaning of this provision is that, if cases of attempted driving are excluded, a constable can only make the request for a breath test while the

---

19. Eg Lord Griffiths, *Francis and Francis (a firm) v Central Criminal Court* [1988] 3 All ER 775 at 790f.

driver is driving. It would therefore have been open to a motorist stopped by a constable who had every reason to suspect him of having alcohol in his body to retort with the subsequent blessing of the court, 'Too late, I am stinking drunk but I am not, by any stretch of the imagination, "driving".'[20]

An illustration of this kind of argument can be found in *Re M (a Minor) (Care Order: Threshold Conditions)*.[1] Under s 31(3) of the Children Act 1989, a court can only make a care order if it is satisfied that the child 'is suffering . . . significant harm' attributable to the care given to him or likely to be given if the order were not made. The local authority applied for a care order in respect of a child whose mother had been recently murdered by his father. Between the application and the date of the hearing, the mother's cousin decided she could look after the child, an arrangement acceptable to the local authority. The judge made a care order at the request of the father and the child's guardian ad litem, but the mother's cousin appealed on the ground that the judge had no jurisdiction to do so because, at the time the order was made the child was no longer suffering significant harm. The argument was accepted by the Court of Appeal but rejected by the House of Lords. Lord Templeman remarked:[2]

'My Lords, this appeal is an illustration of the tyranny of language and the importance of ascertaining and giving effect to the intentions of Parliament by construing a statute in accordance with the spirit rather than the letter of the Act.'

The purpose of the Act could not have been that temporary measures taken to protect the child should preclude a long-term decision about the child's welfare. Accordingly, it was inappropriate to be preoccupied with the present tense used in the statute—as long as the conditions subsisted when the local authority made its application, the court had jurisdiction to determine whether or not a care order should be made for the welfare of the child.

To take a more extreme example, the Appellate Division of the Supreme Court of Alberta was once confronted with an argument in favour of a construction even more literal. The case concerned the construction of a bye-law directing that 'all drug shops shall be closed at 10 pm on each and every day of the week'. It was contended for the defendants that there was no infringement if a drug shop were closed at 10 pm and opened a few minutes later on the same day. This contention was dismissed with the

---

20. Cf W Twining and D Miers *How to do Things with Rules* (3rd edn, 1991) p 7: 'The Case of the Legalistic Child'.
1. [1994] 3 All ER 298.
2. At 309. The reference is to St Paul (2 Corinthians 3,6) 'For the letter killeth, but the spirit giveth life.'

contempt it deserved and with the observation that no-one but a lawyer would ever have thought of imputing such a meaning to the bye-law.[3] Presumably this is the kind of thing which Stephen J had in mind when he said that it is not enough for the drafting of Acts of Parliament to attain to a degree of precision which a person reading them in good faith can understand, 'but it is necessary to attain if possible to a degree of precision which a person reading in bad faith cannot misunderstand'.[4] The words 'if possible' were well chosen. Relatively little of what has to be said in a statute can be said in such a way that it may not be reduced to utter nonsense by a strictly literal and wholly unimaginative construction.

---

3. *R v Liggetts-Finlay Drug Stores Ltd* [1919] 3 WWR 1025.
4. *Re Castioni* [1891] 1 QB 149 at 167.

Chapter 4

The basic rules illustrated

It is now proposed to illustrate the basic rules set out on page 49 by treating some of the more important or more instructive cases on statutory interpretation as involving choices of the different kinds of meaning mentioned in the last section of the previous chapter. Sections A, B and C of this chapter illustrate rule 1 of our basic rules: 'The judge must give effect to the grammatical and ordinary or, where appropriate, the technical meaning of words in the general context of the statute; he must also determine the extent of general words with reference to that context.' Sections D, E and F of the chapter illustrate rules 2, 3, and 5 of the basic rules respectively.

A. CHOICE BETWEEN ORDINARY MEANINGS IN THE CONTEXT

In a number of cases the choice between ordinary meanings in the context is not a very difficult one. These are often criminal appeals in which the point of statutory construction causing the case to be reported was the last resort or forlorn hope of the appellant. In *Abrahams v Cavey*,[1] for example, the Ecclesiastical Courts Jurisdiction Act 1860 was under consideration in a case in which the defendant had caused a disturbance at a Sunday-morning church service at which some leading politicians were present by shouting out criticisms of their policy. The relevant provision penalises 'any person who shall be guilty of riotous, violent, or *indecent* behaviour at divine service'. No doubt 'indecent' often means 'obscene', but it can also be used by ordinary people in the sense of 'unbecoming' and it is difficult to believe that it took the Divisional Court much time to reach the conclusion that, in

---

1. [1967] 3 All ER 179.

the particular context, the word bore the latter meaning. The court treated the word as falling within the general category of creating a disturbance in a sacred place. In *Mills v Cooper*[2] the defendant was charged with a contravention of s 127 of the Highways Act 1959 under which it was an offence 'if without lawful authority or excuse . . . a *gypsy* . . . encamps on a highway'. Some four months earlier the defendant had been acquitted on a similar charge. A plea of issue estoppel might well have succeeded if 'gypsy', in this context, meant a member of the Romany race, but not if it meant a person leading a nomadic life of no fixed employment or abode, because the defendant might have taken to that mode of life between the two charges. The court adopted the second meaning on account of the other provisions of the section, which were solely concerned with interferences with the amenities of the highway. There was a choice between the dictionary and colloquial meanings of the word 'gypsy' and 'it is difficult to think that Parliament intended to subject a man to a penalty in the context of causing litter and obstruction on the highway merely by reason of his race'.[3]

The decision on the appropriate ordinary meaning depends on consideration of the language used within the context of the provision, taking account particularly of the purpose of the enactment. As Professor MacCormick suggests, 'the "obviousness" of an interpretation of enacted words may, perhaps must, depend on an understanding of the principle or principles which are supposed to inform the enactment. . . . What is obvious is, perhaps, obvious only given . . . a theory of the aim and object of the Act'.[4] We have already observed in *Mandla v Dowell Lee*[5] the difficulty of determining the ordinary meaning of the word 'ethnic'. Was it necessary that Sikhs be a biologically separate race or would a distinct social and cultural identity suffice? The differences of view between the Court of Appeal and the House of Lords related essentially to the limits of the purpose of the Race Relations Act 1976—how was racial discrimination to be distinguished from discrimination on religious or other grounds? A similar reference to the context and purpose of an enactment in order to determine the ordinary meaning of a word was seen in *Re C and anor (minors) (parent: residence order)*.[6]

A word may be capable of more than one ordinary meaning. In such a case, the court will have to decide whether they are all admissible, or whether one

---

2. [1967] 2 QB 459.
3. Lord Parker CJ, [1967] 2 QB 459 at 467. The reference to a 'gypsy' was repealed in 1980, but Lord Parker's interpretation is still used: see *Greenwich London Borough Council v Powell* [1989] 1 All ER 65.
4. *Legal Reasoning and Legal Theory*, p 204.
5. Pp 58-59 above.
6. Pp 63-64 above.

particular interpretation is to be preferred. A good example is *Bromley London Borough Council v Greater London Council*.[7] The Transport (London) Act 1969 imposed a duty on the Greater London Council to develop policies and to encourage measures promoting the provision of 'integrated, efficient and *economic* transport facilities and services' for Greater London. Similarly the operator, the London Transport Executive, had to perform its functions with due regard to 'efficiency, *economy* and safety of operation'. The Greater London Council instructed the London Transport Executive to reduce fares by an average of 25% and decided to make up the deficit by levying a supplementary precept on the London boroughs. The instruction and the supplementary precept were challenged by Bromley London Borough Council on the ground that the statutory words 'economic' and 'economy' were confined to acting on business principles, and could not cover the running of the transport services at a large operating loss and balancing the books by means of a subsidy from the rates. The Greater London Council argued that 'economic' and 'economy' meant simply 'not wasteful of resources', and in no way precluded the decision taken. The Divisional Court[8] held that both interpretations were admissible and that the choice between them should be left to politicians. The Court of Appeal and the majority of the House of Lords disagreed, and held that Bromley's interpretation was the only one permissible, and that the decision of the Greater London Council was illegal. The House of Lords based its interpretation on a review of the history of legislation dealing with London transport.

In other cases, the courts have been unwilling to determine the meaning to be ascribed to ordinary words in such circumstances, preferring to leave the choice of the appropriate interpretation to politicians, administrators or tribunals, subject to judicial control only where the interpretation given to the words is unreasonable.[9]

In the past, some judges have placed too much emphasis on the ordinary meaning without due regard to the purpose of the legislation. For example, in *Bourne v Norwich Crematorium Ltd*,[10] Stamp J declined to treat the cremation of human remains as falling within the words 'the subjection of goods or materials to any process' when deciding whether the crematorium operator could claim a tax allowance for industrial buildings or structures under s 271(1)(c) of the Income Tax Act 1952. But, as was seen in *Re M (a*

---

7. [1982] 1 All ER 129 (CA & HL).
8. (1981) Times, 4 November.
9. See *R v Hillingdon London Borough Council, ex p Puhlhofer* [1986] AC 484, p 80 below. See also *R v Preston Supplementary Benefits Appeal Tribunal, ex p Moore* [1975] 2 All ER 807; *R v Boundary Commission for England, ex p Foot* [1983] 1 All ER 1099.
10. [1967] 1 All ER 576.

minor) (care order: threshold conditions),[11] judges today give due weight to the purpose of legislation.

B.   CHOICE BETWEEN AN ORDINARY AND A TECHNICAL MEANING

Many cases bear out the distinction taken by Lord Esher in the following passage which has already been quoted:

> 'If the Act is directed to dealing with matters affecting everybody generally, the words used have the meaning attached to them in the common and ordinary use of language. If the Act is one passed with reference to a particular trade, business, or transaction, and words are used which everybody conversant with that trade, business or transaction knows and understands to have a particular meaning in it then the words are to be construed as having that particular meaning, though it may differ from the common or ordinary meaning of the words.'[12]

To take the second half of the passage first, in *Jenner v Allen West & Co Ltd*[13] the Court of Appeal held that 'crawling boards' within the meaning of the Building (Safety, Health and Welfare) Regulations 1948 meant boards with battens on them to prevent workmen who used such boards when placed over portions of a building from which the roof had been removed from slipping. The trial judge heard evidence on the point and the ordinary meaning of plain boards on which workmen could crawl was rejected. Similarly in *Prophet v Platt Bros & Co Ltd*[14] Harman LJ made the point that the meaning of the word 'fettling' as used in the Schedule to the Protection of Eyes Regulations 1938 was not to be gathered from looking at a dictionary (from which it might have appeared that the word referred to the lining of a furnace). The 'fettling of metal castings' appeared from evidence to be 'a kind of trimming up of the castings as they come from the foundry'.[15]

It will be recollected that Blackstone tells us that, although words are generally to be understood in their 'usual and most known signification', terms of art must be 'taken according to the acceptation of the learned in

11. See p 67 above. See also *Nurse v Morganite Crucible Ltd* [1989] 1 All ER 113, where demolition was held to be a 'process' within the meaning of the Asbestos Regulations 1969.

12. *Unwin v Hanson* [1891] 2 QB 115 at 119, pp 60-61 above.

13. [1959] 2 All ER 115.

14. [1961] 2 All ER 644.

15. At 647-648.

each art, trade and science'.[16] He illustrates this latter point by reference to the Act of Settlement limiting the Crown of England to the Princess Sofia and the heirs of her body, being Protestants: 'It becomes necessary to call in the assistance of lawyers to ascertain the precise idea of the words "heirs of her body" which in a legal sense comprise only certain of her lineal descendants.'[17] In the case of quite a large number of statutes it is clear that words are used in their technical legal sense; but occasionally there are cases in which the point in issue is a choice between a legal and a popular meaning. Thus, in *Re K deceased*[18] the Court of Appeal held that a judge had power to award a widow who had killed her husband a share in his estate, then in the hands of his personal representatives, even though s 2(7) of the Forfeiture Act 1982 prevented orders affecting property 'acquired' by third parties. In law, the personal representatives had acquired the property of the deceased. But it was held that the word 'acquired' was to be interpreted in a non-technical sense. At first instance,[19] Vinelott J supported this interpretation by noting that the Act had resulted from a private Member's Bill and may not have been drafted by Parliamentary Counsel. Furthermore, the wider interpretation best fitted the policy of the Act in permitting the distribution of property from the estate in deserving cases, even if the beneficiary had caused the death of the deceased. A more controversial case is *Fisher v Bell,*[20] in which a shopkeeper was charged with offering a flick-knife for sale contrary to s 1(1) of the Restriction of Offensive Weapons Act 1959 under which 'any person who manufactures, sells or hires or *offers for sale* or hire, or lends or gives to any other person' any knife of the kind sometimes known as a flick-knife was guilty of an offence. The defendant had placed a flick-knife in his shop window, but the Divisional Court held that he had not offered it for sale because Parliament must be taken to have legislated with reference to the general law of contract, according to which the placing of goods in a shop window constitutes an invitation to treat and not an offer. The court had a choice between the technical meaning of the term 'offer', as used in the law of contract, and a popular meaning according to which goods placed in shop windows are offered for sale. It could perhaps be said without undue exaggeration that, being to a large extent addressed to shopkeepers, the Act was passed with reference to a particular trade within the meaning of Lord Esher's dictum quoted at the beginning of this section; but the decision is best regarded as an example of the presumption that penal statutes should be strictly construed in favour of the accused.

---

16. See p 22 above.
17. *Commentaries* vol 1, p 59.
18. [1985] 2 All ER 833.
19. [1985] Ch 85 at 99.
20. [1961] 1 QB 394.

Section 18(5) of the Rent Act 1968 (as originally enacted) accorded a measure of protection against eviction to a sublessee whose protected tenancy has been terminated by the death of his lessor. The subsection protected him against eviction by the head lessor 'where a dwelling house (a) forms part of *premises* which have been let as a whole on a superior letting but do not constitute a dwelling house let on a protected tenancy and (b) is itself let on a protected tenancy or statutory tenancy'. Did the word 'premises' bear its usual legal meaning in the common law context of landlord and tenant of that which constitutes the subject matter of a lease? The House of Lords answered this question in the negative in *Maunsell v Olins*[1] but only by a majority of 3 to 2. The plaintiff owned a farm comprising 100 acres of land on which there was the farmhouse and two tied cottages. He let the farm to B, who was allowed to sublet the cottages. B sublet one of the cottages to the first defendant, and it was not disputed that, as between B and the first defendant, the latter's tenancy was protected by the Rent Act 1968. B died and his tenancy of the farm terminated. The plaintiff claimed possession of the cottage from the first defendant. Obviously he failed if the word 'premises' was to be given its common law meaning in such a context, and Lord Simon of Glaisdale supported this conclusion in a vigorous dissenting speech in which Lord Diplock concurred. From the sociological point of view, the speech derived its strength from the fact that, when problems arise, persons affected by s 18(5) are likely to seek legal advice. The majority reached the conclusion that the subsection only applied to premises which, for the purposes of the 1968 Act, were to be treated as dwelling houses, giving more than one reason. The lease to B was governed by the Agricultural Holdings Act 1948 and it would be odd if the Rent Act had much to do with agricultural lettings; there is a presumption against any greater alteration of the common law than is required by the ordinary meaning of the words of the statute; and, if asked what he understood by the word 'premises', a farmer would probably not include farm land as distinct from farm buildings.

It should be noted that there may be a choice of technical meanings in relation to a particular word. Thus, in *Re McC (A Minor)*,[2] a magistrate was held immune from a suit for damages in that he had not acted 'without jurisdiction or in excess of jurisdiction' within the meaning of s 15 of the Magistrates Courts Act (Northern Ireland) 1964, even though his decision against the plaintiff had been quashed for error of law and want of 'jurisdiction' in the sense given to the term by administrative law. The immunity was intended to protect magistrates in the exercise of their normal functions even where they made decisions wrong in law, and the decision

---

1. [1975] AC 373.
2. [1984] 3 All ER 908.

the defendant had made against the plaintiff came within the normal scope of his functions.

C. FRINGE MEANING AND THE EXTENT OF GENERAL WORDS

Stock examples of the problem of fringe meaning are provided by *Newberry v Simmonds* and *Smart v Allan*. Each case turned on the construction of s 15(1) (as amended) of the Vehicles (Excise) Act 1949: 'if any person uses or keeps on a public road any *mechanically propelled vehicle* for which a licence under this Act is not in force he shall be liable . . .' In *Newberry v Simmonds*[3] a car which was kept standing on a road, and whose engine had been stolen, was held to be a mechanically propelled vehicle requiring a licence. In *Smart v Allan*[4] the defendant bought a car for £2 as scrap and left it on a road. The engine was rusted and did not work; three tyres were flat and one was missing; there was no gear box or electrical accessories and the car could not move under its own power. It was held not to be a mechanically propelled vehicle, Lord Parker CJ saying:[5]

> 'It seems to me as a matter of common sense that some limit must be put, and some stage must be reached, when one can say: "This is so immobile that it has ceased to be a mechanically propelled vehicle." Where, as in the present case, and unlike *Newberry v Simmonds*, there is no reasonable prospect of the vehicle being made mobile again, it seems to me that, at any rate at that stage, a vehicle has ceased to be a mechanically propelled vehicle.'

No useful purpose would be served by providing a multiplicity of illustrations of fringe meaning, but it must be emphasised that the solution of problems of this nature is one of the most common tasks of the courts in relation to statutory interpretation. Is a bicycle a 'carriage'?[6] Is a goldfish an 'article'?[7] Is orange juice pressed from fresh oranges a 'manufactured beverage'?[8] Is a newspaper competition card a 'literary work'?[9] Is a ship, however large, 'equipment'?[10] Conundrums of this sort are part of the daily

---

3. [1961] 2 All ER 318.
4. [1963] 1 QB 291.
5. At 298.
6. *Corkery v Carpenter* [1950] 2 All ER 745.
7. *Daly v Cannon* [1954] 1 All ER 315.
8. *Customs and Excise Comrs v Savoy Hotel Ltd* [1966] 2 All ER 299.
9. *Express Newspapers plc v Liverpool Post & Echo plc* [1985] 3 All ER 680.
10. *Coltman v Bibby Tankers Ltd* [1988] AC 276, p 120 below.

bread of judges and practitioners. In solving them the courts usually pay due regard to the context; but in many instances the answer must, in Lord Parker's words, be treated as a matter of common sense. The fact that a substantial proportion of the problems of statutory interpretation which confront them cannot be answered on principle is something to be borne in mind when the manner in which the courts perform their interpretative function is under discussion. The dictates of common sense are notoriously liable to produce different answers by different people to the same question, but this is not the kind of difficulty which can be overcome by law reform.

In the context of statutory interpretation the expression 'general words' is a broad one. It applies to any word, phrase or provision which refers to actions, persons or things as a class rather than individually. Plowden's report of *Stradling v Morgan* tells us that the sages of the law have construed statutes 'which comprehend all things in the letter . . . to extend but to some things . . . and those which include every person in the letter they have adjudged to reach some persons only'.[11] A good modern example of this process is *Cooper v Motor Insurers' Bureau*,[12] where a person suffered injuries when riding the motor cycle of a friend who had failed to warn him that the brakes were defective. The injured person obtained judgment for damages against the friend who owned the motor cycle, but the latter had not been insured against third-party risks as required by s 143(1) of the Road Traffic Act 1972. The Motor Insurers' Bureau undertakes to satisfy judgments relating to road accidents, among others, against persons who have failed to take out compulsory insurance. The injured person sought a declaration that the Motor Insurers' Bureau was liable to satisfy the judgment he had obtained. Section 145(3)(a) provided that an insurance policy in relation to a motor vehicle 'must insure such person, persons or classes of persons as may be specified in the policy in respect of any liability which may be incurred by him or them in respect of the death of or bodily injury to any person caused by, or arising out of, the use of vehicle on a road'. The plaintiff argued that 'any person' here included the driver of the vehicle and that its owner was legally obliged to be insured in respect of his injuries. The Court of Appeal rejected this argument. Section 145 occurred in Pt VI of the Act, headed 'Compulsory insurance or security against third-party risks', which began in s 143(1) by making it a criminal offence to use, or to cause or permit another to use, a motor vehicle on a road unless an insurance policy in respect of third-party risks was in force relating to the vehicle. The purpose of this Part of the Act was thus limited to protecting third parties and not the driver of a vehicle. Accordingly, read in this context, 'any person' in s 145(3)(a) was restricted to third parties and did not include the driver.

---

11. Pp 10-11 above.
12. [1985] 1 All ER 449.

Another striking illustration of the manner in which the effect of broad general words may be limited by the courts is the interpretation of s 68 of the Education Act 1944 in *Secretary of State for Education and Science v Tameside MBC*.[13] This section empowered the Secretary of State to give directions to a local education authority if he was 'satisfied' that it was acting unreasonably in relation to any power conferred on it. A Conservative council elected in May 1976 sought to modify plans for the introduction of comprehensive education, due to start in September 1976, which had been adopted by its Labour predecessor, and to retain some grammar schools. The Secretary of State considered that the necessary selection process for admission to the grammar schools could not be completed in time for the September entry, and gave directions under s 68 that the council should retain the original plans for comprehensive schooling. The House of Lords quashed the direction on the ground that s 68 applied only where the local education authority was taking action which was so unreasonable that no reasonable authority would take it, and that the Secretary of State had failed to demonstrate that this was the case here. The general purpose of the Act in ensuring local autonomy in the structure and management of education was thus maintained by a limitation on the scope of ministerial supervisory powers, which appeared very general from the wording of the Act itself.

The maxim *generalia specialibus non derogant* (general words do not derogate from special words) expressing the rule, mentioned in the Introduction, that general words in a later statute do not repeal an earlier statute dealing with a special subject, is a further illustration of the cautious approach adopted by the courts to the interpretation of broad provisions. The leading case is *The Vera Cruz* in which Lord Selborne said:[14]

> 'Now if anything be certain it is this, that where there are words in a later Act capable of reasonable and sensible application without extending them to subjects specially dealt with by earlier legislation, you are not to hold that earlier and special legislation indirectly repealed, altered, or derogated from merely by force of such general words, without any indication of a particular intention to do so.'

Of course general provisions are often given their full general effect for in this, as in most other cases, the courts pay due regard to the context. Section 1(1) of the Representation of the People Act 1983 entitles a person to vote in any constituency where he or she is 'resident' on the qualifying date. In *Hipperson v Electoral Registration Officer for the District of*

---

13. [1977] AC 1014.
14. (1884) 10 App Cas 59 at 68.

Newbury[15] it was held that the Greenham Common women were entitled to be registered in the Newbury constituency even though they lived in tents forming a 'peace camp', inhabiting land on which they were not lawfully present. Their presence on the land was sufficiently permanent and its illegal character was not relevant for determining the place in which their fundamental right to vote was to be exercised.

In at least one instance the context and historical background has led to a vast extension of the meaning of general words. Section 1 of the Affiliation Proceedings Act 1957 provided that: 'a *single woman* who is with child, or has been delivered of an illegitimate child, may apply by complaint to a Justice of the Peace for a summons to be served on the man alleged by her to be the father of her child'. The effect of a series of cases going back for 150 years was that a married woman living apart from her husband,[16] even if they occupied the same house,[17] might apply for a summons and obtain an order against another man. The section derived from statutes of Elizabeth I, and the justification for the extended meaning of the phrase 'single woman' was 'public policy'. 'The law, differently interpreted, would fail to reach a very large proportion of illegitimate children.'[18] The basic idea is that the child in respect of whom the order was sought should have been born outside matrimony and this was made clearer in the earlier statutes. It was even held that a woman living apart from her husband under a separation order could obtain an affiliation order against him in respect of a child born a few hours before her previous marriage had been finally dissolved by decree absolute and therefore not legitimated by subsequent marriage.[19] Devlin J said:[20]

> 'The artificiality of the construction which the courts have given to the expression "single woman" is brought into high relief when a wife asserts against her own husband that she is a single woman. Nevertheless once the point is reached when the fact of singleness is determined by looking at the actual state to which the woman has been reduced and not at her status in the eyes of the law, it seems to me that a woman whose husband has deserted her or cast her off can say to him, with as much force as she can say it to anyone else, that he has reduced her to living as a single woman.'

---

15. [1985] 2 All ER 456.
16. *R v Luffe* (1807) 8 East 193.
17. *Whitton v Garner* [1965] 1 All ER 70.
18. Per Lord Denman CJ, *R v Collingwood and Tompkins* (1848) 12 QB 681 at 687.
19. *Kruhlak v Kruhlak* [1958] 2 QB 32. The rule on legitimation was altered by the Legitimacy Act 1959. Affiliation orders were abolished by s 17 of the Family Law Reform Act 1987.
20. [1958] 2 QB 32 at 37.

By the use of some kinds of general words Parliament deliberately confers considerable discretion on those who apply the statute, thus enabling the courts to lay down rules for the exercise of this discretion. Modern examples of general words include judicial powers to declare void exclusion clauses in contracts which are not 'reasonable', to undo consumer credit bargains which are 'unconscionable', or to wind up a company where it appears 'just and equitable' to do so.[1] The use of such phrases may result in a bulk of case law enough to fill a book or make the least prescient reader realise that there is little hope of understanding the statutes in which they occur without a comprehensive reference to the law reports.

Occasionally, the courts propose a test for determining on which side of a line a particular situation falls, but there is then always the danger that the test will become a substitute for the statutory words which it is the judges' duty to apply to the cases that come before them. This is illustrated by the way in which the courts grappled with the Housing (Homeless Persons) Act 1977.[2] Section 1(1) provided that for the purposes of the Act a person is homeless if he has no accommodation, and that—

> 'a person is to be treated as having no accommodation for those purposes if there is no accommodation—(a) which he, together with any other person who normally resides with him as a member of his family or in circumstances in which the housing authority consider it reasonable for that person to reside with him—(i) is entitled to occupy by virtue of an interest in it or of any order of a court, or (ii) has, in England or Wales, an express or implied licence to occupy . . .'[3]

Nothing in the Act defined what was meant by 'accommodation' for this purpose. In *R v Wyre Borough Council, ex p Parr*,[4] the Court of Appeal stated that it meant 'appropriate accommodation' and decided that this did not include accommodation found by the housing authority in the exercise of its duty to house homeless persons which was 150 miles away from where a person lived. Lord Denning MR explained what was meant by 'appropriate accommodation':[5]

> 'That means of course that the house—as a dwelling—must be appropriate for a family of this size. It must have enough rooms to house his wife and five children. If it is in an area with which he has

---

1. See generally P S Atiyah *From Principles to Pragmatism* (1978).
2. Consolidated in Pt III of the Housing Act 1985, and subsequently amended following the decision of the House of Lords in *R v Hillingdon London Borough Council, ex p Puhlhofer*, p 80 below.
3. See now the Housing Act 1985, s 58(1), (2).
4. (1982) 2 HLR 71.
5. At 78.

a local connection, that is good enough. He cannot reasonably refuse
suitable accommodation in his own area. But it is different when the
offer is only accommodation in a far-off area with which he has no
local connection.'

This definition was applied by subsequent judges. However, in *R v Hillingdon
London Borough Council, ex p Puhlhofer*,[6] a different Court of Appeal and
the House of Lords were forced to admit that this judicial definition was too
rigid. Speaking for a unanimous House, Lord Brightman took the view that
'accommodation' meant simply any place which was capable of being
described as accommodation within the ordinary use of that word in the
English language and without a qualifying adjective. This left a greater
discretion to the local authority in determining whether, given the conditions
of their area and the nature of the accommodation occupied, a person was
'homeless' or not. Rather than requiring that the accommodation should be
appropriate in all cases, the court would only intervene where the decision
whether a person occupied 'accommodation' or not amounted to an abuse
of power. For example, Diogenes in his tub could not be described as having
occupied 'accommodation' within the meaning of the Act. Such an approach
better fitted the policy of the Act, determined from the long title, which was
that of providing the homeless with a lifeline of last resort, rather than
providing homes to those who were inadequately housed and giving such
people priority within the local authority's housing waiting list. On the facts,
a local authority was entitled to find that a couple with two children living
in a guest house where they had a bedroom but no cooking facilities were
not without 'accommodation' within the meaning of s 1(1). Overcrowding
was a relevant factor to be considered, but here there was 'accommodation'
within the ordinary meaning of the word. By rejecting a judicial interpretation,
the House of Lords was thus able to preserve the full scope of the local
authority's discretion and evaluation of facts. This book is not concerned
with the labyrinthine details of the Housing (Homeless Persons) Act 1977,
but the cases point clearly to the priority of the statutory text over judicial
elaboration.

For this reason, the courts sometimes prefer to set out guidelines for the
interpretation of the statute, emphasising that these are not to be treated as
hard and fast rules. This is illustrated by the way the courts have interpreted
s 29(3) of the Supreme Court Act 1981, which confers jurisdiction on the
High Court to exercise judicial review over decisions of the Crown Court
except those 'relating to trial on indictment'. In *In Re Smalley* Lord Bridge
noted that:[7]

---

6.   [1986] AC 484.
7.   [1985] AC 622 at 643.

'If the statutory language is, as here, imprecise, it may well be impossible to prescribe in the abstract a precise test to determine on which side of the line any case should fall and, therefore, necessary to proceed . . . on a case by case basis.'

All the same, he did offer some 'helpful pointers'[8] to the meaning of the phrase, which he later amplified in *Sampson v Crown Court at Croydon*[9] where he suggested the phrase covered decisions of the Crown Court which 'are so intimately bound up with the trial process that they must be treated as an integral part of it' and 'affect the conduct of the trial'.[10] But other decisions taken around the trial were not excluded from judicial review. Thus, neither the forfeiture of the recognisance of a surety nor a legal aid order were excluded.[11] Despite the warning that these did not amount to a statutory definition, subsequent decisions of the Divisional Court claimed to exercise judicial review over decisions of the Crown Court to stay criminal proceedings on the ground that they amounted to an abuse of process, or to quash an indictment, which the judges considered did not come within the two phrases of Lord Bridge.[12] Yet the House of Lords overturned these interpretations on the ground that the issues pointed out by Lord Bridge were not the only relevant factors. A further 'helpful pointer' was whether judicial review could delay the trial, which could clearly happen if a ruling on the indictment could be challenged in this way. This pointed in favour of a wider scope for the exclusion from judicial review of decisions of the Crown Court 'relating to trial on indictment'.[13]

D. CHOICE BETWEEN PRIMARY AND SECONDARY MEANING

The second of our basic rules set out on page 49 must now be illustrated: 'If the judge considers that the application of the words in their grammatical and ordinary sense would produce a result which is contrary to the purpose of the statute, he may apply them in any secondary meaning which they are

---

8. At 644.
9. [1987] 1 All ER 609.
10. At 612 and 613.
11. See *In Re Smalley* and *Sampson v Crown Court at Croydon* respectively.
12. *R v Central Criminal Court, ex p Randle* [1992] 1 All ER 370; *R v Crown Court at Norwich, ex p Belsham* [1992] 1 All ER 394; *R v Crown Court at Manchester, ex p DPP* [1993] 1 All ER 804.
13. See *DPP v Crown Court at Manchester and Ashton* [1993] 2 All ER 663; *DPP v Crown Court at Manchester and Huckfield* [1993] 4 All ER 928.

capable of bearing.' To repeat a quotation from one of Lord Reid's speeches:[14]

> 'In determining the meaning of any word or phrase in a statute the first question to ask always is what is the natural or ordinary meaning of that word or phrase in its context in the statute. It is only when that meaning leads to some result which cannot reasonably be supposed to have been the intention of the legislature that it is proper to look for some other permissible meaning of the word or phrase.'

Likewise, Lord Simon of Glaisdale in *Maunsell v Olins* said:[15]

> '... the language is presumed to be used in its primary ordinary sense, unless this stultifies the purpose of the statute, or otherwise produces some injustice, absurdity, anomaly or contradiction, in which case some secondary ordinary sense may be preferred ...'

The question whether words like 'absurdity', 'anomaly' and 'contradiction' are helpful in this context is best considered after the propositions embodied in the above quotations have been illustrated. Certainly, purposive construction most frequently requires giving effect to the ordinary and primary meaning of the words used, since the drafter has chosen them with care to give effect to the purpose for which the legislation is passed. It is only in exceptional cases that a purposive construction requires the judge to seek out a secondary meaning.

There is much to be said for the view that there is no radical discontinuity between primary and secondary meanings. E A Driedger has suggested that:[16]

> 'the adoption of a secondary meaning is not a departure from the literal meaning; the secondary meaning is the literal meaning in the context in which the words are used. I have come to the conclusion that, except where a mistake is corrected or a meaning is given to senseless words, there is no such thing as a literal meaning as distinguished from some other meaning.'

He goes on to point out that the real distinction is between the 'first blush' or 'obvious' meaning of words and the less obvious. This has much in common with the views of Glanville Williams noted in the previous

---

14. *Pinner v Everett* [1969] 3 All ER 257 at 258.
15. [1975] AC 373 at 391, p 49 above.
16. 'Statutes: The Mischievous Literal Golden Rule' (1981) 59 Can Bar Rev 780.

chapter.[17] The appropriate reading of words depends on context, and in particular on the purpose of the statutory provision examined.

It must be emphasised at the outset that it is only when a secondary meaning is available that there can be any question of the courts' abandoning a primary meaning simply because it produces a result which they believe is contrary to the purpose of the Act. No judge can decline to apply a statutory provision because it seems to him to lead to absurd results nor can he, for this or any other reason, give words a meaning they will not bear. We have already seen this point, in connection with *Duport Steels Ltd v Sirs*.[18] It will be recalled that the Court of Appeal considered that the words 'any act done by a person in contemplation or furtherance of a trade dispute' had to be interpreted as qualified by the requirement that the acts should not be too remote from the dispute, because of the undesirable consequences which would flow from admitting as lawful all secondary action. Although expressing sympathy with this concern, the House of Lords considered that it could not but give effect to the plain words of the statute which covered *any act* done in contemplation or furtherance of a trade dispute. Lord Scarman said:[19]

> 'In this field Parliament makes, and un-makes, the law; the judge's duty is to interpret and to apply the law, not to change it to meet the judge's idea of what justice requires. Interpretation does, of course, imply in the interpreter a power of choice where differing constructions are possible. But our law requires the judge to choose the construction which in his judgment best meets the legislative purpose of the enactment. If the result be unjust but inevitable, the judge must say so and invite Parliament to reconsider its position. But he must not deny the statute. Unpalatable statute law may not be disregarded or rejected, merely because it is unpalatable. Only if a just result can be achieved without violating the legislative purpose of the statute may the judge select the construction which best suits his idea of what justice requires.'

The purpose of the Trade Union and Labour Relations Act 1974 was to grant a wide immunity to unions engaged in trade disputes and so the restrictive interpretation proposed by the Court of Appeal could not be acceptable.

In the context of statutory interpretation, the word most frequently used to indicate the doubt which a judge must entertain before he can search for and, if possible, apply a secondary meaning is 'ambiguity'. In ordinary

---

17. See p 65 above.
18. See pp 30-31 above.
19. [1980] 1 All ER 529 at 551.

language this term is often confined to situations in which the same word is capable of meaning two different things; but in relation to statutory interpretation, judicial usage sanctions the application of the word 'ambiguity' to describe any kind of doubtful meaning of words, phrases or longer statutory provisions. It has been suggested that if, in a particular context, words convey to different judges a different range of meanings 'derived, not from fanciful speculations or mistakes about linguistic usage, but from true knowledge about the use of words, they are ambiguous'.[20] The author of the suggestion was not satisfied with the following answer which had already been provided by Viscount Simonds:[1]

'Each one of us has the task of deciding what the relevant words mean. In coming to that decision he will necessarily give great weight to the opinion of others, but if at the end of the day he forms his own clear judgment and does not think that the words are "fairly and equally open to divers meanings" he is not entitled to say that there is an ambiguity. For him at least there is no ambiguity and on that basis he must decide the case.'

There might appear to be a logical problem with this answer, since the mere fact that at least two divergent interpretations can be reached suggests that there is ambiguity. But Viscount Simonds is simply drawing attention to the position of each judge, who must apply what he considers to be the ordinary and natural meaning of statutory words in their context unless that would produce a result which cannot reasonably be supposed to have been intended by the legislature. Of course, there will often be general agreement about the ordinary and natural meaning of statutory words, but such agreement is not universal, a point which is borne out whenever a question of statutory interpretation is litigated. In borderline cases, judges are apt to disagree about the ordinary meaning of words, and they are equally apt to form different opinions on the question whether there is sufficient doubt to warrant the application of a secondary meaning. This point was put very clearly by Lord Reid when dealing, in a later case,[2] with an argument that he should act on the presumption that penal statutes are to be construed strictly:

'But [the presumption] only applies where after full inquiry and consideration one is left in real doubt. It is not enough that the provision is ambiguous in the sense that it is capable of having two meanings. The imprecision of the English language (and, so far as I am

---

20. A L Montrose (1960) 76 LQR 359 at 361.
1. *Kirkness v John Hudson & Co Ltd* [1955] AC 696 at 712.
2. *DPP v Ottewell* [1970] AC 642 at 649.

aware, of any other language) is such that it is extremely difficult to draft any provision which is not ambiguous in that sense. This section [s 37 of the Criminal Justice Act 1967] is clearly ambiguous in that sense, the Court of Appeal (Criminal Division) attach one meaning to it, and your Lordships are attaching a different meaning to it. But if, after full consideration, your Lordships are satisfied, as I am, that the latter is a meaning which Parliament must have intended the words to convey, then this principle does not prevent us from giving effect to our conclusions.'

A secondary meaning may be wider than the ordinary meaning or it may be narrower. The appropriateness of a secondary meaning depends on the purpose of the statute.

The difficulty for a judge in deciding whether the primary meaning or a wider secondary meaning is to be preferred can be illustrated by two cases. In *A-G's Reference (No 1 of 1988)*,[3] the appellant had been acquitted on a charge of dealing in securities of a company as a prohibited person contrary to s 1(3) and (4)(a) of the Company Securities (Insider Dealing) Act 1985. Those provisions prohibited a person from making use of unpublished price-sensitive information which 'he knowingly obtained (directly or indirectly) from another individual' in order to buy or sell shares in a company. In this case, the appellant was in negotiations to acquire a publicly- quoted company which were broken off by the company's merchant bankers when they informed him that it was about to be taken over by another company and that a public announcement of this would be made shortly. Before that public announcement, the appellant purchased shares in that company and made a profit when the take-over bid was publicly announced. The trial judge directed the jury to acquit him of an offence under s 1(3) on the ground that he had not *obtained* the information about the imminent take-over, but had merely *received* it. The primary meaning given in the *Oxford English Dictionary* for 'obtain' was 'to come into possession . . . by one's own effort, or by request', which supported the appellant's case. But referring to the words of Lord Reid just quoted, Lord Lowry said it was necessary to decide whether Parliament intended this primary meaning or the more general secondary meaning given in the dictionary, namely 'to acquire, get'. The purpose of the enactment was to prevent people dealing in shares while in possession of confidential information, and this purpose would be partially defeated by giving the narrower primary meaning to the word 'obtained'. Furthermore, fine distinctions would otherwise have to be drawn between what is and what is not a sufficient effort to satisfy the narrower meaning of 'obtain', whereas

---

3. [1989] 2 All ER 1.

the Act was concerned with the possession of the crucial information, not the way in which it was acquired. Accordingly, the House of Lords answered the point of law by stating that 'obtained' was not restricted in s 1(3) to the narrower meaning of 'acquired by purpose and effort' but had a wider meaning which covered the situation in this case.

A further example is provided by *Wills v Bowley*.[4] Section 28 of the Town Police Clauses Act 1847 (now repealed in this respect) provided that a police officer 'shall take into custody, without warrant, and forthwith convey before a justice, any person who within his view *commits*' any of a list of some 30 offences penalised by the section. The appellant was charged with the offence of using obscene language in a street 'to the annoyance of passengers' contrary to s 28. In resisting arrest, Mrs Wills assaulted three constables. The magistrates dismissed the charge against her under s 28 on the ground that no 'passengers' were annoyed by the language she used; however, they convicted her of assaulting police officers in the execution of their duty. The validity of this conviction depended upon the lawfulness of the arrest under s 28 which, on first sight, might appear to be limited to situations where a person actually 'commits' an offence. Nevertheless, by a majority, the House of Lords affirmed the conviction holding that the wording authorised an arrest where a police officer honestly believed that a person had been committing an offence within his view. This was one of a family of statutes permitting the arrest of people caught in the act of committing an offence and these statutes did not usually contain express language authorising arrest without warrant upon reasonable suspicion that an offence was being committed. It was necessary that the police should have clear guidance, and the legality of an arrest could not be made to depend on whether the person was subsequently convicted. These considerations, and the analogy with police powers in more recent legislation, notably s 2 of the Criminal Law Act 1967 (now repealed), justified rebutting a presumption in favour of individual liberty despite the absence of clear express language. The minority, Lord Elwyn-Jones and Lord Lowry, preferred a narrow construction of the section in favour of the liberty of the subject. A balance had to be struck between the liberty of the subject and the preservation of public order, and Lord Lowry argued:[5]

> 'in such a contest I would require the arguments to be clear and compelling before I could reject the literal meaning, which conduces to the liberty of the subject, in favour of reading into the statute words which it does not contain, with a view to promoting public order.'

---

4.   [1983] 1 AC 57.
5.   At 74.

The majority considered that they were not reading words into the section, but merely giving it a wide construction.

Lord Reid stated on another occasion,[6] in relation to words whose literal application would defeat the obvious intention of the legislation and produce a wholly unreasonable result, that:

> 'The general principle is well settled. It is only where the words are absolutely incapable of a construction which will accord with the apparent intention of the provision and will avoid a wholly unreasonable result that the words of the enactment must prevail.'

In seeking thus to give effect to 'the intention of the provision', a secondary meaning may be chosen in preference to the ordinary meaning of a word. This is clearly illustrated by the controversial case of *Nottinghamshire County Council v Secretary of State for the Environment*.[7] Section 59 of the Local Government, Planning and Land Act 1980, as amended by Pt II of the Local Government Finance Act 1982, empowered the Secretary of State to issue 'guidance ... designed to achieve any reduction in the level of local authority expenditure (or any restriction on increases in that level) which he thinks necessary having regard to general economic conditions', which guidance could be used as a criterion for adjusting the block grant payable to local authorities. Section 59(11A) required that the guidance 'shall be framed by reference to principles *applicable* to all local authorities'. For the financial year 1985-86, the Secretary of State issued guidance which provided for an increase in expenditure according to two criteria, depending on whether the local authority's budget for the then current year (1984-85) exceeded or was below its Grant Related Expenditure assessment (a notional figure of necessary expenditure based on the authority's particular situation and functions). In a challenge by two local authorities to the legality of the guidance issued, the Court of Appeal held that the Secretary of State had unlawfully discriminated between authorities on the basis of their past expenditure records. Being based on budgets for the year which was, by the time of the announcement of the guidance, almost over, the two criteria were not 'applicable', ie capable of being applied, to all local authorities. However, the House of Lords unanimously reversed this decision. The Court of Appeal's interpretation led to two 'startling' consequences. First, the Secretary of State could only issue guidance permitting an overall increase or reduction in local government expenditure without regard to the situations and past records of individual authorities. Second, it would be illegitimate to mitigate the harsh effects of an overall increase or reduction

---

6. *Luke v IRC* [1963] AC 557 at 577.
7. [1986] 1 All ER 199.

in relation to those authorities which had conformed to government policy and kept their spending to a low level. These consequences were contrary to the policy of the Act in achieving a reduction in local government expenditure. Speaking for all their Lordships on this point, Lord Bridge adopted a purposive approach and held that 'applicable' in the context of s 59(11A) meant that the guidance was 'to be applied' to all authorities, rather than only to particular authorities. This interchangeability of 'applicable' and 'to be applied' could be demonstrated by an analysis of other sections of the Act.[8] On this interpretation, the guidance of the Secretary of State was valid since it applied to all local authorities. The ordinary meaning of 'applicable' was set aside in favour of an unusual, secondary meaning appropriate to the context and the purpose of the Act.

A-G's Reference (No 1 of 1988), *Wills v Bowley* and *Nottinghamshire County Council v Secretary of State for the Environment* are examples of the application of an extended meaning of words in order to avoid a result which was considered contrary to the purpose of the statutes in question. In other circumstances, a secondary meaning may have a restrictive character which is required by the purpose of the Act. We have already seen this in the case of *Cooper v Motor Insurers' Bureau*[9] where 'any person' in s 145(3)(a) of the Road Traffic Act 1972 was held to be restricted to third parties and did not include the driver.

In other cases, an 'absurdity' or anomaly is perceived not just from the particular statute under consideration, but from the wider context of the purposes of the law in a particular area of social activity. Since the legislator is presumed to have intended a result which is coherent and consistent with the statutory and common law rules which he has left in force, the judge will seek an interpretation of statutory words which does not produce an incoherence or an inconsistency in the law as a whole and in the policies which the legislator is pursuing in a particular area. For example, *Richard Thomas and Baldwins Ltd v Cummings*[10] was concerned with the construction of s 16 of the Factories Act 1937, which required the fencing of dangerous parts of machines to be 'constantly maintained and kept in position while the parts required to be fenced or safeguarded are *in motion* or use'. There was an exception permitting exposure of the dangerous parts for examination and lubrication or adjustment shown by examination to be immediately necessary, but this clearly did not apply to repairs and Cummings had lost a finger in consequence of an injury sustained while repairing an unfenced machine which had been out of use for three weeks. He had turned the machine by hand in order to get it into position for repairing, and repairs

---

8.   At 213.
9.   [1983] 1 All ER 353, p 76 above.
10. [1955] AC 321.

could not have been effected if the machine were fenced in accordance with the requirements of the Act. Clearly, there was a sense in which the machine could be said to have been 'in motion', but the House of Lords interpreted these words restrictively so as to exclude a mere transitory manual turning. Referring to the impossibility of effecting repairs if 'in motion' were held to include any movement of the parts, however small, however brief and however caused, Lord Reid said:[11]

> 'The fact that the interpretation for which the respondent contends would lead to so unreasonable a result is, in my opinion, sufficient to require the more limited meaning of "in motion" to be adopted unless there is very strong objection to it, and none was suggested. It is true that the Factories Act is a remedial statute and one should therefore lean towards giving a wide interpretation to it, but that does not justify interpreting an ambiguous provision in a way which leads to quite unreasonable results.'

Since the law in general did not hinder the normal running of a factory, it was reasonable to interpret the section in a way which did not lead to such a result.

All the same, the courts will sometimes be reluctant to adopt a restrictive secondary meaning of statutory words. *Jones v Wrotham Park Settled Estates*[12] could be cited as an example of a refusal to do so despite the fact that the result was contrary to the purpose of the statute. But the House of Lords reached its decision in that case with regret that no other interpretation was possible.

We are now in a position to answer two questions which have been left open. (1) Does the word 'absurdity' used in various judicial statements mean something wider than irreconcilability with the rest of the instrument? (2) Do such words as 'anomaly', 'contradiction' and 'absurdity' denote different issues, and how do they relate to a purposive construction of the statute?

It is submitted that the answer to the first question is in the affirmative; 'absurdity' in this context does mean something wider than irreconcilability with the rest of the instrument, although cases of irreconcilability may be subsumed under the conception of absurdity.[13] *Richard Thomas and Baldwins Ltd v Cummings*[14] seems to afford conclusive support for this submission,

---

11. At 334-345.
12. See pp 19-20 above.
13. This view was once contested by E A Driedger, but he now supports the view stated in the text: see his 'Statutes: The Mischievous Literal Golden Rule' (1981) 59 Can Bar Rev 780 at p 784.
14. Pp 88-89 above.

since a holding, contrary to that of the House of Lords, to the effect that the machine was in motion would, far from being irreconcilable with the rest of the statute, have furthered its purpose, the protection of workmen. There are many similar cases. For example, in *Mallinson v Secretary of State for Social Security*[15] an anomaly would have resulted if a partially sighted person could have obtained an attendance allowance for help with reading or walking in unfamiliar surroundings, but a completely blind person could not, and this would have been contrary to the purpose of the relevant provisions of the Act. As Lord Hailsham remarked extra-judicially, 'There is nothing necessarily arbitrary or improper if judges select restricted or extended interpretations of an Act based less on language than on the nature and purpose of the legislation.'[16] But, as has been pointed out,[17] the context of a statutory provision includes the place which it occupies in relation to other legal provisions and values in the legal system as a whole. Accordingly, a secondary meaning of a statutory provision may be chosen to avoid an anomaly or irreconcilability in relation to those other provisions or values. Both the majority and the minority in *Wills v Bowley*[18] adopted this approach, differing merely on which legal value, public order or the liberty of the citizen, was to be given priority in the interpretation of the section.

Although the judge may proceed in this way with a view to securing coherence and consistency within the law as a whole, this approach is limited by the texts under consideration. This is clearly shown by the case of *R v Barnet London Borough Council, ex p Nilish Shah*.[19] Section 1(1) of the Education Act 1962 requires local education authorities to make grants to students who are 'ordinarily resident' in their area, so that they can attend courses of higher education. Regulations made under the Act required the student to have been 'ordinarily resident' in the United Kingdom for three years prior to his application. The question arose whether persons who had come to the United Kingdom for secondary or other education could count the period so spent as 'ordinary residence' so as to qualify for a mandatory grant under the Act. The Court of Appeal held that they could not.[20] Lord Denning MR and Eveleigh LJ were impressed by the need to relate this Act to the policy of the Commonwealth Immigrants Act 1962 and its successor, the Immigration Act 1971. Under the latter Act, students coming only for study had a conditional leave to stay in the country limited to the purpose of study and this did not involve ordinary residence for the general purposes of everyday life. They considered that consistency with this Act required the

---

15. Pp 59-60 above.
16. *Hamlyn Revisited: the British Legal System Today* (1983) p 68.
17. See p 50 above.
18. Pp 86-87 above.
19. [1983] 2 AC 309.
20. [1982] QB 688.

term 'ordinarily resident' in the Education Act to be interpreted as living as an ordinary member of the community would, which could not include residence for the limited purpose of study. Lord Denning MR argued that 'We must do our best to legislate for a state of affairs for which Parliament has not legislated. We must say what is the meaning of the words "ordinarily resident" in the context of the situation brought about by the Immigration Act 1971'.[1] The House of Lords unanimously reversed this decision. In its opinion, the Court of Appeal had given too much weight to the arguments drawn from the purposes of the Immigration Act 1971. Parliament's purpose expressed in the Education Act gave no hint of any restriction on the eligibility for a mandatory award other than ordinary residence in the United Kingdom for three years and a satisfactory educational record. There was nothing expressed in the Immigration Act which gave guidance as to the interpretation of the Education Act and, indeed, despite a series of immigration measures since 1962, nationality had not formed part of the regulations under the Education Act until 1980. Accordingly, the ordinary natural meaning of the Education Act prevailed to make the students eligible for a mandatory grant if they had resided in the United Kingdom for the purposes of study.[2] Lord Scarman stated that, 'It cannot be permissible in the absence of a reference (express or necessarily to be implied) by one statute to the other to interpret an earlier Act by reference to a later Act.'[3] The role of the judge is not to reconcile legislative provisions unless it is reasonable to infer that this is what the legislator intended.

If the answer to the first question on p 89 is in the affirmative, then there would not appear to be a substantial difference in what is denoted by the words 'irreconcilability', 'anomaly', 'contradiction', and 'absurdity' as used by the judges. Our rules of interpretation have fortunately not reached such a degree of sophistication as to require distinctions of so great a subtlety to be drawn. The construction of s 59 of the Local Government, Planning and Land Act 1980 adopted by the House of Lords in *Nottinghamshire County Council v Secretary of State for the Environment* [4] avoided an irreconcilability between the requirement that guidance be determined by reference to criteria 'applicable to all local authorities' and the purpose of the Act in trying to reduce the expenditure of high-spending local authorities; the construction of s 35(1)(a) of the Social Security Act 1975 adopted in *Mallinson v Secretary of State for Social Security* [5] avoided an anomaly; and the construction of s 145(3)(a) of the Road Traffic Act 1972

---

1. At 721.
2. The law was altered on this point by the Education (Fees and Awards) Act 1983.
3. [1983] 2 AC 309 at 348-349.
4. Pp 87-88 above.
5. Pp 59-60 above.

in *Cooper v Motor Insurers' Bureau*[6] avoided an internal contradiction. In such cases the judges could also be described as avoiding an absurd result. Bennion argues[7] that 'repugnancy, inconsistency and contradiction (all as between different enactments) raise conceptual problems different to those where the "absurdity" lies within a single provision'. Certainly, problems of the internal consistency of a statute read as a whole may appear more readily soluble than those requiring consistency between a statutory provision and other legal provisions or values, where the choice of solutions may be greater and it may be more doubtful whether an attempt at consistency is appropriate. However, problems of internal consistency are sometimes resolved by reference to the scheme of legislation in the same area of the law. For example, in *Re C and anor (minors) (parent: residence order)*,[8] the decision that a father whose child had been freed for adoption was no longer a 'parent' within s 8 of the Children Act 1989 was consistent with the approach of the Adoption Act 1976 to natural parents after an adoption order had been made. Other legal values, such as those expressed in the presumptions discussed in Chapter 7, are also often used to arbitrate between different possible meanings of statutory words. To this extent, the issues of internal and external consistency are not easily dissociated. Consistency with other provisions of the Act is but one instance of the wider obligation of judges to ensure that the provisions of the law are, as far as possible, interpreted in a way which is coherent and consistent.

Since these various words denote substantially the same issue, the use of different words may appear confusing. In the end, the issue always amounts to asking whether a construction is inconsistent with the purpose of the statute. Of course, the judge must have in view not merely the specific purpose of the statute, but also the general purposes of the law into which the purpose and provisions of the statute are presumed to have been intended to fit coherently. Given this double aspect of the consistency which the judge strives to achieve, it might be thought that a general word such as 'absurdity' best describes all the conditions which permit the judge to depart from the primary meaning of statutory words. However, such a term has the inconvenience of failing to make it clear that it is only inconsistency with the purpose of the statute, understood in the light of other legal provisions and values, that justifies this departure and not a judge's more general views of what is an 'absurd' result. For this reason, the second basic rule speaks of 'a result which is contrary to the purpose of the statute', rather than of 'an absurd result'.

---

6. See p 76 above.
7. *Bennion* p 680.
8. Pp 63-64 above.

E. READING WORDS IN AND OUT OF A STATUTE

This brings us to the illustration of the third of the basic rules set out on p 49: The judge may read in words which he considers to be necessarily implied by words which are already in the statute; and he has a limited power to add to, alter or ignore statutory words in order to prevent a provision from being unintelligible, absurd or totally unreasonable, unworkable, or totally irreconcilable with the rest of the statute.

Words may be said to be necessarily implied by other words when their express statement merely clarifies a secondary meaning of those other words. Several instances of necessary implication have already been given. In *Adler v George*[9] the court took the view that, in the context of the obstruction of airfields, the words 'in the vicinity of' were apt to cover someone on a field; the words 'in or' were implied with the result that an offence could be committed by someone 'in or in the vicinity of'. Similarly, in *Wills v Bowley*[10] words permitting the arrest of someone reasonably believed to be committing the offence were treated as a necessary implication in the text. In many cases it is possible to apply the secondary meaning of a single word or phrase without there being any question of implying further words. This was the nature of the interpretation of 'obtained' in *A-G's Reference (No 1 of 1988)*.[11]

The reason why the process is mentioned in rule 3 is that there are inevitably cases in which it is debatable whether the court is giving effect to a secondary meaning or adding words in order to prevent unreasonable results. For example, *Re K (a minor) (adoption: nationality)*[12] concerned the interpretation of s 1 of the British Nationality Act 1981, subsection (5) of which provides that a minor acquires British citizenship as a result of an adoption order if the adopter is a British citizen. Section 1(6) further provides:

> 'Where an order in consequence of which any person became a British citizen by virtue of subsection (5) ceases to have effect, whether on annulment or otherwise, the cesser shall not affect the status of that person as a British citizen.'

In this case, an adoption order was made in respect of K just before her eighteenth birthday, but the making of the order was opposed by the Home Secretary who appealed against it. Counsel for K argued that the effect of

---

9. See pp 36-37 above.
10. See pp 86-87 above.
11. See pp 85-86 above.
12. [1994] 3 All ER 553.

s 1(6) was that, even if the appeal were allowed and the adoption order ceased to have effect, the child would not lose the British citizenship acquired under s 1(5) by virtue of that order. The Court of Appeal refused to accept the argument. Balcombe LJ argued that 'the right of a party to proceedings to be entitled to appeal against any order made in those proceedings is so fundamental a right that I would expect Parliament to have used express language if it intended to abrogate or limit that right'.[13] Section 1(6) could not be interpreted so as to deny the Home Secretary any effective right of appeal, and so the word 'order' had to be limited to mean 'an order made subsequently to the adoption proceedings' and not an order made on appeal in the adoption proceedings themselves.[14] The Court of Appeal did not specifically state that it was adding words to the text, but its interpretation had a similar effect.

An example of the exercise of the power to add to the words of a statute in order to prevent a provision from having a result clearly contrary to the plain intention of the rest of the statute was the decision of the Court of Appeal in *Deria v General Council of British Shipping*.[15] There s 8(1) of the Race Relations Act 1976 was read as providing that 'employment is to be regarded as being at an establishment in Great Britain unless the employee does *or is to do* his work wholly outside Great Britain', the italicised words being necessary to prevent initially permissible discrimination from being rendered unlawful by changes in the location of employment several months later. Such a case demonstrates that the criticisms of judicial legislation in *Duport Steels*[16] and *Ex p Shah*[17] should not be treated as precluding a judicial power to read words into statutes beyond those which are already there by necessary implication. A more elaborate attempt to lay down the limits of the power to read words into a statute was made in *Western Bank Ltd v Schindler*.[18] The defendant had entered into a mortgage under which he was liable to repay the capital, with interest, after ten years, but was under no obligation to pay any interest until then. The mortgagee applied to the court to take possession of mortgaged property under his common law right to possession, exercisable irrespective of any default. Section 36(1) of the Administration of Justice Act 1970 gives the court a power to defer a possession order 'if it appears to the court that in the event of its exercising the power the mortgagor is likely to be able within a reasonable period to pay any sums due under the mortgage or to remedy a default consisting of a breach of any other obligation arising under or by virtue of the mortgage'.

---

13. At 557.
14. Ibid.
15. See pp 37-38 above.
16. *Duport Steels Ltd v Sirs* [1980] 1 All ER 529.
17. See pp 90-91 above.
18. [1977] Ch 1.

A literal reading would suggest that the court's powers are limited to cases where the mortgagor is in default under the mortgage agreement. Here, the defendant mortgagor was held not to be in default under the mortgage, because the ten years had not elapsed at the end of which the repayment of the capital with interest was required; and the mortgagee argued that, there being no default, s 36 was inapplicable. The Court of Appeal rejected this argument. Both Buckley and Scarman LJJ considered that it would be manifestly unfair if the court were to have a discretionary power to defer an order for possession where the mortgagor was in default, but no such power where he was not. They considered that the conditional clause in the subsection must be read as applying only in cases involving a default, and that its meaning would be clear if it had read 'but, if any sum is due under the mortgage or the mortgagor is in default . . . [the court may exercise its power to defer possession] only if it appears to the court . . .' Scarman LJ distinguished this approach from judicial legislation:

> 'Judicial legislation is not an option open to an English judge. Our courts are not required, as are, for instance, the Swiss courts (see the Swiss Civil Code, articles 1 and 2), to declare and insert into legislation rules which the judge would have put there, had he been the legislator. But our courts do have the duty of giving effect to the intention of Parliament, if it be possible, even though the process requires a strained construction of the language used or the insertion of words in order to do so. . . . The line between judicial legislation, which our law does not permit, and judicial interpretation in a way best designed to give effect to the intention of Parliament is not an easy one to draw. Suffice it to say that before our courts can imply words into a statute the statutory intention must be plain and the insertion not too big, or too much at variance with the language used by the legislature. The courts will strain against . . . leaving unfilled the "casus omissus".'[19]

This approach seems to go further than what might be added to a text by necessary implication.

Some allowance must at least be made for obvious drafting errors. For example, s 33 of the Fines and Recoveries Act 1833 provided that, if the protector of a settlement should be convicted of felony, or an infant, the Court of Chancery should be the protector in lieu of the infant. The convicted felon was obviously omitted in error, and, in *Re Wainewright*,[20] Lord Lyndhurst held that the omission should be made good by supplying

---

19. At 18.
20. (1843) 1 Ph 258.

the words 'in lieu of the person who shall be convicted' before the reference to the infant.

Although most of the cases happen to be concerned with the substitution rather than the addition of words, modern judges are generally prepared to describe what they are doing in more realistic terms than their predecessors. All the same, many of them will prefer not to express what they are doing as a rectification of the statutory words. For example, *Johnson v Moreton*[1] concerned the interpretation of s 24 of the Agricultural Holdings Act 1948, which, unlike other sections in the Act, did not provide that 'this section shall have effect notwithstanding any agreement to the contrary'. Nevertheless, the House of Lords held that a tenant could exercise his right under the section to apply to the Agricultural Land Tribunal, despite his agreement with his landlord to the contrary. Their Lordships based their interpretation on the policy which the Act was designed to serve, namely the protection of tenants in the interests of promoting agricultural efficiency. In this instance, all their Lordships preferred to say that the granting of the right to apply to the Agricultural Lands Tribunal should be construed as a mandatory provision of the Agricultural Holdings Act 1948, rather than to say that they were adding words to the section.

One of the frankest statements concerning the power to go further than merely giving a statutory provision a secondary meaning and stating expressly what was already implied is that of MacKinnon LJ in *Sutherland Publishing Co Ltd v Caxton Publishing Co Ltd*:[2]

> 'When the purpose of an enactment is clear, it is often legitimate, because it is necessary, to put a strained interpretation upon some words which have been inadvertently used, and of which the plain meaning would defeat the obvious intention of the legislature. It may even be necessary, and therefore legitimate, to substitute for an inept word or words that which such intention requires. The most striking example of this I think is one passage in the Carriage of Goods by Sea Act 1924, where to prevent a result so nonsensical that the legislature cannot have intended it, it has been held necessary and legitimate to substitute the word "and" for the word "or". The violence of this operation has, I think, been minimised by saying that in this place the word "or" must be taken to mean "and". That is a cowardly evasion. In truth one word is substituted for another. For "or" can never mean "and".'

---

1. [1980] AC 37.
2. [1938] Ch 174 at 201.

MacKinnon LJ was presumably referring to *R F Brown & Co Ltd v T and J Harrison*[3] where, as MacKinnon J, he had held that, in a provision of the Carriage of Goods by Sea Act 1924, 'or' could not be read as conjunctive, although he was prepared to treat 'and' as substituted for 'or'. He omitted to say that, although the Court of Appeal affirmed his decision, they did so on the ground that 'or' could sometimes be construed conjunctively in order to avoid an absurdity, Atkin LJ feeling constrained to characterise the argument that 'or' could never mean 'and' as the worst point that had ever been taken in the Court of Appeal in his time. MacKinnon LJ was partially vindicated by the decision of the House of Lords in *Federal Steam Navigation Co Ltd v Department of Trade and Industry*,[4] where Lord Reid agreed that 'or' can never mean 'and', adding that decisions suggesting that, as a matter of construction, it could do so were wrong; but he reaffirmed the existence of a power to substitute 'and' for 'or' although he was one of the two dissentients who thought that it ought not to have been exercised on the particular facts. Both defendants were charged with contravening s 1 of the Oil in Navigable Waters Act 1955 which read in part as follows: 'If any oil . . . is discharged from a British ship . . . into a part of the sea which is a prohibited sea area . . . *the owner or master* of the ship shall be guilty of an offence.' The defendants were respectively the owner and master of a British ship from which oil had been discharged into a prohibited sea area. Both of them were convicted and they appealed unsuccessfully to the Court of Appeal. In the House of Lords a majority of 3 to 2 was in favour of dismissing their appeals. All the Law Lords agreed that the House had power to treat the section as though the relevant words were 'the owner and the master or each of them' or, to put it more shortly, 'the owner and/or the master'. What divided the House was the question whether the concept of a criminal offence, with regard to which the prosecution had an unfettered discretion to select which of two persons should be proceeded against, was such a legal monstrosity that it had to be avoided by the application to the section of what Lord Wilberforce, a member of the majority, regarded as 'surgery rather than therapeutics'.[5] MacKinnon LJ's vindication has been described as partial because Lord Salmon expressly, and Lord Morris and Lord Simon by implication, did not commit themselves on the linguistic question whether 'or' could ever mean 'and'. Granted that a court has power to substitute 'and' for 'or' in the reading of a statute the linguistic question is legally irrelevant.

---

3.   (1927) 43 TLR 394, affirmed by the Court of Appeal at 633.
4.   [1974] 2 All ER 97.
5.   At 111.

R v Oakes[6] is the converse of *Federal Steam Navigation Co Ltd v Department of Trade and Industry*, for 'or' was substituted for 'and'. Oakes was charged with doing an act preparatory to the commission of an offence under the Official Secrets Act 1911. Section 7 of the Official Secrets Act 1920 reads:

> 'Any person who attempts to commit any offence under the Official Secrets Act 1911, or this Act, or solicits or incites or endeavours to persuade another, or aids or abets *and* does any act preparatory to the commission of an offence under the Official Secrets Act 1911 or this Act shall be guilty . . . '

It was unsuccessfully argued at first instance and on appeal that the indictment disclosed no offence because Oakes was not charged with attempting, inciting, aiding or abetting the commission of an offence in addition to doing a preparatory act. Lord Parker's answer was:[7]

> 'It seems to this court that where the literal reading of a statute, and a penal statute, produces an intelligible result, clearly there is no ground for reading in words or changing words according to what may be the supposed intention of Parliament. But here we venture to think that the result is unintelligible.'

The courts seem to have had fewer inhibitions about ignoring statutory words than about adding to and altering them. For example, in *McMonagle v Westminster City Council*[8] the words 'are not unlawful' were ignored in the interpretation of requirements for a licence for a sex encounter establishment under the Greater London Council (General Powers) Act 1986. Another clear example is *R v Registrar General, ex p Smith*.[9] Section 51(1) of the Adoption Act 1976 provides:

> ' . . . the Registrar General shall on an application made in the prescribed manner by an adopted person a record of whose birth is kept by the Registrar General and who has attained the age of 18 years supply to that person on payment of the prescribed fee (if any) such

---

6.   [1959] 2 QB 350.
7.   At 354.
8.   See p 38 above.
9.   [1990] 2 All ER 170. Another example of qualifying apparently absolute entitlements on grounds of public policy is *R v National Insurance Commr, ex p Connor* [1981] 1 All ER 769, where the provisions of s 24 of the Social Security Act 1975 that '[a] woman who has been widowed shall be entitled to a widow's allowance' were held not to apply where the woman in question had killed her husband.

information as is necessary to enable that person to obtain a certified copy of the record of his birth.'

Smith was such a person, but the Registrar General refused to give him the necessary information because he was a patient in a secure mental hospital (Broadmoor), having been convicted, inter alia, of the manslaughter of a cellmate whom he mistook for his adoptive mother. The Registrar was afraid that Smith would use the actual record of his birth to trace his real mother and perhaps to do violence to her. The Divisional Court had no difficulty in upholding the decision of the Registrar General. The grammatically mandatory words of s 51(1) were ignored so as to deny the applicant a statutory right where there was a real risk that it would be used for future criminality. To treat the right as absolute would outrage the public. Watkins LJ considered that it did not matter that there was no precedent for the Registrar General's argument:[10]

'If what we deem to be an appropriate head of public policy is apparently novel and wanting until now of expression being given to it, that is no reason at all to deny it a place in the relevant law.'

Although this might be seen as an example of ellipsis, in reality this case exemplifies not the deliberate omission of the obvious by a drafter, but his inability to foresee all contingencies.

The power to add to, alter or ignore statutory words is an extremely limited one. Generally speaking, it can only be exercised where there has been a demonstrable mistake on the part of the drafter or where the consequence of applying the words in their ordinary, or discernible secondary, meaning would be utterly unreasonable. Even then the mistake may be thought to be beyond correction by the court, or the tenor of the statute may be such as to preclude the addition of words to avoid an unreasonable result. In the past, Lord Macmillan argued that, where Parliament had 'plainly missed fire'[11] by using language which failed to achieve its objective, then the courts could do nothing. But this has been criticised more recently. Lord Diplock retorted extra-judicially that, if the courts can identify the target of Parliamentary legislation, 'their proper function is to see that it is hit; not merely to record that it has been missed'.[12] Lord Diplock's approach has been supported more recently in *BBC Enterprises Ltd v Hi-Tech Xtravision Ltd.*[13] Section 298(2)

---

10. [1990] 2 All ER 170 at 175.

11. Lord Macmillan, *IRC v Ayrshire Employers' Mutual Insurance Association Ltd* [1946] 1 All ER 637 at 641.

12. *Courts and Legislators* (1965) p 10, reprinted in B Harvey (ed) *The Lawyer and Justice* (1978) p 274.

13. [1991] 3 All ER 257.

of the Copyright, Designs and Patents Act 1988 gave to a person making charges for the reception of programmes the same rights and remedies as a copyright holder against any person making, importing, selling or letting any apparatus or device 'to enable or assist persons to receive the programmes or other transmissions when they are not entitled to do so'. In this case the defendants made and sold decoders to enable television viewers to watch satellite programmes produced by the plaintiffs who had authorised another company to sell decoders for its programmes. BBC Enterprises sought an injunction to prevent the defendants continuing to make and sell their decoders. At first instance, Scott J held that no action lay since s 298 was limited to where the people receiving the programmes were acting unlawfully, but simply watching programmes without the authorisation of the broadcaster did not infringe any of that person's rights. The Court of Appeal and House of Lords considered that such an interpretation would render s 298 ineffective. Staughton LJ argued that:[14]

> 'Save perhaps in revenue and penal enactments, I consider that the courts should now be very reluctant to hold that Parliament has achieved nothing by the language it used, when it is tolerably plain what Parliament wished to achieve.'

Sir Nicolas Browne-Wilkinson V-C noted that the White Paper preceding the Act had acknowledged that unauthorised viewing of programmes did not infringe any rights of the broadcaster, so that it could not be presumed that Parliament had made a mistake in choosing its words. Instead, he and the House of Lords preferred to interpret the words 'when they are not entitled to do so' as meaning 'when they are not authorised by the providor of the programmes . . . to do so'. Such an interpretation gave effect to the provision and to the purpose of the provision, which was to strengthen the protection available to the broadcaster in relation to satellite and cable transmissions. This principle of effectiveness is also used in the interpretation of European Community law which we consider in section F of this chapter.

Lord Diplock's approach implies that it is the courts' sole function to ascertain the intention of Parliament and give effect to it. No doubt this is true so far as most statutes are concerned; but in the case of some statutes, notably those creating crimes but possibly also those imposing taxes, surely the courts have the further function of ensuring that citizens are only deprived of their liberty or their money by reasonably clearly worded provisions or at least by provisions which, though poorly phrased, are susceptible of comparatively easy rectification. Lord Diplock's own speech

---

14. [1990] 2 All ER 118 at 123.

in *Jones v Wrotham Park Settled Estates*[15] should sound a note of caution here. In that case it was clear that the legislation had failed to cover a possible method of evasion, yet their Lordships refused to rectify the Act in the absence of a clear indication of what the substituted words should be.

R v Northampton Borough Council, ex p Quietlynn Ltd[16] is a case in which the clear wording of express provisions of a statute precluded any addition to its words in order to avoid an unreasonable result. Paragraph 29 of Sch 3 to the Local Government (Miscellaneous Provisions) Act 1982 applies to applications for licences to use premises as a sex establishment made before 'the appointed day' (the day on which the Schedule comes into force in the area of the local authority concerned). Subparagraph (2) prohibits the local authority from considering any application to which the paragraph applies before the appointed day, and sub-para (3) prohibits them from granting any such application 'until they have considered all such applications'. In two cases, because of administrative difficulties, local authorities had granted licences to use premises as sex establishments in respect of applications made *after* the appointed day, but had refused to grant licences in respect of applications made *before* that day until they could consider all these latter applications. A company which had made applications before the appointed day sought judicial review to quash these refusals to grant licences. The Court of Appeal concluded that Parliament had assumed that, on the appointed day, the local authority would gather up and consider all the applications for licences received before that day and decide on them, so that subsequent applications would necessarily be processed at a later date. This assumption had been falsified by the administrative difficulty of having to consider all the applications received before the appointed day prior to a determination on any of them. The lack of a provision requiring priority to be given to applications made before the appointed day over those made later resulted from a failure of Parliament to foresee the situation which arose, and not just from a failure to spell out its intentions clearly. The Court of Appeal thus felt constrained to construe the wording of para 29(3) according to its plain terms which required the local authority to delay granting any licences to those who had applied before the appointed day until all such applications could be decided upon together. Accordingly, the local authorities had acted properly and the applications for judicial review failed. A clear objection to action by the courts in such a situation is the difficulty of specifying the precise words which should be added. Should the local authorities have granted no licences at all until they had decided on all the applications made before the appointed day?

---

15. [1980] AC 74, see pp 19-20 above.
16. (1986) 85 LGR 249.

Were it not for a passage in Lord Reid's speech in *Federal Steam Navigation Co Ltd v Department of Trade and Industry*[17] no attempt would have been made in the formulation of rule 3 of the basic rules set out on p 49, above to classify the cases to which it applies. It confers a wholly exceptional power of what is in effect rectification of a statute, and the wiser course might have been to refrain from further formulation. Lord Reid said:[18]

> 'Cases where it has properly been held that a word can be struck out of a deed or statute and another substituted can as far as I am aware be grouped under three heads: where without such substitution the provision is unintelligible or absurd or totally unreasonable; where it is unworkable; and where it is totally irreconcilable with the plain intention shown by the rest of the deed or statute.'

Perhaps it is permissible to extend these remarks to cases of addition and alteration. Examples have been given of all three of the categories mentioned by Lord Reid. Section 7 of the Official Secrets Act 1920 is unintelligible without the substitution of 'or' for 'and' adopted in *R v Oakes*;[19] the addition of the reference to a convicted felon in *Re Wainewright* [20] prevented an absurdity; and the effect of s 36 of the Administration of Justice Act 1970 would have been totally unreasonable without the emendation agreed by Buckley and Scarman LJJ in *Western Bank Ltd v Schindler*.[1] *Wills v Bowley*[2] may properly be regarded as adding words to s 28 of the Town Police Clauses Act 1847 in order to prevent it being unworkable for police officers. Section 1(6) of the British Nationality Act 1981 would have been at variance with the rest of the Act and general principles of law if the word 'order' had not been restricted in *Re K (a minor)*.[3]

Lord Reid also made the point that it would not always be proper to strike words out even when the case fell within one of the above categories. In this context it is worth recalling the three conditions for the exercise of the analogous power of adding words to a statute laid down by Lord Diplock in *Jones v Wrotham Park Estates Ltd*:[4]

---

17. [1974] 2 All ER 97, see p 97 above.
18. At 100.
19. P 98 above.
20. Pp 95-96 above.
1. Pp 94-95 above.
2. See pp 86-87 above, but see the contrary views of Lord Lowry in the same case, [1983] 1 AC at 89. It is not sufficient that the result is merely inconvenient: *Pollway Nominees Ltd v Croydon London Borough Council* [1985] 3 All ER 24; and *Bennion* s 314.
3. See pp 93-94 above.
4. Pp 19-20 above. *Bennion* p 661, argues that the third condition set out by Lord Diplock is wrong, citing *R v Schildkamp* [1971] AC 1, p 56 above. The cases mentioned in this section are all ones in which the missing words were formulated, and the editors consider Lord Diplock's statement to be correct.

'First, it [must be] possible to determine from a consideration of the provisions of the Act read as a whole what the mischief was that it was the purpose of the Act to remedy; secondly, it [must be] apparent that the draftsman and Parliament had by inadvertence overlooked, and so omitted to deal with, an eventuality that required to be dealt with if the purpose of the Act was to be achieved; and thirdly, it [must be] possible to state with certainty what were the additional words that would have been inserted by the draftsman and approved by Parliament had their attention been drawn to the omission before the Bill passed into law.'

To these might be added a fourth condition drawn from the judgment of Scarman LJ in *Western Bank Ltd v Schindler*,[5] namely that the insertion should not be 'too big, or too much at variance with the language used by the legislature'. In omitting or inserting words the judge is not really engaged in a hypothetical reconstruction of the intentions of the drafter or the legislature, but is simply making as much sense as he can of the text of the statutory provision read in its appropriate context and within the limits of the judicial role.

There can be little doubt that different judges have taken different views with regard to the exercise of the exceptional power of rectification. It is far from clear that all judges would give their blessing to the emendation of s 8(1) of the Race Relations Act 1976 approved by the Court of Appeal in *Deria v General Council of British Shipping*.[6] On the other hand, there are reported decisions in which the power was not exercised although other judges might have acted differently. For instance, Lord Halsbury argued in *Income Tax Special Purposes Commrs v Pemsel* that:[7]

'Whatever the real fact may be I think a court of law is bound to proceed on the assumption that the legislature is an ideal person that does not make mistakes. It must be assumed that it has intended what it has said, and I think any other view of the mode in which we must approach the interpretation of a statute would give authority for the interpretation of the language of an Act of Parliament which would be attended with the most serious consequences.'

But would Lord Halsbury have acquitted the accused in *R v Vasey and Lally*[8] on the ground that the statutory provision under which they were charged was gibberish which did not define a crime in relation to salmon rivers? Section 13 of the Salmon Fisheries Act 1873 read:

---

5. Pp 95 above.
6. See p 38 above.
7. [1891] AC 531 at 549. For a draftsman's view of his own fallibility compare Bennion *Statute Law* (3rd edn, 1990), Ch 19.
8. [1905] 2 KB 748.

'The provisions of s 32 of the Malicious Injuries to Property Act 1861 so far as they relate to poisoning any water with intent to kill or destroy fish shall be extended and apply to salmon rivers, as if the words "or in any salmon river" were inserted in the said section in lieu of the words "private rights of fishery" after the words "noxious material in any such pond or water".'

Unfortunately, the words 'any private rights of fishery' did not follow the words 'noxious material in any pond or water' but occurred at a point in the verbiage of s 32 before the putting of noxious material into water with intent to kill or destroy fish had been reached. The Court for Crown Cases Reserved did not care whether the words in s 13 of the 1873 Act from 'as if' on were ignored or whether the proposed amendment was inserted at a point at which it made sense. But the court did carry out the obvious intention of the legislature and held that, in consequence of s 13 of the 1873 Act, it was a misdemeanour under s 32 of the 1861 Act unlawfully and maliciously to put noxious materials into any salmon river with intent to destroy fish.

Would Lord Halsbury have concluded that, on the true construction of the Criminal Appeal Act 1907, an accused who pleaded guilty could appeal against sentence although the Court of Criminal Appeal had no power to substitute another sentence if the original one were quashed? This certainly appeared to be the effect of the words of the Act. Under s 3 a person convicted on indictment might appeal against a sentence passed on his conviction. Section 4(3) provided that 'on an appeal against sentence the Court of Criminal Appeal shall, if they think that a different sentence should have been passed, quash the sentence passed at the trial, and pass such other sentence warranted in law by the *verdict* (whether more or less severe) in substitution therefor as they think ought to have been passed'. Plainly, no other sentence is warranted in law 'by the verdict' in the case of someone who pleaded guilty, but the Court of Criminal Appeal avoided this difficulty in *R v Ettridge*[9] by 'striking out' those words.

Similarly, in the recent case of *R v Moore*[10] the Court of Appeal had no hesitation in giving a 'rectifying construction' to s 1C(1)(a) of the Powers of Criminal Courts Act 1973 by treating it as ending with the words 'under the preceding provisions of this Act' instead of the words 'under the following provisions of this Act'. Sections 1A to 1C were inserted into the 1973 Act by s 8(3) of the Criminal Justice Act 1991 'for the purpose of rearranging Part I of that Act in consequence of the amendments made by [s 8(1) and (2)]', and it was 'manifest' that the reference to the *following* provisions of the 1973 Act, as amended, 'did not correspond with the end

---

9. [1909] 2 KB 24.
10. (1994) Times, 26 December.

clearly posited by subsections 8(2) and (3)'. Loyalty to the literal wording of s 1C would 'frustrate the plain legislative intent' and 'involve a failure to recognise the inconsistency with s 8 of the 1991 Act'. Sedley J, giving the judgment of the court, said that in such a situation the court 'was affirmatively required to give the enactment a "rectifying construction" '.

The cases thus demonstrate that both today and in Lord Halsbury's time, judges have not been slow to correct mistakes which the legislature has made. Of course there must be an exceptionally strong case for the exercise of the wholly exceptional power of rectification, and of course it is essential that the courts should so far as possible stick to the ordinary meaning of statutory words, but this does not mean that they should throw their hands up in despair, not always unmingled with satisfaction, when the ordinary meaning produces a preposterous result. As often as not it is a matter of taste whether such results are avoided by the technique of necessary implication or by rectification, but avoided they should be like the plague.

F. EUROPEAN COMMUNITY LAW

We now proceed to the illustration of the fifth of our basic rules stated on p 49: the judge must interpret a statute so as to give effect to directly applicable European Community law, and, in so far as this is not possible, must refrain from applying the statutory provisions which conflict with that law.

The European Community treaties not only create obligations in international law between the Member States but also legal provisions which are directly applicable in their domestic laws. By virtue of the European Communities Act 1972, European Community law is an integral part of the national laws of the United Kingdom. Whether because they are directly effective or because they have been incorporated into domestic legislation, provisions of European Community law pose frequent problems of interpretation for lawyers in the United Kingdom. Many provisions of the various treaties establishing the European Union (notably the treaties of Paris (1951), Rome (1957), and Maastricht (1992)) have direct effect, that is to say they affect the legal position of citizens and public authorities in Member States without the need for national implementing legislation. Community regulations normally have similar direct effect. According to art 189 of the EC Treaty,[11] 'a directive shall be binding, as to the result to be achieved, upon each Member State to which it is addressed, but shall leave to the national authorities the choice of form and methods'. While

---

11. Formerly called the 'EEC Treaty'.

implementing national legislation is normally necessary in order to give such a directive legal effect in a Member State, some provisions will have direct effect against organs of the state.[12] This will occur where a provision in a directive is sufficiently clear and precise, establishes an unconditional obligation which does not require for its implementation measures to be taken by Community institutions or Member States, and the deadline for implementing the directive has passed.[13] Although the national courts may (and sometimes must) refer questions of the interpretation of rules of European Community law to the European Court of Justice under art 177 of the EC Treaty, they will frequently be required to interpret them themselves.[14] This is not a treatise on European Community law, however, and discussion of EC methods of interpretation is provided in other works.[15] It is sufficient here to draw attention to the key features of the Community approach to interpreting its legislation and how this differs from the approach outlined in the rest of this chapter.

The general approach which national courts should adopt to the interpretation of European Community law can be seen through the issue of the relationship between directives and national law. Whether the provisions have direct effect or not, art 189 is clear that member states have an obligation to implement the result envisaged by a directive in their national laws. This obligation to achieve the purpose of the directive is not limited to the legislature but applies equally to the courts. As the European Court of Justice stated in *Marleasing SA v La Comercial Internacional de Alimentaciòn SA* Case C-106/89:[16]

> 'the Member States' obligation arising from a directive to achieve the result envisaged by the directive and their duty under art 5 of the Treaty to take all appropriate measures, whether general or particular,

---

12. See *Foster v British Gas Ltd* Case 188/89 [1990] 3 All ER 897; *Marshall v Southampton and South West Hampshire Area Health Authority (Teaching)* Case 152/84 [1986] 2 All ER 584.

13. See D Lasok and J W Bridge *Law and Institutions of the European Communities* (6th edn, 1994) pp 114-131. Even where this is not the case, an action for damages may sometimes be brought by a citizen against the Member State for failure to implement the directive: *Francovich v Italian Republic* Case C-6/90 [1992] IRLR 84.

14. See eg *Equal Opportunities Commission v Secretary of State for Employment* [1994] 1 All ER 910; *R v Secretary of State for the Environment, ex p Greenpeace Ltd* [1994] 4 All ER 352. C Barnard and R Greaves, [1994] CMLR 1055 at 1063-1080.

15. See J Bengoetxea *The Legal Reasoning of the European Court of Justice* (1993) pp 233-262; T Millett 'Rules of Interpretation of E.E.C. Legislation' [1989] Stat LR 163; Lord Slynn of Hadley 'Looking at European Community Texts' [1993] Stat LR 12; L N Brown and T Kennedy *Brown and Jacob's The European Court of Justice* (4th edn, 1994) Ch 14.

16. [1990] ECR I-4135. English courts have stressed that this principle applies only in so far as it is possible to interpret the British legislation in this way without distortion: Lord Keith, *Webb v EMO Air Cargo (UK) Ltd* [1992] 4 All ER 929 at 939-940; Potts J, *R v Secretary of State for the Environment, ex p Greenpeace Ltd* [1994] 4 All ER 352 at 365-366.

to ensure the fulfilment of that obligation, is binding on all the
authorities of the Member States including, for matters within their
jurisdiction, the courts. It follows that, in applying national law,
whether the provisions in question were adopted before or after the
directive, the national court called upon to interpret it is required to do
so, as far as possible, in the light of the wording and purpose of the
directive in order to achieve the result pursued by the latter and thereby
comply with the third paragraph of article 189 of the Treaty.'

In that case, a Spanish court was required to interpret restrictively long-
established provisions in the Civil Code which regulated the nullity of
companies in order to give effect to a directive which had yet to be
implemented in Spanish law, even though the directive did not have direct
effect. Thus, even where the provision of Community law does not have
direct effect, judicial interpretation achieves at least an indirect effect on the
national law of the Member State. The ruling of the European Court of
Justice in that case emphasises the general duty of the courts of Member
States to give priority to an interpretation which achieves the objectives of
Community law. Indeed, where such interpretation is not possible and there
is a clear conflict between national law and Community law, the European
Court of Justice has laid down that the national court must refuse to apply
the conflicting national provision, and the English courts have now accepted
that this obligation requires them to refuse to apply an Act of Parliament
where it conflicts with a provision of Community law.[17]

As with English law, there is no single authoritative statement of the
principles for interpreting European Community law. Judge Kutscher, a
former member of the European Court of Justice, has however given a useful
guide to its approach:[18]

'You have to start with the wording (ordinary or special meaning). The
Court can take into account the subjective intention of the legislature
and the function of a rule at the time it was adopted. The provision has
to be interpreted in its context and having regard to its schematic
relationship with other provisions in such a way that it has a reasonable
and effective meaning. The rule must be understood in connexion with
the economic and social situation in which it is to take effect. Its
purpose, either considered separately or within the system of rules of
which it is a part, may be taken into consideration. Considerations

17. *Amministrazione delle Finanze dello Stato v Simmenthal (No 2)* Case 106/77 [1978]
3 CMLR 263; *Factortame Ltd v Secretary of State for Transport* [1989] 2 All ER 692, HL;
Factortame Ltd v Secretary of State for Transport (No 2) [1991] 1 All ER 70, ECJ and HL.
18. H Kutscher 'Methods of Interpretation as Seen by a Judge at the Court of Justice'
(Judicial and Academic Conference, Luxembourg, 1976) part 1, ss 5- 6.

based on comparative law are admissible if necessary. In new fields of
law the court must feel its way from case to case (continental legal
thought is fully conversant with reasoning from case to case).'

This passage identifies four methods of interpretation: literal, historical,
schematic and teleological. The most important of these is the last.

The teleological approach involves both ensuring that a provision 'has a
reasonable effect and meaning' — the principle of effectiveness (*effet utile*)
— and that its purpose is achieved. This can be clearly seen from one of the
Court's earliest decisions in *Van Gend en Loos v Nederlandse Administratie
der Belastingen* Case 26/62.[19] Article 12 of the EC Treaty provides that:

'Member States shall refrain from introducing between themselves
any new customs duties on imports or exports or any charges having
equivalent effect, and from increasing those which they already apply
in their trade with each other.'

Until 1958, when the Treaty came into force, Van Gend en Loos had been
paying a 3% customs duty on glue imported from Germany. In 1959, the
Netherlands ratified a Benelux customs protocol under which the customs
duty on this item rose to 8%. Although the Treaty says nothing about the
rights of citizens and art 12 only talks of the obligations of Member States,
the European Court of Justice ruled that a citizen of a Member State could
rely on it in order to resist the claim to an increased customs duty.

'To ascertain whether the provisions of an international treaty extend
so far in their effects it is necessary to consider *the spirit, the general
scheme, and the wording* of those provisions. *The objective of the EEC
Treaty*, which is to establish a Common Market, the functioning of
which is of direct concern to interested parties in the Community,
implies that this Treaty is more than an agreement which merely
creates mutual obligations between the contracting states. This view
is confirmed by the preamble to the Treaty which refers not only to
governments but to peoples. . . . In addition the task assigned to the
Court of Justice under Article 177, the object of which is to secure
uniform interpretation of the Treaty by national courts and tribunals,
confirms that the states have acknowledged that Community law has
an authority which can be invoked by their nationals before those
courts and tribunals. The conclusion to be drawn from this is that the
Community constitutes a new legal order of international law for the
benefit of which the states have limited their sovereign rights, albeit

---

19. [1963] ECR 1.

within limited fields, and the subjects of which comprise not only Member States but also their nationals. Independently of the legislation of Member States, Community law therefore not only imposes obligations on individuals but is also intended to confer upon them rights which become part of their legal heritage. . . . With regard to *the general scheme of the Treaty* as it relates to customs duties and charges having equivalent effect it must be emphasized that Article 9, which bases the Community upon a customs union, includes as an essential provision the prohibition of these customs duties and charges. . . . A restriction of the guarantees against an infringement of Article 12 by Member States to the procedures under Articles 169 and 170 [enforcement proceedings before the European Court of Justice brought by the Commission and by other Member States] would remove all direct legal protection of the individual rights of their nationals. There is a risk that recourse to the procedure under these Articles would be *ineffective* if it were to occur after the implementation of a national decision contrary to the provisions of the Treaty.'[20]

Article 12 was thus interpreted by reference not only to the words used, but also in relation to the 'general scheme of the Treaty', as is seen from the discussion of arts 9 and 177, as well as its preamble. These were related to the 'objective of the EEC Treaty' and to its 'spirit' so as to prevent an 'ineffective' implementation of European Community obligations. The decision laid the foundations of what Judge Kutscher described as 'the principle of the progressive integration of the Member States in order to attain the objectives of the Treaty',[1] as a Community legal principle. That principle identifies the active role which judicial interpretation plays in the creation of the European legal order, a role which contrasts with the subordinate role which the judiciary in the United Kingdom plays in relation to Parliament.

Literal interpretation, with its emphasis on the ordinary meaning of words, is of limited importance in a system with multiple official languages. Words may have been chosen in a precise way, but linguistic nuances in one language may not translate into another. For example, in *Marleasing*[2] Advocate General Van Gerven argued for a restrictive interpretation of the scope of the directive based on the wording of the German and Dutch texts; but this was not adopted by the Court, which based its argument solely on the purpose of the directive. The European Court of Justice drew attention

---

20. [1963] ECR 1 at 12-13 (emphasis added).
1. Op cit (see p 107, n 18 above) at p 39.
2. Pp 106-107 above.

to some of the peculiarities of Community law in this area in its *CILFIT* decision:[3]

> 'it must be borne in mind that Community legislation is drafted in several languages and that the different language versions are all equally authentic. An interpretation of a provision of Community law thus involves a comparison of the different language versions.
>
> It must also be borne in mind, even where the different language versions are entirely in accord with one another, that Community law uses terminology which is peculiar to it. Furthermore, it must be emphasised that legal concepts do not necessarily have the same meaning in Community law and in the law of the various Member States.'

It should be noted that, unlike most UK statutes, EC legislation contains preambles which specifically recite its purposes. Thus, in an important sense, to give effect to the purpose so stated is to give effect to the words of the provision read in the context of the legislation as a whole.

Historical interpretation is of more limited value. The legislative process in the European Union is more complex than in the United Kingdom. Depending on its nature, a measure may have to be considered not only by the Commission, the Council of Ministers, and the Parliament, but also by the Economic and Social Committee or the Committee of the Regions. The deliberations of the Commission and the Council are not published, although reasons are given for the decisions reached by each organ. In this setting, it is difficult to discern an intention of the legislature based on historical records of a heterogenous set of institutions. In addition, the Community is a dynamically developing body, with the result that the historical setting of a provision will often be inappropriate to determine how its objective should be implemented today. As the European Court of Justice stated in the *CILFIT* decision:[4]

> 'every provision of Community law must be placed in its context and interpreted in the light of the provisions of Community law as a whole, regard being had to the objectives thereof and to its state of evolution at the date on which the provision in question is to be applied.'

That quotation and the *Van Gend en Loos* case[5] illustrate clearly that an examination of the context of a provision within the scheme of legislation

---

3.   *CILFIT v Ministry of Health* Case 283/81 [1982] ECR 3415 at 3430, paras 18 and 19.
4.   Para 20.
5.   Pp 108-109 above.

is central to determining its purpose and meaning. Schematic interpretation focuses on this feature and requires the judge to look not only at the measure as a whole, but also the way the provision fits into the general scheme of Community legislation in the relevant area.

Bennion argues that 'the British doctrine of purposive construction is more literalist than the European variety, and permits a strained construction only in comparatively rare cases'.[6] In the sense that the judicial role in the European context is more activist than in the national context, this is undoubtedly correct. The British judge therefore has to be wary when contemplating the application of British methods of interpretation to the case in hand. This is illustrated by the case of *R v Henn and Darby*.[7] The appellants were convicted of fraudulently evading the prohibition on the importation of obscene articles imposed by s 42 of the Customs Consolidation Act 1876. They argued that this prohibition was no longer in force as it conflicted with art 30 of the EC Treaty which prohibits 'quantitative restrictions on imports'. Lord Widgery CJ rejected this argument in the Court of Appeal on the ground that, linguistically, 'quantitative restrictions' did not cover a total ban on imports, but only quotas. Following a line of previous authorities, the European Court of Justice focused on the purpose of art 30 and held that it covered all measures capable of hindering intra-Community trade. The House of Lords applied the ruling of the European Court of Justice, and Lord Diplock drew the lesson that the very doubt that Lord Widgery CJ held whether art 30 covered the case in hand 'shows the danger of an English court applying English canons of statutory construction to the interpretation of the Treaty or, for that matter, of Regulations or Directives'.[8]

A more typical example of the British approach to EC legislation is provided by *Litster v Forth Dry Dock Co Ltd*.[9] Under reg 5(1) and (3) of the Transfer of Undertakings (Protection of Employment) Regulations 1981, the transfer of a business did not operate to terminate the contracts of employment of employees who were employed in the business 'immediately before the transfer'. In this case, the employees had been dismissed with immediate effect at 3.30 pm on 6 February 1984 and the business had been transferred at 4.30 pm on the same day. The House of Lords held that reg 5 applied not only to employees who were employed in the business at the point in time immediately before the transfer, but also to those who, but for an unfair dismissal, would have been so employed. Thus, since the employees

---

6. *Bennion* s 311. (He defines a 'strained' meaning as any meaning other than the literal (ie grammatical) meaning of an enactment: see s 157.)
7. [1978] 3 All ER 1190, CA; Case 34/79 [1979] ECR 3795, ECJ; [1980] AC 850, HL.
8. [1981] AC 850 at 904-905.
9. [1989] 1 All ER 1134.

in this case had been unfairly dismissed, they were covered by reg 5. Such a construction gave effect to the result which the EC Council Directive 77/187 was designed to achieve and in implementation of which the 1981 Regulations had been made. As Lord Oliver stated:[10]

> 'If the legislation can reasonably be construed so as to conform to [the United Kingdom's] obligations [under the EC Treaty], obligations which are to be ascertained not only from the wording of the relevant directive but from the interpretation placed on it by the Court of Justice of the European Communities, such a purposive construction will be applied even though, perhaps, it may involve some departure from the strict and literal application of the words which the legislature has elected to use.'

Before leaving the topic, it is worth noting that teleological interpretation does not always involve expansive interpretation as in *Van Gend en Loos* and *R v Henn and Darby*. Thus in *Owens Bank Ltd v Bracco (No 2)*,[11] the European Court of Justice was concerned with art 22 of the Brussels Convention on Jurisdiction and the Enforcement of Judgments in Civil and Commercial Matters (incorporated into English law by the Civil Jurisdiction and Judgments Act 1982). Article 22 provided that 'where related actions are brought in the courts of different Contracting States, any court other than the court first seised may . . . stay its proceedings'. This was held not to apply to a case where proceedings were brought first in Italy and then in England to enforce a judgment of a court in St Vincent. The purpose of the convention had been to enhance the legal protection of persons established in the Community and it therefore had no application to the judgments of courts of non-contracting states. The phrase 'related actions' was thus limited to actions concerning the enforcement of judgments of the courts of Member States.

---

10. [1989] 1 All ER 1134 at 1140.
11. Case 129/92 [1994] 1 All ER 336.

Chapter 5
Internal aids to construction

We saw in Chapter 3 that statutory words must be interpreted in their context. To quote Viscount Simonds, 'context' includes not only 'other enacting provisions of the same statute', but also 'its preamble'.[1] Such features constitute the internal context for the statutory words to be interpreted. The internal aids to construction discussed briefly in this chapter are the enacting parts of the same statute (its sections and schedules), other parts of the same statute (the preamble, long and short titles, headings, side-notes and punctuation), and rules of language, (such as the *ejusdem generis* rule). Each of these contributes to the interpretation of the text, but they are not all of equal status.

A. ENACTING PARTS OF THE SAME STATUTE

It is scarcely necessary to cite authority for the proposition that Acts must be construed as a whole. Guidance with regard to the meaning of a particular word or phrase may be found in other words and phrases in the same section or in other sections, although the utility of an extensive consideration of other parts of the same statute will actually vary from case to case. Speaking of the Income Tax Act 1952 (which consolidated a large number of enactments passed between 1918 and 1951), Lord Reid said:[2]

'It is no doubt true that every Act should be read as a whole, but that is, I think, because one assumes that in drafting one clause of a Bill the draftsman had in mind the language and substance of other clauses,

---

1. See pp 55-56 above.
2. *IRC v Hinchy* [1960] AC 748 at 766.

and attributes to Parliament a comprehension of the whole Act. But where, as here, quite incongruous provisions are lumped together and it is impossible to suppose that anyone, draftsman or Parliament, ever considered one of these sections in the light of another, I think it would be just as misleading to base conclusions on the different language of different sections as it is to base conclusions on the different language of sections in different Acts.'

The consolidating Income and Corporation Taxes Act 1988 contains 845 sections and 31 schedules, occupying 1037 pages. To read an Act of this size literally 'as a whole' is a practical impossibility.

Changes of language do, however, frequently have a decisive effect on the construction of a statutory provision. For example, s 102 of the Mental Health Act 1959 empowered the judge to do or secure the doing of all such things with respect to the property and affairs of a patient as appear necessary or expedient:

'(*b*) for the maintenance or other benefit of members of the patient's family; or (*c*) for making provision for other persons or purposes for whom or which the patient might be expected to provide if he were not mentally disordered.'

In *Re D M L*[3] Cross J said:

'The contrasting language of sub-clauses (*b*) and (*c*) suggests to my mind that the legislature considered that the word "family" consisted of persons for all of whom the patient might *prima facie* be expected to make some provision. This, I think, indicates that the word does not include collateral relatives'.

The result was that a scheme to avoid death duties under which benefits were conferred on the patient's nephews and nieces could not be sanctioned under s 102(*b*) although it was sanctioned under s 102(*c*).

There is a presumption that the same word or phrase bears the same meaning throughout the same statute. For example, in *Dixon v British Broadcasting Corpn*,[4] para 5(2) of Sch 1 to the Trade Union and Labour Relations Act 1974[5] provided that an employee was to be treated as dismissed by his employer only if—

---

3. [1965] Ch 1133 at 1137.
4. [1979] 2 All ER 112.
5. Now s 55 of the Employment Protection (Consolidation) Act 1978.

'(a) the contract under which he is employed by the employer is terminated by the employer, whether it is terminated by notice or without notice, or (b) where under that contract he is employed for a fixed term, that term expires without being renewed under the same contract.'

In an earlier case, *British Broadcasting Corpn v Ioannou*,[6] the Court of Appeal had expressed the opinion in relation to para 12 of the same Schedule[7] that a 'fixed term contract' was one whose term could not be unfixed by notice. If applied to paragraph 5(2), such an interpretation would mean that a contract for a stated period which contained a clause permitting either party to terminate it upon notice would not be a 'fixed term' contract, which would stultify the purpose of the Act in protecting employees against the premature or unfair termination of their employment. Accordingly, in deciding that contracts of two months and four weeks respectively, containing a clause permitting termination on notice, were 'fixed term' contracts, the Court of Appeal in *Dixon* felt obliged to declare the interpretation given in *Ioannou* as wrong, for both para 5 and para 12 were in the same Part II of the Schedule and the phrase should have the same meaning in each. The presumption is, however, of the mildest kind for it is easy to point to cases in which the same word has been held to have different meanings in different sections, or even the same section, of a single statute. A stock example of the first type of case is provided by the different meanings of the word 'premises' in the Landlord and Tenant Act 1954. Sometimes it is used in its popular sense of buildings, while at other points in the statute it bears the technical meaning of that which may form the subject matter of the habendum of a lease with the result that even land with no buildings on it, such as land used as gallops for training racehorses, may be included.[8] The stock example of the use of the same verb in different senses in the same section is s 57 of the Offences Against the Person Act 1861 which provides that: 'whosoever, being *married*, shall *marry* any other person during the life of the former husband or wife' shall be guilty of bigamy. Although 'being married' means being validly married, 'shall marry' necessarily means no more than 'go through a marriage ceremony'.[9]

Bennion[10] raises the corollary that different words, should, prima facie, be given a different meaning. The drafter should never be presumed to have been gratuitous in his changes of wording. However, the *Nottinghamshire*

---

6. [1975] 2 All ER 999.
7. Now s 142 of the Employment Protection (Consolidation) Act 1978.
8. *Bracey v Read* [1962] 3 All ER 472.
9. *R v Allen* (1872) LR 1 CCR 367.
10. *Statutory Interpretation* (2nd edn) p 808.

County Council[11] case shows that this is merely a presumption, for there the House of Lords treated 'applicable' and 'to be applied' as being interchangeable expressions. That case well illustrates the problems that may be caused by provisions textually inserted into an Act by subsequent legislation. The controversial word 'applicable' occurred in a subsection inserted into the Local Government Planning and Land Act 1980 by the Local Government Finance Act 1982. The various judges in the case had to consider whether the word was intended to be different from 'to be applied' used in the original section. As Balcombe J put it in *Chaudhary v Chaudhary*:[12]

> 'the principle of giving a word or phrase the same construction when it appears in different sections of the same Act, which in any event is not an absolute rule, is of limited application when the section relied on for the purpose of comparison has been introduced by subsequent legislation.'

It would be pointless to multiply examples of the effect of a change of language, or the use of identical language, within the same section or statute. Everything depends on the context, and it is impossible to make useful generalisations; but something must be said about the effect that one section of a statute may have on the construction of another section of the same statute as a matter of substance rather than language.

Where an Act covers a number of different topics in separate parts, consistency of provisions in those different parts will not necessarily be expected any more than consistency of language. For example, in *R v Huntingdon District Council, ex p Cowan*,[13] the Divisional Court considered that the three parts of the Local Government (Miscellaneous Provisions) Act 1982 dealing respectively with the licensing of public entertainment, sex shops, and take-away food shops really amounted to three separate codes. Parts II and III had detailed procedures for the making of objections, notifications, and representations in connection with the grant of a licence, but the absence of such provisions in Part I was not considered to be a deliberate exclusion of similar non-statutory rights of objectors in relation to public entertainments licences.

There may well, however, be provisions which are apparently repugnant to each other. If the repugnancy is total and wholly inescapable, it was suggested in the past that a later section prevails over an earlier one in accordance with the maxim 'later laws repeal earlier contrary laws' (*'leges posteriores priores contrarias abrogant'*); but this approach has been

---

11. Pp 87-88 above.
12. [1984] 3 All ER 1017 at 1035.
13. [1984] 1 All ER 58.

criticised by Nicholls LJ as 'mechanical' and 'altogether out of step with the modern, purposive, approach to the interpretation of statutes'[14] Typically, the courts are able to use various techniques in order to construe apparently conflicting provisions so as to avoid repugnancy. One of these, the technique of finding a secondary meaning for one or more of the words or phrases in question, has already been discussed. Two others are the technique of treating apparently conflicting provisions as dealing with distinct matters, and the technique of holding that one section apparently in conflict with another merely provides for an exception to the general rule contained in that other. The first is illustrated by *Windsor and Maidenhead Royal Borough Council v Brandrose Investments Ltd*, the second by *Steeples v Derbyshire County Council*, both cases concerning the interpretation of the Town and Country Planning Act 1971.[15]

Windsor and Maidenhead Royal Borough Council v Brandrose Investments Ltd[16] concerned the relationship between ss 52 and 277A of the Act. The former conferred on a local planning authority power to enter into an agreement with any person regulating the use of that person's land. The Windsor & Maidenhead Council entered into such an agreement with a landowner allowing it to develop its site, which could not be done without the demolition of the buildings then on it. Section 52(3) expressly provided that:

> 'Nothing in this section or in any agreement made thereunder shall be construed—(a) as restricting the exercise, in relation to land which is the subject of any such agreement, of any powers exercisable by any Minister or authority under this Act so long as those powers are exercised in accordance with the provisions of the development plan, or in accordance with any directions which have been given by the Secretary of State . . .'

There was no development plan or direction of the Secretary of State affecting the site. Subsequently, the authority included the site within a conservation area and invoked the provision in s 277A(2) of the Act that no building in the area could be demolished without its consent. The Court of Appeal held that the two powers were distinct and that the power to create a conservation area was not limited by the exercise of the power under s 52. Accordingly the council was entitled to insist that no demolition on the site took place without its consent.

---

14. *Re Marr (a Bankrupt)* [1990] Ch 773 at 784. For criticism, see *Bennion* p 810.
15. Repealed by the consolidating Town and Country Planning Act 1990.
16. [1983] 1 All ER 818.

In *Steeples v Derbyshire County Council*,[17] two further sections of the
same Act were in conflict. Section 26 set out the procedure for applications
for planning permission relating to 'any class of development' designated
under that section. Section 270(1) provided that, 'in relation to land of local
planning authorities and to the development by local authorities of land in
respect of which they are the local planning authorities', certain specified
sections (not including s 26) should have effect, subject to any exceptions
or modifications prescribed in regulations. In a challenge to a planning
application by a local planning authority for the creation of an amusement
park on its own land, it was argued that the application was invalid, inter alia,
because the authority had not complied with the formalities specified in s 26.
Webster J rejected the argument on the ground that s 270(1) should be
construed as exempting local planning authorities from the obligations of
the Act except in respect of the sections which it expressly mentions.

One section may affect the construction of another as a matter of
substance when account is taken of the fact that a particular construction of
the section before the court, which does not produce a result inconsistent
with the purpose of the statute, would lead to a construction of other sections
which would produce such a result. Whether considerations of this nature
are proper in a criminal case is perhaps questionable, but the outstanding
instance is undoubtedly *R v Prince*.[18] Prince was charged with abduction
contrary to s 55 of the Offences Against the Person Act 1861 according to
which it was an offence to 'unlawfully take . . . any unmarried girl, being
under the age of 16 years, out of the possession and against the will of her
father or mother. . . .' He was found by the jury to have believed on
reasonable grounds that the girl he abducted was over 16, but by a majority
of 14 to 1, the Court for Crown Cases Reserved held that this was no defence.
Under s 50 of the 1861 Act it was a felony to 'carnally know and abuse any
girl under the age of 10 years', and s 51 made it a misdemeanour to 'carnally
know and abuse any girl being above the age of 10 years and under the age
of 12 years'. The principal argument used in the leading majority judgment
delivered by Blackburn J is contained in the following passage:[19]

> 'It seems impossible to suppose that the intention of the legislature in
> those two sections [ss 50 and 51] could have been to make the crime
> depend upon the knowledge by the prisoner of the girl's actual age. It
> would produce the monstrous result that a man who had carnal
> connection with a girl, in reality not quite 10 years old, but whom he
> on reasonable grounds believed to be a little more than 10, was to

---

17. [1984] 3 All ER 468.
18. (1875) LR 2 CCR 154.
19. At 171-172.

escape altogether. He could not, in that view of the statute, be convicted of the felony, for he did not know her to be under 10. He could not be convicted of the misdemeanour because she was in fact not above the age of 10. It seems to us that the intention of the legislature was to punish those who had connection with young girls, though with their consent, unless the girl was in fact old enough to give a valid consent. . . . The 55th section, on which the present case arises, uses precisely the same words as those in ss 50 and 51, and must be construed in the same way.'

In a sense *Prince* was the victim of bad drafting, for, quite apart from any issue concerning the niceties of mens rea, there is something seriously wrong with two such provisions as ss 50 and 51 of the Offences Against the Person Act 1861 if a man charged with unlawful intercourse with a girl above 10 and under 12 should have the cast-iron defence that she was in fact under 10. Section 51 should simply have prohibited intercourse with girls under 12. Allowing for the substitution of the ages of 13 and 16 for 10 and 12, this is the result achieved by ss 5 and 6 of the Sexual Offences Act 1956, as amended by the Criminal Law Act 1967. Section 5 punishes intercourse with girls under 13 with a maximum of imprisonment for life, and s 6 punishes intercourse with girls under 16 with a maximum of two years' imprisonment. The failure of the drafter of the 1861 Act to appreciate the merits in certain situations of a statutory overlap may have been a significant cause of the proliferation of offences of strict liability.

Three types of provision to be found in the enacting parts of many statutes require special consideration as aids to interpretation. They are the interpretation (or definition) section, the proviso and the saving.

1. Interpretation sections

Modern statutes frequently contain (usually, in the case of English statutes, at the end) a set of provisions with the marginal note 'Interpretation'. These usually take one of two forms, stating either that a particular word or phrase 'means . . .' (or 'has the meaning hereby assigned to it') or that a particular word or phrase 'includes . . .'. Both forms are found in s 62(1) of the Sale of Goods Act 1979: ' "buyer" means a person who buys or agrees to buy goods'; ' "goods" includes all chattels personal other than things in action and money'. There are usually qualifying words such as 'unless the context otherwise requires', nevertheless the distinction is important because, when an interpretation section states that a word or phrase 'means . . .', any other meaning is excluded, whereas the word 'includes' indicates an extension of the ordinary meaning which continues to apply in appropriate cases.

'The word "include" is very generally used in interpretation clauses in order to enlarge the meaning of words or phrases occurring in the body of the statute; and when it is so used these words or phrases must be construed as comprehending, not only such things as they signify according to their natural import, but also those things which the interpretation clause declares that they include.'[20]

The distinction is illustrated by the Employers' Liability (Defective Equipment) Act 1969. Section 1(1) provides that an employer is liable to an employee who suffers personal injury in the course of his employment 'in consequence of a defect in equipment provided by the employer for the purposes of the employer's business'. Section 1(3) states that ' "equipment" includes any plant and machinery, vehicle, aircraft and clothing'. In *Coltman v Bibby Tankers Ltd,*[1] the crew of a ship was drowned allegedly because of its unseaworthiness. The personal representatives of a member of the crew sued the employer under s 1(1) of the Act. In the Court of Appeal, Glidewell LJ held that the definition of equipment in s 1(3) expressly included means of conveyance by land ('vehicle') or air ('aircraft') and should be taken to specifically exclude conveyance on the sea in a ship.[2] The House of Lords rejected this interpretation. Lord Oliver stated that 'includes' in s 1(3) could not be construed as 'means and includes' so as to restrict the scope of the word 'equipment' to the examples given. That subsection merely served to clarify that all kinds of plant and machinery were covered. The purpose of the Act was 'manifestly to saddle the employer with liability for defective plant of every sort with which the employee is compelled to work in the course of his employment'[3] and liability to crew members for a ship clearly came within this.

Interpretation sections may bring the most incongruous things within the operation of a statute. This point was made by Channell J in the course of holding that the Savoy Hotel was a shop.[4] In spite of its seeming oddity, the effect of the decision was beyond criticism for it brought persons under 18 within the protection against excessive working hours accorded by the Shops Act 1892 under which 'shop' included 'licensed public houses and refreshment houses of any kind'. Despite the occasional bizarre conclusion of this sort, interpretation sections are a common feature of modern British statutes and are responsible for a great deal of economy in drafting. They are

---

20. *Dilworth v Stamps Commrs* [1899] AC 99 at 105-106, per Lord Watson.
1. [1988] AC 276, CA and HL.
2. At 288.
3. At 301.
4. *Savoy Hotel Co v London County Council* [1900] 1 QB 665 at 669. For a more recent example, see *Dunsby v British Broadcasting Corpn*, (1983) Times, 25 July (a film studio is a 'factory' within s 175(1)(c) of the Factories Act 1961).

also a common feature of EC legislation not only for this reason, but also to achieve uniformity of interpretation and application.

2. Provisos

A proviso is frequently not an aid to construction, although the terms of the provision to which it is a proviso are usually of considerable aid to its construction. To discuss the subject under the head of aids to construction is rather like putting the cart before the horse. But the adoption of this course has its conveniences. The reason why the main provision affects the construction of the proviso is that there is a presumption based on the ordinary use of language that the scope of the proviso is affected by the scope of the main provision. The leading case is *Thompson v Dibdin*.[5] After enacting that no marriage between a man and his deceased wife's sister should be, or be deemed to have been, void or voidable as a civil contract by reason of such affinity, s 1 of the Deceased Wife's Sister's Marriage Act 1907[6] continued:

> 'Provided always that no clergyman in holy orders of the Church of England shall be liable to any suit, penalty or censure, whether civil or ecclesiastical, for anything done or omitted to be done by him in the performance of the duties of his office to which suit, penalty or censure he would not have been liable if this Act had not been passed.'

Did this mean that a clergyman could refuse holy communion to a man and his deceased wife's sister who had intermarried, as he could have done before the Act? Read without reference to what preceded it, this would have been the effect of the proviso, but, having regard to the fact that s 1 was solely concerned with the contract of marriage, the Court of Appeal and House of Lords held that a clergyman was not entitled to refuse holy communion in the circumstances:

> '. . . A proviso must *prima facie* be read and considered in relation to the principal matter to which it is a proviso, that is the marriage contract. It is not a separate or independent enactment. The words are dependent on the principal enacting words to which they are tacked as a proviso. They cannot be read as divorced from their context.'[7]

---

5. [1912] AC 533.
6. See now Marriage (Enabling) Act 1960.
7. [1912] AC 533 at 544, per Lord Ashbourne.

It has been said that if Parliament had in plain terms stated in the proviso that a clergyman might do just what the clergyman in *Thompson v Dibdin* had claimed to do, the courts would not have been entitled to refuse to give effect to that enactment on the ground that the drafter had broken a rule which he should have observed. This is of course perfectly true, but such drafting invites misunderstanding. The point is that the ordinary reader would expect a proviso to qualify in some way the words which precede it.

Enactments containing provisos must be construed as a whole and it is not permissible to separate the principal part of the enactment from the proviso.[8] Nevertheless, the ordinary reader would not expect the proviso to control the construction of the main provision. Warnings have from time to time been given against allowing a proviso to exercise an undue influence over the construction of the main section. To quote Lord Watson:[9]

> 'I am perfectly clear that if the language of the enacting part of the statute does not contain the provisions which are said to occur in it, you cannot derive those provisions by implication from a proviso, . . .
> I perfectly admit that there may be and are many cases in which the terms of an intelligible proviso may throw considerable light on the ambiguous import of the statutory words.'

In recent years, provisos have become increasingly rare in English statutes. But the words 'provided that', in the sense of 'on condition that' are occasionally used.

3. Savings

A saving resembles a proviso in its function of qualifying the main provision, but has no particular form.[10] It often begins with a phrase such as 'Nothing in this section shall be construed as . . .'. Section 52(3) of the Town and Country Planning Act 1971, discussed in the *Windsor and Maidenhead* case,[11] is an example. Being, like a proviso, a qualification of the generality of the main provision, it is subject to similar principles of interpretation. In

---

8. See *Gubay v Kington (Inspector of Taxes)* [1984] 1 All ER 513, HL.
9. *West Derby Union v Metropolitan Life Assurance Society* [1897] AC 647 at 652. *Bennion* p 494 suggests that such warnings resulted from the fact that provisos in the 19th century were frequently added by a Bill's opponents and were not an integral part of the original scheme of the Bill.
10. *Bennion* pp 494-496.
11. P 117 above.

Ealing London Borough Council v Race Relations Board,[12] Lord Simon of Glaisdale expressed some hesitation about savings:

> '. . . considerable caution is needed in construing a general statutory provision by reference to its statutory exceptions. "Saving clauses" are often included by way of reassurance, for avoidance of doubt or from abundance of caution. Section 27(9)(a) [of the Race Relations Act 1968] itself provides a striking example: it provides that nothing in the Act shall invalidate certain rules restricting certain classes of employment to "persons of particular birth, citizenship, nationality, descent or residence", and "residence", at least, is not conceivably within the ambit of s 1(1).'

The function of a saving provision is not to alter existing rights or powers, but to preserve them. All the same, this may lead to surprising results. Thus, in *R v Brent Health Authority, ex p Francis*,[13] s 1(8) of the Public Bodies (Admission to Meetings) Act 1960 was successfully used to justify the exclusion of the public from a meeting which the Act required to be open. The subsection provided that:

> 'The provisions of this section shall be without prejudice to any power of exclusion to suppress or prevent disorderly conduct or other misbehaviour at a meeting.'

The applicant claimed that this did not include a power to exclude the public altogether. Drawing on a precedent of 1866 in relation to a colonial legislature, it was held that the common law conferred on a body all powers without which it could not perform its functions, and that this included a power to remove people for obstructing debates. On this basis, the common law power to exclude the public from meetings, where members of the public create a disorder, was held to be preserved by the saving, even though the legislature had probably been unaware of the existence of such an obscure common law power.

B. OTHER PARTS OF THE SAME STATUTE

A distinction is usually drawn between the enacting parts of the statute (those which create operative rules of law) and other parts of the Act which

---

12. [1972] AC 342 at 363.
13. [1985] 1 All ER 74.

surround or introduce them. Items falling within this second head are the long title, the preamble (if any), and the short title on the one hand, and cross-headings, side-notes (or marginal notes) and punctuation on the other. Nowadays it is probably true to say that each one of the above items has some value as an aid to construction in some circumstances, but they all have less value than the items mentioned in the previous section simply because they do not enact anything. Certainly the provisions of Lord Scarman's Interpretation of Legislation Bills of 1980 and 1981 which sought to give statutory effect to the admissibility of such items as aids to interpretation encountered no objections.[14] There is a distinction between the first and second groups of non-enacting items because the first three items can be amended by Parliament when dealing with a Bill whereas this is not true of the last three. All the same, the content of the last three is determined by the Parliamentary clerks, on the advice of the drafter, in accordance with Parliamentary practice, and is fixed before royal assent. Thus, in their different ways, all of the items listed can fairly be regarded as representing the intention of Parliament, and it would be wrong to reject the last three as merely indicating the intention of the drafter.[15]

There is a bewildering mass of conflicting dicta on the question whether some of the above items can be treated as aids to construction at all and, when it is conceded that they may be so treated, upon their weight. This is due to a failure to distinguish between two stages in the process of interpretation at which the aids may be relevant. The first stage is that at which the judge has to decide whether he has any real doubt about the meaning of the word, phrase or passage which he is called upon to interpret. At this point it is hard to believe that he can or should have any inhibitions concerning the parts of the statute which he will read. No doubt he will begin with the section containing the word, phrase or passage in dispute. He can hardly help taking account of the punctuation and side-note. If he is to fulfil his duty of reading the whole Act, when it is necessary to do so in order to determine whether there is an ambiguity, he must look at the long title, preamble (if any), short title and cross-headings. If, after this performance, the judge is satisfied that the word, phrase or passage the meaning of which is in dispute really only has one meaning in the context, he must apply that meaning; but if he has doubts on the subject he will think again. It is at this point that the distinction between the enacting parts of a statute and the other parts becomes crucial. If the sole cause of doubt is a disparity between the otherwise clear and unambiguous words and a title, preamble, heading or

---

14. See 405 HL Official Report (5th series) cols 276-306 (13 February 1980); 418 HL Official Report (5th series) cols 64-83 (9 March 1981).
15. See *Bennion* pp 484-485. A contrary view was expressed in the first edition of this work at p 107.

side-note, the judge must disregard his doubts and apply the otherwise clear and unambiguous words. This is because there is a rule of law according to which, although the parts of the statute which do not enact anything may be consulted as a guide to Parliamentary intent and hence to the meaning of the enacted words, effect must not be given to any doubts which they may raise about the meaning of those words. If, however, the judge has doubts about the meaning of the statutory provision he is considering for some other reason such as its lack of clarity or apparent pointlessness, he may take the title, preamble, heading or side-note into consideration in determining how those doubts should be resolved. As we shall see, reservations have been expressed about the propriety of taking any of the above items into consideration, but it is submitted that the following remarks of Lord Upjohn in *DPP v Schildkamp*[16] amply justify the above general account of the relevance of the items mentioned at the beginning of this section to the judicial process of interpretation. The remarks were made with special reference to cross-headings:

> 'When the court construing the statute is reading it through to understand it, it must read the cross-headings as well as the body of the statute and that will always be a useful pointer to the intention of Parliament in enacting the immediately following sections. Whether the cross-heading is no more than a pointer or label, or is helpful in assisting to construe, or even in some cases to control, the meaning or ambit of those sections must necessarily depend on the circumstances of each case, and I do not think it is possible to lay down any rules.'

The matter must now be considered in slightly greater detail.

1. Long title and preamble

The long title of an Act is set out at the beginning and usually contains a general indication of the legislative purpose. For example the long title of the Social Security (Incapacity for Work) Act 1994 reads:

> 'An Act to provide for incapacity benefit in place of sickness benefit and invalidity benefit; to make provision as to the test of incapacity for work for the purposes of that benefit and other social security purposes; to make provision as to the rate of statutory sick pay; to make other amendments as to certain allowances payable to a person who is or has been incapable of work; and for connected purposes.'

---

16. [1971] AC 1 at 28.

Rules of Parliamentary procedure require no more than that the long title should cover everything in the Bill as introduced; and, if necessary, it is amended to accommodate changes made in the content of the Bill before it is enacted. In modern times all Acts have long titles, but preambles have for a long time been something of a rarity. An exception is the Canada Act 1982, the preamble to which reads:

> 'Whereas Canada has requested and consented to the enactment of an Act of the Parliament of the United Kingdom to give effect to the provisions hereinafter set forth and the Senate and the House of Commons of Canada in Parliament assembled have submitted an address to Her Majesty requesting that Her Majesty may graciously be pleased to cause a Bill to be laid before the Parliament of the United Kingdom for that purpose'.

When there is a preamble, it sets out the facts and assumptions upon which the statute is based. The long title and preamble are discussed together because the law with regard to the use which may be made of each is the same. It is worth noting that what is strictly a long title is sometimes erroneously referred to as a preamble.

Preambles are regularly to be found in EC legislation and contain fairly extensive statements of the purpose of and reasons for a regulation or directive. For example Regulation 2257/94 EC of 16 September 1994[17] laying down quality standards for bananas has the following preamble which is actually longer than the three articles of the Regulation:

> 'Whereas Regulation (EEC) No 404/93 makes provision for laying down common quality standards for bananas intended for consumption fresh, not including plantains; whereas the purpose of these standards is to ensure that the market is supplied with products of uniform and satisfactory quality, in particular in the case of bananas harvested in the Community, for which efforts to improve quality should be made;
>
> Whereas, given the wide range of varieties marketed in the Community and of marketing practices, minimum standards should be set for unripened green bananas, without prejudice to the later introduction of standards applicable at a different marketing stage; whereas the characteristics of fig bananas and the way in which they are marketed are such that they should not be covered by the Community standards;
>
> Whereas the banana-producing Member States already apply national standards within their territory at different stages in the

---

17. OJ 1994 L 245/6 (20 September 1994).

marketing of bananas; whereas it seems appropriate, in view of the objectives pursued, to allow these existing rules to continue to apply to their own production but only at stages subsequent to unripened green bananas, provided those rules are not in conflict with the Community standards and do not impede the free circulation of bananas in the Community;

Whereas account should be taken of the fact that, because climatic factors make production conditions difficult in the Community regions of Madeira, the Azores, the Algarve, Crete and Lakonia, bananas do not develop to the minimum length laid down; whereas in these cases such bananas may still be marketed, but only in Class II; . . .'

In considering EC legislation, the Court of Justice makes frequent reference to the preamble as an indication of the broad policy underlying an act. Its consideration forms an integral part of telelogical interpretation which was discussed above on pp 108-109. Unlike English courts, the Court of Justice does not refer to a preamble as part of teleological interpretation only where there is ambiguity in the enactment. The preamble is part of the legislation taken as a whole and, for example, may contribute to a teleological interpretation which displaces a wholly unambiguous literal reading of a particular article of a regulation.[18]

The commonly accepted position as regards the use that may be made of the long title was succinctly stated by Donovan J in *R v Bates*:[19]

'In many cases the long title may supply the key to the meaning. The principle, as I understand it, is that where something is doubtful or ambiguous the long title may be looked to resolve the doubt or ambiguity, but, in the absence of doubt or ambiguity, the passage under construction must be taken to mean what it says, so that, if its meaning be clear, that meaning is not to be narrowed or restricted by reference to the long title.'

However, this has been challenged by some other judicial statements and is rejected by Bennion as too restrictive. On this wider view, the long title may always be consulted as 'the plainest of all guides to the general objectives of a statute. But it will not always help as to particular provisions'.[20]

---

18. See T Millett 'Rules of Interpretation in EEC legislation' [1989] Stat LR 163 at 171-172, citing *Franz Grad v Finanzamt Traunstein* Case 9/70 [1970] ECR 825 at 839, and *Fellinger v Bundesanstalt für Arbeit* Case 67/79 [1980] ECR 535.

19. [1952] 2 All ER 842 at 844; also *Manuel v A-G* [1982] 3 All ER 822 at 831, per Slade LJ. See also *R v Galvin* [1987] QB 862 at 869, per Lord Lane CJ, discussed at p 129 below.

20. *Black-Clawson International Ltd v Papierwerke Waldhof-Aschaffenberg AG* [1975] AC 591 at 647, per Lord Simon of Glaisdale; *Bennion* pp 598-599.

If this refers to the first stage mentioned on p 124, then this is clearly true. But this does not contradict the fundamental point made by Donovan J that, once their full context is considered in the light of the purposes of the Act, it is the unambiguous words of a section which will prevail over the long title.

The accepted position as regards the use that may be made of a preamble of an Act of Parliament was stated by Lord Normand in the following terms in *A-G v Prince Ernest Augustus of Hanover:*[1]

> 'When there is a preamble it is generally in its recitals that the mischief to be remedied and the scope of the Act are described. It is therefore clearly permissible to have recourse to it as an aid to construing the enacting provisions. The preamble is not, however, of the same weight as an aid to construction of a section of the Act as are other relevant enacting words to be found elsewhere in the Act or even in related Acts. There may be no exact correspondence between preamble and enactment, and the enactment may go beyond or it may fall short of the indications that may be gathered from the preamble. Again, the preamble cannot be of much or any assistance in construing provisions which embody qualifications or exceptions from the operation of the general purpose of the Act. It is only when it conveys a clear and definite meaning in comparison with relatively obscure or indefinite enacting words that the preamble may legitimately prevail. The courts are concerned with the practical business of deciding a *lis*, and when the plaintiff puts forward one construction of an enactment and the defendant another, it is the court's business in any case of some difficulty, after informing itself of what I have called the legal and factual context including the preamble, to consider in the light of this knowledge whether the enacting words admit of both the rival constructions put forward. If they admit of only one construction, that construction will receive effect even if it is inconsistent with the preamble, but if the enacting words are capable of either of the constructions offered by the parties, the construction which fits the preamble may be preferred.'

Lord Normand was speaking in a case in which the section of the statute of Anne which conferred British citizenship on the lineal descendants of the Electoress Sofia 'born or hereafter to be born' was held to be unaffected by the reference to naturalisation in Queen Anne's lifetime in the preamble. The preamble itself was none too clear, but the *Hanover* case is clear authority for the proposition that the fact that the enacting words under

---

1.   [1957] AC 436 at 467; see pp 54-55 above.

consideration go beyond the scope of the purposes mentioned in the preamble is not a reason for declining to give effect to otherwise unambiguous statutory words.[2] It will be recollected that the case is also authority for the proposition that no one is entitled to assert that statutory words are unambiguous until he has read them in their full context which includes the long title and, if there is one, the preamble.[3]

A further illustration of the rule that these parts of a statute cannot control otherwise unambiguous enacting words merely because those words fall outside their scope is provided by *R v Galvin*.[4] The relevant provisions of section 2(1) of the Official Secrets Act 1911 provided that:

> 'If any person having in his possession or control any . . . document . . . which he has obtained owing to his position as a person who holds . . . a contract made on behalf of [Her] Majesty . . . (a) communicates the . . . document . . . to any person, other than a person to whom he is authorised to communicate it, . . . that person shall be guilty of [an offence].'

In this case the appellant was convicted under s 2(2) of unlawfully receiving a document knowing or having reason to believe it to have been communicated to him in breach of s 2(1). The document in question was an aircraft manual which was classified as 'restricted' and was passed to him from a serviceman. The appellant argued that, although still classified, the manual had been disseminated by the Ministry of Defence as part of tender documents for a defence contract, and it was thus put into the public domain and no longer secret. The long title of the Official Secrets Act 1889, which preceded the 1911 Act, was 'An Act to prevent the Disclosure of Official Documents and Information'. The appellant argued that once information came into the public domain it was no longer 'official' in this sense. The Court of Appeal refused to let the title restrict the otherwise plain meaning of the words of the 1911 Act which unambiguously stated that it was an offence to communicate a document to someone to whom the official was not authorised to communicate it.

This case may be contrasted with *Brett v Brett*[5] which shows that the long title and preamble may be allowed to play their part in controlling apparently unambiguous enacted words when doubts about the meaning of those words arise from some other source. The Wills Act 1751 provided that beneficiaries who attested 'any will or codicil' should be good witnesses but that gifts made to them in the will or codicil should be void. The words 'any will or

---

2. See also *The Norwhale* [1975] 2 All ER 501.
3. See pp 55–56 above.
4. [1987] QB 862, criticised in *Bennion* p 498.
5. (1826) 3 Add 210.

codicil' were of course apt to cover wills of personalty as well as realty, but the then state of the law naturally gave rise to doubts about their applying to wills of personalty because such wills did not require attestation at all. These doubts, coupled with the terms of a later section of the Act, and a reference to the long title and preamble both of which spoke only of wills and codicils of real estate were held by Sir John Nicholl to warrant the reading in of the words 'of real estate' after the word 'codicil'.

One of several examples of modern cases in which reference was made to the long title as something which resolved a doubt about the meaning of an enacted word is *R v Wheatley*.[6] The appellant was charged with the unlawful possession of an 'explosive substance', namely a metal pipe bomb filled with fire-dampened sodium chlorate mixed with sugar, contrary to s 4 of the Explosive Substances Act 1883. While expert evidence for the Crown contended that the bomb was capable of producing an explosive effect, expert evidence for the accused contended that it would only produce a pyrotechnic effect and was therefore not an 'explosive substance'. In his direction to the jury, the trial judge held that the words 'explosive substance' were to be construed by reference to the definition of 'explosive' in s 3(1) of the Explosives Act 1875 which covered substances 'used or manufactured with a view to produce a practical effect by explosion or a pyrotechnic effect'. The Court of Appeal upheld the conviction on the ground that the 1883 Act had properly been construed in the light of the 1875 Act. The long title of the 1883 Act was 'An Act to amend the law relating to Explosive Substances', and that of the 1875 Act was 'An Act to amend the law with respect to manufacturing, keeping, selling, carrying, and importing Gunpowder, Nitro-glycerine, and other Explosive Substances'. From a comparison of these long titles, it was clear that they dealt with the same subject matter, and this sufficed to justify the judge's application of the definition of 'explosive substance' contained in the earlier Act.

2. Short title

The short title is usually stated in a separate subsection towards the end of the statute. For example s 36(1) of the Theft Act says 'This Act may be cited as the Theft Act 1968'. As it is contained in the body of the Act and is, like the long title and preamble, subject to amendment during the Bill's passage through Parliament, one might think that the short title should be treated in the same way as a guide to interpretation. However, its sole purpose being to serve as a brief identifying label, it is by no means as helpful as the long

---

6. [1979] 1 All ER 954.

title or a preamble. The need for brevity often results in a short title that does not cover everything in the Act. Thus, for example, in *R v Galvin*,[7] the short title of the Official Secrets Act 1911 did not prevent s 2(1) being construed as including the communication of a document which was arguably neither 'official' nor 'secret'. The drafter may occasionally seek to make the title formally comprehensive, as in the 'Health and Safety at Work etc Act 1974', but this is not usual. However, despite its limitations, there is no reason why the short title should not sometimes be used as a guide to interpretation. As Scrutton LJ put it, with reference to the issue whether the Vexatious Actions Act 1896 applied to criminal proceedings:[8]

> 'I agree that the court should give less importance to the title than to the enacting part, and less to the short title than to the full title, for the short title being a label, accuracy may be sacrificed to brevity; but I do not understand on what principle of construction I am not to look at the words of the Act itself to help me to understand its scope in order to interpret the words Parliament has used, by the circumstances in respect of which they were legislating. It is by no means conclusive, but it is striking that if they were intending to deal with criminal proceedings they should call their Act the Vexatious Actions Act.'

3. Headings

Headings are not voted upon by Parliament, but they are included in the Bill and form part of the text entered on the Parliament Roll. A new Part or schedule added to a Bill by amendment during the Bill's passage through Parliament will contain headings in the same way as a Part or schedule contained in the Bill as introduced. Despite dicta to the contrary, headings have parliamentary authority and are appropriately consulted to resolve an ambiguity in the text. Thus, in *Dixon v British Broadcasting Corpn*[9] both Shaw and Brandon LJJ referred to the heading 'Unfair Dismissal' of Part II of Sch 1 to the Trade Union and Labour Relations Act 1974 and to the heading 'Right of employee not to be unfairly dismissed' underneath as giving the purpose in the light of which paras 5 and 12 were to be interpreted. Equally, we have already seen that great importance was attached to the headings in the Companies Act 1948 by the majority of the House of Lords

---

7. P 129 above.
8. *Re Boaler* [1915] 1 KB 21 at 40-41.
9. Pp 1114-115 above.

in *DPP v Schildkamp*.[10] The fact that the heading of the group of sections which included s 332 was 'Offences antecedent to or in the course of Winding-Up' supported the conclusion that the offence under s 332(3) could only be charged in a case in which a winding-up order had been made. The uncertainty concerned the scope rather than the meaning of the statutory words.

4. Side-notes

Side-notes (frequently referred to as 'marginal notes') have a similar status to headings. In the words of Upjohn LJ: 'While the marginal note to a section cannot control the language used in the section, it is at least permissible to approach a consideration of [the section's] general purpose and the mischief at which it is aimed with the note in mind.'[11] Thus in *Tudor Grange Holdings Ltd v Citibank NA*[12] it was argued that a deed of release signed by a bank and companies having claims against it was invalid under s 10 of the Unfair Contract Terms Act 1977. That section provided that:

> 'A person is not bound by any contract term prejudicing or taking away rights of his which arise under or in connection with the performance of another contract, so far as those rights extend to the enforcement of another's liability which [Part I] of this Act prevents that other from excluding or restricting.'

The rights extinguished by the release related to the bank's liability for negligence, a matter covered in Part I of the Act. Browne-Wilkinson VC found assistance from the side-note 'Evasion by means of a secondary contract'. This clearly indicated that the section was aimed at the use of a secondary contract as a way of evading the restrictions on limitation of liability imposed by Part I of the Act. It did not cover a contract to settle existing claims relating to the performance of another contract, and so s 10 had no application to the deed of release in this case.

By contrast, Lord Reid took the view in *Chandler v DPP*[13] that 'side-notes cannot be used as an aid to construction. They are mere catch-words . . .' In that case anti-nuclear protestors who demonstrated on a military

---

10. See p 56 above.
11. *Stephens v Cuckfield RDC* [1960] 2 QB 373 at 383.
12. [1991] 4 All ER 1.
13. [1964] AC 736 at 789. But see his subsequent remarks in *DPP v Schildkamp* [1971] AC 1 at 10 where he suggested that the side-notes (in common with the punctuation and cross-headings) represent the intention of Parliament.

airfield were convicted of an offence under s 1(1) of the Official Secrets Act 1911 which punishes those who approach prohibited places for a purpose prejudicial to the interests of the state. The side-note reads 'Penalties for spying' and it was conceded that the defendants were not spying, but their appeal was dismissed on the ground that they were acting for a purpose prejudicial to the interests of the state within the meaning of s 1(1). Rather as in *R v Galvin*[14] on the same Act, the side-note could not restrict the plain meaning of the enacting words. As Bennion remarks, 'If the side-note contradicts the text this puts the interpreter on inquiry; but the answer may be that the drafter chose an inadequate signpost, or neglected to alter it to match an amendment made to the clause during the passage of the Bill'.[15] But this does not deprive the side-note of all value as an aid to construction.

5. Punctuation

Punctuation forms part of the statute and, even if the reader has to be wary of older Acts, in which punctuation was inserted after enactment by the printer, the punctuation of modern statutes must be given the significance it has to the ordinary user of the English language. As Lord Lowry put it:[16]

'I consider that not to take account of punctuation disregards the reality that literate people, such as Parliamentary draftsmen, punctuate what they write, if not identically, at least in accordance with grammatical principles. Why should not other literate people, such as judges, look at the punctuation in order to interpret the meaning of the legislation as accepted by Parliament?'

Or, as Thornton more trenchantly observes:[17]

'It is a curious paradox that judges, whose entire reading is punctuated, should, in carefully punctuated judgments, consider themselves obliged to proclaim that the punctuation in carefully punctuated statutes is no part of the law.'

---

14. See p 129 above.
15. *Bennion* p 513.
16. *Hanlon v Law Society* [1981] AC 124 at 198.
17. *Legislative Drafting* (3rd edn) pp 33-34.

While older dicta[18] suggested that the punctuation should not be regarded as decisive of meaning, this does not represent the modern view. All the same, the judge may in some cases be compelled to correct errors in punctuation, a course which the courts are prepared to adopt more readily than amendment of the wording of the statute.

For example, in *Luby v Newcastle-under-Lyme Corpn*,[19] s 113(4) of the Housing Act 1957 provided that 'the local authority shall from time to time review rents and make such changes, either of rents generally or of particular rents, and rebates (if any) as circumstances may require'. The comma after the word 'rents' where it occurs for the third time suggests that the authority has power to make rebates rather than to make changes in rebates, but the subsection was read as though the comma was not there. As Bennion points out, the obscurity really results from the omission of the word 'of' before 'rebates' and not so much from the comma used.[20] Nevertheless, by focusing on the punctuation, the judges are able to appear to be interfering less with the Parliamentary text than if words were added.

C. RULES OF LANGUAGE

Statutes are drafted with care and it is reasonable to apply to their wording ordinary grammatical rules for the use of language. Four such rules are of particular importance—the *ejusdem generis* ('of the same kind') rule, the maxim *noscitur a sociis* ('a thing is known by its associates'), the rule of rank and the maxim *expressio unius exclusio alterius* ('the mention of one thing is the exclusion of another'). *Noscitur a sociis* and the rule of rank can, roughly speaking, be respectively regarded as extended and attenuated versions of the *ejusdem generis* rule. These rules or maxims have attracted an unduly large quantity of case law because they are neither legal principles nor legal rules. It is hardly correct to speak of them as rules of language, for they simply refer to the way in which people speak in certain contexts. They are no more than rough guides to the intention of the speaker or writer. To update an example of E A Driedger:[1] ordinarily a parent who authorised a teenage daughter to buy a dress coat, shoes and 'anything else you need' would not expect her to buy anything but clothes. To exemplify the *expressio unius* maxim by the words of an even more generous hypothetical speaker, if someone were to say 'I am going to give you my houses in

---

18. Eg *Duke of Devonshire v O'Connor* (1890) 24 QBD 468 at 478, per Lord Esher MR.
19. [1964] 3 All ER 169.
20. *Bennion* pp 519-520.
1. 'A New Approach to Statutory Interpretation' (1951) 29 Can Bar Rev 838 at p 841.

London and York and the fixtures in my London house', the prospective donee could hardly hope for the fixtures in the York house.

1. Ejusdem generis ('of the same kind')[2]

E A Driedger also provides a full formulation of the *ejusdem generis* rule:[3]

> 'Where general words are found, following an enumeration of persons or things all susceptible of being regarded as specimens of a single genus or category, but not exhaustive thereof, their construction should be restricted to things of that class or category, unless it is reasonably clear from the context or the general scope and purview of the Act that Parliament intended that they should be given a broader signification.'

In *Quazi v Quazi*, Lord Diplock explained the rule in the following way:[4]

> 'The presumption then is that the draftsman's mind was directed only to [the genus indicated by the specific words] and that he did not, by his addition of the word "other" to the list, intend to stray beyond its boundaries, but merely to bring within the ambit of the enacting words those species which complete the genus but have been omitted from the preceding list either inadvertently or in the interests of brevity.'

An example is s 2(4) of the Land Charges Act 1972 which requires the registration as a Class C(iv) land charge of any 'estate contract', 'including a contract conferring either expressly or by statutory implication, a valid option to purchase, a right of pre-emption *or any other like right*'. The italicised words have been held to cover a conditional contract,[5] a contract to transfer land to any third person the contracting party specifies,[6] an obligation on the tenant to offer to surrender the lease before requesting the landlord's consent to its transfer,[7] and the right of a council to repurchase a council house it had sold.[8] However, the words have been held not to cover a notice to treat served under a compulsory purchase order,[9] nor an equitable

---

2. See G Williams, 'The Origin and Logical Implications of the *Ejusdem Generis* Rule' (1943) 7 Conv (NS) 119; A Samuel 'The Ejusdem Generis Rule in Statutory Interpretation' [1984] Stat LR 180.
3. *Construction of Statutes* (2nd edn) p 116.
4. [1980] AC 744 at 807-808.
5. *Haselmere Estates Ltd v Baker* [1982] 3 All ER 525.
6. *Turley v Mackay* [1943] 2 All ER 1.
7. *Green v Church Commrs for England* [1974] 3 All ER 609.
8. *First National Securities Ltd v Chiltern District Council* [1975] 2 All ER 766.

right to re-entry,[10] nor a proprietary estoppel.[11] They are concerned with rights created voluntarily by contract, and not with rights created in other ways. Although, as Lord Diplock indicated, one reason for the rule is that the drafter must be taken to have inserted the general words in case something which ought to have been included among the specifically enumerated items had been omitted; a further reason is that, if the general words were intended to have their ordinary meaning, the specific enumeration would be pointless. For instance, in *Re Stockport Ragged, Industrial and Reformatory Schools*[12] the question was whether Industrial Schools fell within the proviso to s 62 of the Charitable Trusts Act 1853. If they did not, the consent of the Charity Commissioners to their mortgages was required. The proviso referred to 'any cathedral, collegiate, chapter, or *other* schools'; but it was held to be applicable only to schools of the specified kinds and those of a similar type. Lindley MR said that he could not conceive why the legislature should have taken the trouble to specify particular kinds of schools except in order to show the type of school to which reference was being made.

For the rule to apply, it must be possible to construct a category (commonly called a 'genus') out of the specific words to delimit what is to be considered as 'of the same kind'. *Quazi v Quazi*[13] concerned s 2 of the Recognition of Divorces and Legal Separations Act 1971, which requires recognition to be given to foreign divorces and legal separations obtained by means of 'judicial or other proceedings'. The House of Lords considered that 'other proceedings' was not limited to a procedure akin to a judicial proceeding, but could apply to *talaq* divorces which were essentially religious ceremonies. Lord Scarman remarked:[14]

> 'If the legislative purpose of a statute is such that a statutory series should be read ejusdem generis, so be it; the rule is helpful. But, if it is not, the rule is more likely to defeat than to fulfil the purpose of the statute. The rule, like many other rules of statutory interpretation, is a useful servant but a bad master.'

The purpose of the legislation was to give recognition in Britain to divorces validly obtained abroad, and the methods adopted by a foreign country in granting divorces were not a concern of the English courts.

---

9. *Capital Investments Ltd v Wednesfield UDC* [1964] 1 All ER 655.
10. *Shiloh Spinners Ltd v Harding* [1973] 1 All ER 90.
11. *E R Ives Investments Ltd v High* [1967] 1 All ER 504.
12. [1898] 2 Ch 687.
13. [1980] AC 744.
14. At 824.

Although it has been said that a single species followed by general words cannot create a genus,[15] the speeches in *Quazi v Quazi* lend no support to this view and there are numerous examples to the contrary. For instance, in *Parkes v Secretary of State for the Environment*,[16] the Court of Appeal held that in the phrase 'building or other operations' in s 290 of the Town and Country Planning Act 1971 'other operations' must be read as akin to building.

There is no need for the genus to be of an obvious kind, and the courts are willing to limit general words by reference to a fairly heterogeneous set of words. Thus in *R v Staniforth, R v Jordan*,[17] s 4(1) of the Obscene Publications Act 1959 provided a defence to proceedings relating to the possession for gain of obscene articles 'if it is proved that publication of the article in question is justified as being for the public good on the ground that it is in the interests of science, literature, art or learning, or of other objects of general concern'. Section 4(2) permitted expert evidence to be admitted on such questions. The trial judge ruled inadmissible expert evidence purporting to show the psychotherapeutic benefit of the pornographic material to its readers. The House of Lords upheld this decision on the ground that 'other objects of general concern' were limited to matters of a kind similar to science, literature, art or learning and this was not the case here. Lord Wilberforce stated:[18]

> 'even if this is not strictly a case for applying a rule of *ejusdem generis* (the genus being one of intellectual or aesthetic values), the structure of the section makes it clear that the other objects, or, which is the same argument, the nature of the general concern, fall within the same area, and cannot fall in the totally different area of effect on sexual behaviour and attitudes. . . .'

This statement shows that the rule of *ejusdem generis* should not be too narrowly interpreted and that the notion of a 'genus' simply indicates a reasonably identifiable category of items or values.

The cases show that the application of the *ejusdem generis* rule is limited by the basic duty of the courts to have regard to the purpose of the statutory provisions under consideration. The *Quazi* case shows that the purpose of legislation may require general words to be construed in their most general sense in spite of the fact that they are preceded by specific words. In that case, the purpose was established by reference to an international convention to which the Act gave effect. However, even if a wide meaning does have to be given, the purpose will still restrict the scope.

---

15. Eg *Alexander v Tredegar Iron & Coal Co Ltd* [1944] KB 390 at 396, per Scott LJ.
16. [1979] 1 All ER 211.
17. [1977] AC 699.
18. At 719.

2.   Noscitur a sociis ('A thing is known by its associates')

The *ejusdem generis* rule is an example of a broader linguistic rule or practice to which reference is made by the Latin tag *noscitur a sociis*. Words, even if they are not general words like 'or any other' preceded by specific words, are liable to be affected by other words with which they are associated. To quote Stamp J:[19]

> 'English words derive colour from those which surround them. Sentences are not mere collections of words to be taken out of the sentence, defined separately by reference to the dictionary or decided cases, and then put back into the sentence with the meaning which you have assigned to them as separate words. . . .'

Two illustrations show that the meaning of a word may be coloured by the context of the words used either in the same sentence or within the same Act read as a whole. An example of the former is *Westminster City Council v Ray Alan (Manshops) Ltd*.[20] Section 14(1) of the Trade Descriptions Act 1968 penalised the making of a false statement as to the nature of 'any services, accommodation or facilities provided'. A company announced a 'Closing Down Sale' at one of its shops, but continued trading normally and did not intend to close the shop. The Divisional Court held that the word 'facilities' was limited by the preceding words to things made available for use by customers and so did not include the broader notion of shopping facilities.

The second situation is illustrated by *Bromley London Borough Council v Greater London Council*.[1] Section 1(1) of the Transport (London) Act 1969 required the Greater London Council to develop policies and to encourage measures for 'the provision of integrated, efficient and *economic* transport facilities and services for Greater London'. In discussing the sense to be given to the word 'economic', Lord Scarman observed:[2]

> 'As a matter of English usage, the term "economic" . . . has several meanings. They include both that for which the appellants contend and that for which Bromley contends. It is a very useful word, chameleon-like, taking its colour from its surroundings.'

In the context, and especially in the light of s 7(3) which imposed a duty on the London Transport Executive 'as far as practicable' to make up any

---

19. *Bourne v Norwich Crematorium Ltd* [1967] 2 All ER 576 at 578.
20. [1982] 1 All ER 771.
1. Pp 70-71 above.
2. [1982] 1 All ER 129 at 174.

deficit emerging at the end of an accounting period, the word 'economic' meant 'being run on business principles'.

No useful purpose would be served by multiplying examples. It is sufficient to stress that, as in the case of the construction of a genus, the context may prevent words from being coloured by their associates. Thus in *Coltman v Bibby Tankers Ltd*,[3] 'plant and machinery' was not restricted by the associated words 'vehicle' and 'aircraft'.

3. The rule of rank

The rule of rank is the second of the rules for the construction of statutes mentioned by Blackstone at the end of the third section of his *Commentaries*, where it is formulated as follows:[4]

> 'A statute, which treats of things or persons of an inferior rank, cannot by any *general words* be extended to those of a superior. So a statute, treating of "deans, prebendaries, parsons, vicars, *and others having spiritual promotion*" is held not to extend to bishops, though they have spiritual promotion; deans being the highest persons named, and bishops being of a still higher order.'

The rule is treated with contempt by Bentham:

> 'and who can be sure in such an assemblage what is a superior and what inferior? Suppose deans had been omitted, and prebendaries had been the first word, would canons have been to stand included or excluded?'[5]

Yet there are cases where, as a matter of ordinary language, an omission is so striking that one would pause to treat it as included in general words although there is no question of the specific words constituting a relevant genus to which the general words might be limited. Surely most people would hesitate before including the Thames in a prohibition on salmon fishing in 'the waters of the Humber, Ouse, Trent . . . and all other waters in the realm wherein salmon be taken'?[6] If this type of problem can be solved by a rule of language, the *expressio unius* maxim is at least a safer guide than the uncertain rule of rank; but can the *expressio unius* maxim be applied to exclude the literal sense of general words?

---

3. Pp 120 above.
4. *Commentaries on the Laws of England* (1st edn) vol 1 p 88.
5. *A Comment on the Commentaries* p 140.
6. Coke 2 Inst 478.

4.   Expressio unius ('The mention of one thing is the exclusion of another')

The effect of the Latin maxim *expressio unius est exclusio alterius*, sometimes stated in the form *expressum facit cessare tacitum* (that which is expressed puts an end to that which is unspoken) is that mention of one or more things of a particular class may be regarded as by implication excluding all other members of the class. An example is provided by *Dimbleby & Sons Ltd v National Union of Journalists.*[7] Section 17(3) of the Employment Act 1980 conferred an immunity from suit for actions taken during a trade dispute against 'a party to the dispute'. Section 17(4) granted an immunity for a limited number of actions (not including those in the case) taken against an 'associated employer', defined as meaning an employing company controlled by the employer in the dispute or by a third person also having control of that employer. Here a newspaper publisher sought an injunction to prevent a union from instructing its members not to produce copy to be printed by TBF Printers Ltd. The union was in dispute with TB Forman Ltd, which was an associated company of TBF Printers Ltd having the same shareholders. The House of Lords refused to hold that the action was covered by the immunity under s 17(3), since TBF Printers was a separate legal person from the 'party to the dispute', TB Forman Ltd. While not excluding the possibility of lifting the corporate veil in an appropriate case should the purpose of the statute so require, the creation of a separate immunity for actions against 'associated employers' in s 17(4) precluded such a wide construction of 'a party to the dispute' in s 17(3). A similar approach has been seen in *Re DML.*[8] The same applies to a series of words. The word 'land' is usually apt to include all kinds of mine, but a reference to 'lands, houses and coalmines' may mean that no mines are included in the word 'lands'.[9]

Yet, although it would be possible to multiply the above examples considerably, it is doubtful whether the maxim does any more than draw attention to a fairly obvious linguistic point, viz that in many contexts the mention of some matters warrants an inference that other cognate matters were intentionally excluded. Allowance must always be made for the fact that the '*exclusio*' may have been accidental, still more for the fact that there may have been good reason for it. This last point is well illustrated by *Dean v Wiesengrund.*[10] Section 14 of the Increase of Rent and Mortgage Interest (Restrictions) Act 1920 provided that excess rent should be recoverable by the tenant by whom it was paid from the landlord or his personal

---

7. [1984] 1 All ER 751.
8. P 114 above.
9. *R v Sedgley Inhabitants* (1831) 2 B & Ad 65.
10. [1955] 2 QB 120.

representative. It was held that the omission of any reference to the tenant's personal representative did not prevent him from suing. The excess rent was made recoverable retrospectively, and the intention may have been to ensure that the personal representatives of landlords who died before the Act came into force could be sued. Jenkins LJ said:[11]

> 'The argument for the landlord is summed up in the maxim *expressio unius est exclusio alterius* which, applied to the present case, is said to compel the conclusion that the express reference to the legal personal representative of one of the parties excludes any implied reference to the legal personal representative of the other. But this maxim is after all no more than an aid to construction and has little, if any, weight where it is possible, as I think it is in the present case, to account for the *inclusio unius* on grounds other than an intention to effect the *exclusio alterius*.'

But, as J M Keyas remarks in his careful review of the topic,[12]

> 'The fact that *expressio unius* does not render answers with mathematical certainty is no more reason for dismissing it as an interpretative aid than it is for dismissing grammar or logic.'

---

11. At 130.
12. J M Keyas 'Expressio unius' [1989] Stat LR 1 at 25.

Chapter 6
External aids to construction

In Chapter 2 we noted that a judge will often base an interpretation on the 'obvious' purpose of an enactment gathered from reading the text in the light of the rest of the law and of what Lord Denning once described as 'matters generally known to well-informed people'.[1] This unresearched context is the subject of judicial notice but as has already been stated on p 59, evidence is often admitted to confirm an interpretation. In section A of this chapter, a little is said about this process of taking judicial notice of matters generally known to 'well-informed people' and the extent to which these matters, when judicially noticed, may be used as aids to statutory interpretation. Section B will consider the use of legislative history, an area much affected by the decision of the House of Lords in *Pepper v Hart*,[2] which has sought to improve the ability of the courts to discover the purpose of legislation. Nothing need be said about the process of taking judicial notice of the previous state of the law. It is simply a matter of consulting the relevant statutes, decisions and textbooks.

A. INFORMED INTERPRETATION

An informed interpretation involves the use, as aids to construction, of the historical setting of the statute, dictionaries and other literary sources, the practices of classes of the community to which the statute applies, contemporary exposition, and other statutes on the same subject. The last three of these items come mainly within the cognisance of lawyers, and the

---

1. *Escoigne Properties Ltd v IRC* [1958] AC 549 at 566. See generally pp 32-33, above.
2. Pp 18-19 above.

aid to be derived from dictionaries tends to be subordinated to that to be gained from judicial statements concerning the meaning of words.

1. Historical setting

The historical setting of the statute has been invoked as an aid to its construction in several cases which have already been mentioned. The following remark was made by Lord Reid in *Chandler v DPP*[3] in support of the conclusion that members of the Committee of 100 who obstructed an airfield acted for a 'purpose prejudicial to the safety or interests of the State' within the meaning of s 1 of the Official Secrets Act 1911, although they believed that nuclear disarmament would be beneficial to this country:

> 'The 1911 Act was passed at a time of grave misgiving about the German menace, and it would be surprising and hardly credible that the Parliament of that date intended that a person who deliberately interfered with vital dispositions of the armed forces should be entitled to submit to a jury that government policy was wrong and that what he did was really in the best interests of the country, and then perhaps to escape conviction because a unanimous verdict on that question could not be obtained.'

The examination of the historical setting of a statutory provision sometimes produces a conflict between the literal meaning and a purposive reading of the text. For example, in *Johnson v Moreton*[4] the historical setting of the Agricultural Holdings Act 1948 showed that it had been passed to promote general agricultural efficiency in the national interest during the post-war period. The protection of agricultural tenants was part of this policy, and this gave support to the view that the tenant's right to appeal against eviction to the Agricultural Lands Tribunal could not be excluded by agreement with the landlord. This interpretation was adopted despite the absence in s 24 of the formula 'this section shall have effect notwithstanding any agreement to the contrary'.

The historical setting is relevant even for very recent Acts. For instance, in *Nottinghamshire County Council v Secretary of State for the Environment*[5] s 59(11A) of the Local Government, Planning and Land Act 1980 required that expenditure guidance 'shall be framed by reference to principles applicable to all local authorities'. On a literal reading, this appeared to

---

3. [1964] AC 763 at 791, pp 132-133 above.
4. P 96 above.
5. Pp 87-88 above.

exclude the adoption of principles which discriminated between high-spending and low-spending authorities. However, Lord Bridge of Harwich noted that 'as is well known, it has been government policy since 1979 to reduce or restrain the level of public expenditure, which includes, of course, expenditure by local authorities'.[6] The Act formed part of this policy and, indeed, in its other dispositions it introduced mechanisms for discriminating between high-spending and low-spending authorities in the distribution of rate support grant. Against this setting, a literal reading would be manifestly contrary to the purpose of the Act, since it would have the consequence that expenditure guidance could not be adapted to take account of the past records of authorities in reducing their expenditure.

These cases demonstrate that the historical setting is often a matter of general knowledge and that this can be established without recourse to documents evidencing the legislative history of the Act.

2. Dictionaries and other literary sources

Reference has already been made to the use of dictionaries and other literary sources in aid of interpretation.[7] The example given was the definition of the word 'ethnic' in *Mandla v Dowell Lee*[8] for which the 1972 Supplement to the *Oxford English Dictionary* was referred to. However, the value of such sources is limited. It has been pointed out that dictionaries must be used with caution in certain situations—when, for example, the court is concerned with the meaning of a word at a particular date[9] or of a two-word phrase like 'unfair competition'.[10]

On the whole, definitions offered in previous judicial opinions are more influential, even if they do not constitute binding precedents. Thus in *Mandla v Dowell Lee*, Lord Fraser of Tullybelton relied heavily on a New Zealand decision on a similar statutory phrase.[11] Similarly in *National Westminster Bank plc v IRC*,[12] both the majority and the minority of the House of Lords relied predominantly on judicial pronouncements (though also on textbooks) to determine when shares were 'issued' for the purposes of s 299A of the Income and Corporation Taxes Act 1988.

---

6. [1986] AC 240 at 252.
7. See pp 61-62 above.
8. See pp 61-62 above; see also *A-G's Reference (No1 of 1988)*, pp 85-86 above.
9. *Hardwick Game Farm v Suffolk Agricultural and Poultry Producers Association Ltd* [1966] 1 All ER 309 at 323, per Davies LJ.
10. *Lee v Showman's Guild of Great Britain* [1952] 2 QB 329 at 338, per Somervell LJ.
11. *King-Ansell v Police* [1979] 2 NZLR 531, cited at [1983] 2 AC 563-4.
12. [1994] 3 All ER 1.

The *National Westminster Bank* case illustrates the use of opinions of contemporary legal writers, but older works, such as those of Coke, are also accorded respect where relevant. Literary sources may be consulted,[13] as may specialist works, such as books on political economy which were consulted in aid of the interpretation of the expression 'direct taxation' used in the British North America Act 1867.[14]

3. Practice

As long ago as 1744 Lord Hardwicke said: 'The uniform opinion and practice of eminent conveyancers has always had great regard paid to it by all courts of justice,'[15] and nothing has occurred during the intervening years to suggest a change of attitude on the part of the courts. The practice of conveyancers is of assistance in cases calling for the application of a technical meaning, and it may, presumably, be the subject either of evidence or of judicial notice. In *Jenkins v IRC* the meaning of the phrase 'irrevocable settlement', used in s 21(10) of the Finance Act 1936, was in issue. It was suggested that the phrase extended to a case in which, although the settlement itself was irrevocable, it would have been terminated in effect if the settlor had gone through a variety of processes such as putting various companies into liquidation. Lord Greene said:

'It seems to me quite illegitimate to take a word which has a technical and precise meaning in conveyancing and then to argue that it has some extended meaning. If the legislature wished to give to the word "irrevocable" some unusual and extended meaning of this sort, I ask myself why in the world did it not do so.'[16]

Conveyancers are not, of course, the only class of specialists whose practice may, in appropriate cases, be an aid to statutory interpretation. Commercial usage is, and for a long time has been, at least as important. For example, in *United Dominions Trust Ltd v Kirkwood*, the Court of Appeal had to construe the phrase 'any person *bona fide* carrying on the business of banking' used in s 6(d) of the Moneylenders Act 1900. Lord Denning said: 'In such a matter as this, when Parliament has given no guidance, we cannot do better than look at the reputation of the concern amongst intelligent men of commerce.'[17]

---

13. See *London and North-Eastern Rail Co v Berriman* [1946] AC 278.
14. *Bank of Toronto v Lambe* (1887) 12 App Cas 575 at 581, per Lord Hobhouse.
15. *Bassett v Bassett* (1744) 3 Atk 203 at 208.
16. [1944] 2 All ER 491 at 495.
17. [1966] 2 QB 431 at 454.

Recourse to previous practice is not confined to situations in which a word has acquired a technical meaning among a relevant body of specialists such as conveyancers. It also includes the previous practice of a relevant government body which may provide evidence of the background against which a statute was enacted. Thus in *Greenwich London Borough Council v Powell*,[18] policy guidance published in circulars issued in 1977 by the Department of the Environment encouraged local authorities to use their powers under the Caravan Sites Act 1968 to provide accommodation for the long-term needs of gypsies, and these were used as aids to the interpretation of their obligations in relation to gypsies under the Mobile Homes Act 1983. This situation must be distinguished from cases where the post-enactment practice of an official body is drawn to the court's attention as a possible aid to interpretation. In general, the post-enactment practices and statements of such bodies are only relevant if they provide contemporary exposition as discussed in the next section. What is said or done long after the enactment of legislation will typically reveal current policies of such bodies rather than the intentions of the legislature. However, there are some situations where this material can be appropriately influential in interpretation. For example, in *Wicks v Firth (Inspector of Taxes)*,[19] the House of Lords considered the tax liability of higher-paid employees for the scholarships received by their children and provided by a fund created by their employer. The Revenue argued that such scholarships were not exempt from tax under s 375 of the Income and Corporation Taxes Act 1970. However, the Revenue had issued a press release stating that it would treat as exempt scholarships awarded from a fund open to all to scholars who happened to be children of employees of the firm by which the fund was financed, which was not the case here. Lord Bridge of Harwich noted that, if the Revenue's arguments on s 375 were correct, there would be a legal liability to tax even in the cases covered by the press release. He continued:[20]

'This is not a decisive consideration, but in choosing between competing constructions of a taxing provision it is legitimate, I think, to incline against a construction which the Revenue are unwilling to apply in its full rigour, but feel they must mitigate by way of extra-statutory concession, recognising, presumably, that in some cases their construction would produce a result which Parliament can hardly have intended.'

---

18. [1989] 1 All ER 65.
19. [1983] 2 AC 214.
20. At 231; cf Lord Templeman at 236. See further Bennion *Statute Law* pp 294-295, and *Statutory Interpretation* s 232.

Modern
usage)
Explanation

4. Contemporary exposition (often referred to by its Latin name, 'contemporanea expositio')

The justification for using contemporary expositions of the meaning of a statute is given in the following extract from *Maxwell*,[1] cited in the judgment of the Court of Criminal Appeal in *R v Casement*:[2]

'It is said that the best exposition of a statute or any other document is that which it has received from contemporary authority . . . where this has been given by enactment or judicial decision, it is of course to be accepted as conclusive. But, further, the meaning publicly given by contemporary or long professional usage is presumed to be the true one, even where the language has etymologically or popularly a different meaning. It is obvious that the language of a statute must be understood in the sense in which it was understood when it was passed, and those who lived at or near the time when it was passed may reasonably be supposed to be better acquainted than their descendants with the circumstances to which it had relation, as well as with the sense they attached to legislative expressions. Moreover, the long acquiescence of the legislature in the interpretation put upon its enactment by notorious practice may, perhaps, be regarded as some sanction and approval of it.'

It is necessary to distinguish two forms of the contemporary exposition of a statute. Contemporary exposition may refer, firstly, to the way a text was interpreted by courts, legal writers and others in the period following its enactment. This shows how the statute was understood by those to whom it was addressed. Contemporary exposition may refer, secondly, to statements or statutory instruments issued by the government contemporaneously with the Act. This shows how the Act was understood by those responsible for its enactment.

An example of the former is *Mark Rowlands Ltd v Berni Inns Ltd.*[3] Section 2 of the Life Assurance Act 1774 provides that a policy must name the person whose life is insured under it. The Court of Appeal held that this provision did not invalidate an indemnity insurance policy taken out by a landlord and covering, among other things, the risk of death or personal injury to any person using a building, even though the persons covered were not specifically named. The Act, originally without a short title, was long known as the

---

1. *On the Interpretation of Statutes.* This passage is now on p 264 of the 12th edn.
2. [1917] 1 KB 98 at 138-139.
3. [1985] 3 All ER 473.

Gambling Act 1774, and in 1854 a judge had acknowledged the settled understanding that it did not apply to indemnity insurance, being confined to contracts to pay money on the occurrence of a specific insured event, eg if the king died within the year. Courts will tend to respect previous judicial decisions on the interpretation of a particular statute even when they are not bound by them and may be reluctant to depart from them because of the undesirability of disturbing past transactions. But in the absence of such a danger, courts seem willing to overrule decisions on the interpretation of a statute no less than decisions on the common law.[4] Similarly, great respect is paid to the opinion of writers such as Coke and Hale with regard to the construction of a statute, but no more so than is the case with regard to their opinions concerning the common law. The House of Lords has made it plain that reliance can only be placed on this form of contemporary exposition as an aid to the interpretation of ambiguous language in very old statutes.[5]

As regards contemporary official statements and statutory instruments, the courts are willing to use this form of contemporary exposition as an aid to interpret even very recent statutes. For example, in *Nottinghamshire County Council v Secretary of State for the Environment*,[6] the House of Lords in 1985 used the Rate Support Grant Report for 1982-83, submitted to the House of Commons on 5 February 1982 and approved by resolution of the House, to interpret a subsection inserted by the Local Government Finance Act 1982, which received the Royal Assent on 13 July 1982. The Act was intended to give retrospective force to the guidance contained in that report and so could be construed in the light of the report. As Lord Bridge of Harwich explained:[7]

'The reality is that the Rate Support Grant Report for 1982-83, which contained the relevant guidance and secured the approval of the House of Commons, was submitted to the House by the Secretary of State whose department was concurrently promoting the money Bill which became the 1982 Act. Is there any principle which requires us to put on blinkers and ignore this reality? I know of none. If we can regard the reality, then it seems to me that, to the extent that the meaning of provisions given retrospective force is open to doubt, the nature of the guidance by reference to which those provisions will operate, having been set out in a report submitted to and approved by the House of

---

4. See *R v Shivpuri* [1986] 2 All ER 334; *Vestey v IRC* [1980] AC 1148; see p 175 n 2 and pp 181-182 below. See generally, J W Harris 'Towards Principles of Overruling—When Should a Final Court of Appeal Second Guess?' (1990) 10 OJLS 135 at pp 156ff.
5. *Campbell College, Belfast (Governors) v Valuation Comr for Northern Ireland* [1964] 2 All ER 705 at 727.
6. [1986] AC 240, see pp 87-88 above.
7. At 264.

Commons before the enactment of the statute, is available as a
contemporanea expositio of the draftsman's purpose.'

A similar approach was adopted in *Hanlon v Law Society*,[8] where regulations
made in 1976 and 1977 were used to interpret the reference in s 9(6) of the
Legal Aid Act 1974 to 'property recovered or preserved' in proceedings
involving legal aid. That subsection began 'Except insofar as regulations
otherwise provide . . .' and this was considered by the House of Lords as
justifying the use of the regulations to interpret the meaning of the parent
Act. Lord Lowry suggested:[9]

> 'A study of the cases and of the leading textbooks . . . appears to me
> to warrant the formulation of the following propositions.
> (1) Subordinate legislation may be used in order to construe the
>   parent Act, but only where power is given to amend the Act by
>   regulations or where the meaning of the Act is ambiguous.
> (2) Regulations made under the Act provide a Parliamentary or
>   administrative contemporanea expositio of the Act but do not
>   decide or control its meaning: to allow this would be to substitute
>   the rule-making authority for the judge as interpreter and would
>   disregard the possibility that the regulation relied on was
>   misconceived or ultra vires.
> (3) Regulations which are consistent with a certain interpretation of
>   the Act tend to confirm that interpretation.
> (4) Where the Act provides a framework built on by con-
>   temporaneously prepared regulations, the latter may be a reliable
>   guide to the meaning of the former.
> (5) The regulations are a clear guide, and may be decisive, they are
>   made in pursuance of a power to modify the Act, particularly if
>   they come into operation on the same day as the Act which they
>   modify.
> (6) Clear guidance may also be obtained from regulations which are
>   to have effect as if enacted in the parent Act.'

More recently, the House of Lords has pointed out that these propositions
apply only where the regulations are roughly contemporaneous with the Act
and do not apply where they were made four years later to counteract an
identified loophole.[10]

---

8. [1981] AC 124.
9. At 193-194.
10. Lord Browne-Wilkinson, *Deposit Protection Board v Dalia* [1994] 2 All ER 577 at 585.

Important as contemporary exposition may be, this does not prevent the courts from adopting an 'updating' or 'ambulatory' interpretation where the wording or the purpose of an enactment so requires.[11]

5. Other statutes on the same subject

As we have seen,[12] the external context of a statute includes its place within the general scheme of statutory and common law rules and principles. In particular, this context includes statutes on the same subject (known as statutes *in pari materia*). A later statute may expressly provide that it is to be read (or construed) as one with earlier legislation. In that event the court must construe all the statutes directed to be read together as though they were one Act. The result can sometimes be a surprising one. In *Phillips v Parnaby*[13] a conviction under s 21 of the Weights and Measures Act 1889 for delivering less coal than that shown on the weight ticket had to be quashed because the defendant had not been served with notice of prosecution. No such notice was required by the Act, but notice of prosecution had to be given under s 12(6) of the Sale of Food (Weights and Measures) Act 1926, s 15 of which provided that it was to be construed as one with former Weights and Measures Acts, including that of 1889.

Where new statutory provisions are inserted in the text of an existing statute, it is intended that the old and the new provisions should be read as one. But, as the *Nottinghamshire County Council* case shows,[14] problems can arise when the terminology used is not identical with that of the original Act and caution is required with the notion that statutes of different dates should be read as one.

When an earlier statute is *in pari materia* with a later one, it is simply part of its context to be considered by the judge in deciding whether the meaning of a provision in the later statute is plain.[15] Like the preamble and long title, it may not be allowed to raise an ambiguity, although it may help to resolve an ambiguity raised by other considerations. For example, in *Re C and anor (minors) (parent: residence order)*,[16] the Court of Appeal referred to the provisions of the Adoption Act 1976 on the status of the natural parent after an adoption order had been made in order to assist the interpretation of the word 'parent' in the Children Act 1989.

---

11. See pp 51-54 above.
12. See p 50 above.
13. [1934] 2 KB 299.
14. See pp 87-88 above.
15. Viscount Simonds referred to statutes *in pari materia* in this way in *A-G v Prince Ernest Augustus of Hanover* [1957] AC 436 at 461.
16. See pp 63-64 above.

There is no authoritative definition of the expression *in pari materia*. It is said to be not enough that the statutes should deal with the same subject matter, but a lot depends on how narrowly the latter term is defined. It is not very helpful to say that they must form part of a 'system', and, with respect, it is difficult to believe that any greater assistance is to be derived from the oft-quoted statement of an American judge, made as long ago as 1829, that statutes are *in pari materia* if they relate to the same person or thing, or to the same class of persons or things.[17]

However much an earlier and later statute may be *in pari materia*, the later one cannot be treated as part of the context of the earlier; but it may be used as an aid to the construction of the earlier statute if the two of them can be described as 'laws on the same subject' and if the part of the earlier Act which it is sought to construe may be 'fairly and equally open to different meanings'.[18] The mere fact that a particular construction of the earlier provision would mean that the later one is surplusage may be of no great significance, for it might have been enacted out of an abundance of caution. However, the courts are loath to regard a subsequent Act as unnecessary, since 'Parliamentary time is sufficiently precious for Parliament not to pass unnecessary Acts of Parliament'.[19] That remark was made by Forbes J in a case concerning the refusal by a Chief Constable to grant a pedlar's certificate under the Pedlars Act 1871 to a sales representative for goods made by the disabled on the ground, among others, that his hawking of goods from house to house would constitute an offence under the House to House Collections Act 1939. The court's attention was drawn to the Trading Representatives (Disabled Persons) Act 1958, which makes it an offence for an unregistered person, in selling or soliciting orders for goods, to represent that disabled persons are employed in their production. Had the Chief Constable's interpretation been correct, the 1958 Act would have been unnecessary to regulate an activity already prohibited by the 1939 Act. The court preferred to give the 1939 Act an interpretation that left room for a useful interpretation of the later Act. Equally, if a later Act has proceeded on the assumption that an earlier statute has a certain effect, the courts will prefer a construction which accords with Parliament's understanding.[20]

The foregoing discussion of statutes *in pari materia* as aids to interpretation has, of course, been solely concerned with the assistance to be derived in the construction of one statutory provision from the terms of another. Guidance by contrast or analogy may sometimes be derived from a provision of a statute other than that under consideration although there is no question of the two of them being *in pari materia*, but there is no obligation on the judge

---

17. Hosmer J, *United Society v Eagle Bank*, 7 Conn 457 at 469.
18. *Re MacManaway* [1951] AC 161 at 177.
19. *Murphy v Duke* [1985] 2 All ER 274 at 280.
20. Browne-Wilkinson LJ, *Re Billson's Settlement Trusts* [1984] 2 All ER 401 at 406.

to consider such statutes as there is in the case of those *in pari materia*.[1] So far as judicial decisions are concerned, although those with regard to the meaning of words in one statute are not binding so far as words in another statute are concerned (unless the second statute consolidates the first), they often have great persuasive force.

B. LEGISLATIVE HISTORY

'Legislative history' means (i) the legislative antecedents of the statutory provision under consideration, ie corresponding provisions in previous enactments since repealed and re-enacted with or without modification;[2] (ii) pre-parliamentary materials relating to the provision or the statute in which it is contained, eg reports of committees and commissions reviewing the existing law and recommending changes; and (iii) parliamentary materials, ie the text of a Bill as first published and successively amended in its passage through Parliament, explanatory memoranda, proceedings in committees and parliamentary debates. All three of these items have claims to be regarded as part of the context of a statute but special rules, which are none too easy to state with confidence, apply to the use which a judge may make of them when giving reasons for his decision. In the first place, reference to legislative history is only permissible when he is in doubt about the meaning of the provision under consideration after considering it in its general context as defined by Viscount Simonds in *A-G v Prince Ernest Augustus of Hanover*.[3] Secondly, as will be seen, a distinction has to be drawn between situations in which judges ought to have regard to legislative history which may then provide reasons for the interpretation adopted, and situations in which judges receive such information to confirm an interpretation justified by the meaning of the words read in context. In the latter case, legislative history plays a supporting role similar to that played by dictionaries in relation to matters which are the subject of judicial notice.

The principle underlying the dominant contemporary judicial approach to the use of legislative history as an aid to interpretation was clearly stated by Lord Diplock in *Fothergill v Monarch Airlines Ltd*:[4]

---

1. See pp 44-46 above.
2. These are not the same thing as statutes *in pari materia*. Those are considered as forming part of the legislative scheme, whereas legislative history is considered in order to see how a particular provision reached its present position on the statute book.
3. [1957] AC 436 at 461, see pp 55-56 above.
4. [1981] AC 251 at 279-280.

'The constitutional function performed by courts of justice as interpreters of the written law laid down in Acts of Parliament is often described as ascertaining "the intention of Parliament"; but what this metaphor, though convenient, omits to take into account is that the court, when acting in its interpretative role, ... is doing so as mediator between the state in the exercise of its legislative power and the private citizen for whom the law made by Parliament constitutes a rule binding upon him and enforceable by the executive power of the state. Elementary justice or, to use the concept often cited by the European Court, the need for legal certainty demands that the rules by which the citizen is to be bound should be ascertainable by him (or, more realistically, by a competent lawyer advising him) by reference to identifiable sources that are publicly accessible. The source to which Parliament must have intended the citizen to refer is the language of the Act itself. These are the words which Parliament has itself approved as accurately expressing its intentions. If the meaning of those words is clear and unambiguous and does not lead to a result that is manifestly absurd or unreasonable, it would be a confidence trick by Parliament and destructive of all legal certainty if the private citizen could not rely upon that meaning but was required to search through all that had happened before and in the course of the legislative process in order to see whether there was anything to be found from which it could be inferred that Parliament's real intention had not been accurately expressed by the actual words that Parliament had adopted to communicate it to those affected by the legislation.'

This principle must, however, be qualified by that stated by Lord Griffiths in *Pepper v Hart*;[5]

'The courts now adopt a purposive approach which seeks to give effect to the true purpose of legislation and are prepared to look at much extraneous material that bears upon the background against which the legislation was enacted.'

The rules adopted by the courts represent a compromise between the requirements of the rule of law and legal certainty on the one hand, and of fidelity to the intention of Parliament on the other.

---

5. [1993] 1 All ER 42 at 50.

1. The plain meaning rule

It would be possible to place a restrictive interpretation on Lord Diplock's ban on consulting legislative history so as to confine it to cases where the words of the Act are 'clear and unambiguous'; but it accords more with judicial practice to extend it to cases where the judge is satisfied that one of two or more possible meanings of statutory words, read in a context bereft of their legislative history, best fits the purpose of the legislation.

This priority of the plain meaning remains unaffected by the admissibility of legislative history after *Pepper v Hart*. Such material is only admissible where the wording of the enactment is ambiguous, obscure or leads to an absurdity.[6] As N S Marsh has observed,[7] in contrast to other jurisdictions in Europe, the English judge:

> 'does not generally feel himself under the same obligation to search as deeply as possible for the most satisfactory meaning of the statute, if he has to hand an interpretation which accords with the normal usage of language as employed in the text of the statute, and of the more obvious and immediate contextual implications of the text.'

The reference to the normal usage of language gives the clue to the justification of the English practice. To quote Lord Diplock again:[8]

> 'The acceptance of the rule of law as a constitutional principle requires that a citizen, before committing himself to any course of action, should be able to know in advance what are the legal consequences that will flow from it. Where those consequences are regulated by a statute the source of that knowledge is what the statute says. In construing it the court must give effect to what the words of the statute would be reasonably understood to mean by those whose conduct it regulates.'

It is quite right that the courts should take such internal matters as the preamble and long title into account because they would be taken into account by the normal user of the English language, but there are limits to the extent to which he, or (and this is where we approach the realities of the situation) his legal adviser, can be expected to consider non-statutory materials. We have seen that the long title and preamble can only serve in

---

6. See Lord Oliver and Lord Browne-Wilkinson, pp 156-157 below.
7. *Interpretation in a National and International Context* p 75.
8. *Black-Clawson International Ltd v Papierwerke Waldhof-Aschaffenburg AG* [1975] AC 591 at 638; see also Lord Oliver (second quotation) p 157 below.

the first instance as pointers to a plain meaning, they cannot be allowed to raise an ambiguity, although they may, at a later stage, resolve ambiguities in the enacting words. No greater force should be accorded to legislative history, hence it would be preposterous to expect those acting on the statute extrajudicially to refer to that history when they consider the meaning of the statutory words to be plain without its aid. This justification of the English practice is unanswerable provided the distinction between plain meaning and ambiguity is as clear cut and workable as the practice assumes it to be.

2. Parliamentary materials

Until *Pepper v Hart*[9] was decided in 1992, the rule had been that, for practical reasons, Parliamentary debates reported in *Hansard* could not be cited as an aid to the construction of a statute.[10] But there are a number of cases studied in this book where the problem posed to the court had been raised in Parliament and answered by the Minister, who considered the Bill clear enough not to require further elaboration on the point. For example, that Sikhs were protected by the phrase 'ethnic' was expressly agreed by the Minister at the time when the Bill for the Race Relations Act 1976 was before Parliament.[11] The result in *Mandla*[12] was in accord with what the Minister had considered implicit, even though the courts did not refer to parliamentary debates. By contrast, there was divergence between the House of Lords and the reply of the Minister on the question of whether the Transport (London) Act 1969 permitted the subsidy of fares by the Greater London Council. As has been shown by J Dignan, the decision in *Bromley London Borough Council v Greater London Council* on the interpretation of that Act was clearly contrary to a ministerial statement made during the passage of the Bill.[13] As Lord Goff remarked:[14]

---

9. [1993] 1 All ER 42, pp 18-19 above.
10. *Beswick v Beswick* [1968] AC 58; *Davis v Johnson* [1979] AC 264; *Hadmor Productions Ltd v Hamilton* [1983] 1 AC 191: see the 2nd edition of this work pp 154-158.
11. See St John A Robilliard [1983] PL 348.
12. *Mandla v Dowell Lee* [1983] 2 AC 438, pp 58-59 above.
13. 'Policy-making, Local Authorities and the Courts: the "GLC Fares" Case' (1983) 99 LQR 605, 622-624: pp 70-71 above.
14. In a House of Lords debate on statutory interpretation, 503 HL Official Report (5th series) col 280 at 282 (18 January 1989). Similarly, Lord Griffiths said (at col 286):
'I have long thought that our courts have placed an unreasonable fetter on themselves by refusing to look at the parliamentary history of an Act. We profess to attempt to give effect to the intention of Parliament when we are construing a statute and yet we refuse to check whether Parliament said what its intention was, what it intended to cover or what a particular word was perhaps intended to mean.'

'It is strange that a court, even the appellate committee of your Lordship's House, should deliberately blindfold itself and as a result interpret a statute in a manner which is clean contradictory to the way in which Parliament heard the Bill introduced.'

Pepper v Hart was a case which nearly produced a result contrary to the intention of Parliament. This was avoided only because it was re-argued before seven Law Lords after the original committee had the Minister's statement drawn to their attention. That statement made it clear that under what became s 63(2) of the Finance Act 1976 the benefit to the teacher under arrangements for the children of staff in private, fee-paying schools to be taught at less than the commercial fee would be assessed by reference to the cost to the employer (which in that case would be very small indeed) and not by reference to the full commercial fee.[15]

A new practice has been instituted by this decision, although in some respects it does not represent a radical departure from what has gone before. The normal rule remains that *Hansard* should not be used in the interpretation of statutes. But, as Lord Browne-Wilkinson stated:[16]

'the exclusionary rule should be relaxed so as to permit reference to parliamentary materials where: (a) legislation is ambiguous or obscure, or leads to an absurdity; (b) the material relied on consists of one or more statements by a minister or other promoter of the Bill together if necessary with such other parliamentary material as is necessary to understand such statements and their effect; (c) the statements relied on are clear.'

In the case before the House, the statements made by the minister in Parliament clearly resolved an ambiguity in the language of the statute, and were therefore appropriate to be used.

The restrictive approach adopted by Lord Browne-Wilkinson is also reflected in the concurring speeches of Lords Bridge and Oliver. Lord Bridge suggested that *Hansard* should be used 'only . . . in the rare cases where the very issue of interpretation which the courts are called on to resolve has been addressed in parliamentary debate and where the promoter of the legislation has made a clear statement directed to that very issue'.[17] Lord Oliver remarked:[18]

---

15. See p 19 above.
16. [1993] 1 All ER 42 at 69.
17. At 49.
18. At 52.

'It can only apply where the expression of the legislative intention is genuinely ambiguous or obscure or where a literal or *prima facie* construction leads to a manifest absurdity and where the difficulty can be resolved by a clear statement directed to the matter in issue.'

The justification for such a restricted approach remains legal certainty. As Lord Oliver stated, 'A statute is, after all, the formal and complete intimation to the citizen of the particular rule of law which he is enjoined . . . to obey and by which he is both expected and entitled to regulate his conduct'.[19] Thus, only when the ordinary language of the statute is ambiguous or absurd and thereby puts ordinary citizens on notice that they need to look further, is it appropriate to permit research into parliamentary debates to find the meaning and purpose of legislation.

The new approach has been much used by the courts since *Pepper v Hart* was decided. As Lord Mackay LC warned extrajudicially, there are many instances where *Hansard* does not provide assistance to the court.[20] Nevertheless, there are a number of cases in which the courts have found considerable assistance from parliamentary materials. To take just one example, in *R v Warwickshire County Council, ex p Johnson*,[1] Lord Roskill relied on the words of Lord Beaverbrook, the minister presenting the Bill, at the Report Stage, as to whom might be prosecuted under what became the Consumer Protection Act 1987. In that case, the manager of a Dixons retail shop was prosecuted under s 20 of the Consumer Protection Act 1987 for giving a misleading price indication 'in the course of [a] business of his'. He argued that, as a manager, he did not have a business, and the person who should have been prosecuted was the company, Dixons Stores Group Ltd. The House of Lords upheld this argument and directed that his conviction be set aside. Relying on clear statements in parliamentary debate on this phrase, a 'business of his', Lord Roskill demonstrated that it was never intended to apply to individual shop assistants or store managers, but only to businesses. In *Pickstone v Freemans plc*,[2] the House of Lords had already drawn upon the speech of the minister presenting the Equal Pay (Amendment) Regulations to demonstrate that these were intended to bring English law into line with Community law following the judgment of the European Court of Justice in Case 61/81, *Commission v UK*.[3] Lord Keith justified this

---

19. At 52.
20. 'Finishers, Refiners, and Polishers: the Judicial Roles in the Interpretation of Statutes' [1989] Stat LR 151: see eg *Scher v Policyholders Protection Board (No 2)* [1993] 4 All ER 840 at 852.
1. [1993] 1 All ER 299. See also *Steele Ford & Newton (a firm) v Crown Prosecution Service* [1993] 2 All ER 769.
2. [1989] AC 66.
3. [1982] ECR 2601.

departure from practice by stating that, since the draft regulations were not subject to the parliamentary process of consideration and amendment in committee, as a Bill would have been, it was entirely legitimate for the purpose of ascertaining the intention of Parliament to take into account the terms in which the draft was presented by the responsible minister.[4]

Three major concerns have been expressed by opponents of the use of *Hansard*. First, Lord Mackay LC argued in his dissenting speech that, if *Hansard* were potentially admissible in court, lawyers would feel obliged to consult it and this would increase the cost of legal advice, as well as prolonging cases in court.[5]

Other Law Lords recognised this difficulty but did not think it was insuperable. For a start, modern technology permits the collation of relevant material from *Hansard* with some speed, thus reducing cost. Furthermore, experience in Australia and New Zealand, where the rule excluding parliamentary debates had been relaxed, did not suggest that there would be a significant increase in the expense and complexity of litigation or legal advice. In their view, the amount of research into parliamentary debates which lawyers would actually do was probably exaggerated. Lord Templeman preferred to rely on the common sense of judges and counsel not to engage in fruitless researches. If excessive or unnecessary use of *Hansard* were made and prolonged litigation, this could be penalised by the award of costs.

It seems likely that in reality very few practising lawyers would embark on a speculative search of *Hansard*. They will look there when they are led to believe that *Hansard* contains some useful material. Such 'leads' for a search will be found in annotations to the Act in, for instance, *Current Law Statutes Annotated*, or in textbooks or articles written on the Act. If that is the reality of the matter, then the dangers involved are considerably less than opponents would expect. The image of unprompted research fails to reflect the real character of the legal community, with its interdependence between academics and practitioners. All the same, it has to be recognised that lawyers are potentially liable to their clients for negligent advice. This fact may encourage them to engage in research into *Hansard* when there is only a slim chance that it will contain useful material, and even when they would not commonly be regarded as professionally negligent in having decided not to undertake such research.

A second difficulty is the reliability of what is said. The American authority on statutory interpretation, Reed Dickerson, commented that '[i]n general, little legislative history is helpfully relevant. Much of it is unreliable or unreliably revealed'.[6] Furthermore, he suggests that, if debates in the

---

4.   [1989] AC 66 at 112.
5.   [1993] 1 All ER at 47-48.
6.   'Statutory Interpretation in America: Dipping into Legislative History' [1984] Stat LR 76 at 80.

legislature did become admissible, they would become less reliable if the experience of debates on the floor of Congress is any guide:

> 'Not only are they laden with sales talk, but their frequent reference to what a provision means is an unconscious effort to finesse [ie delicately manipulate] the courts in performing their constitutional function of having the last word on what the statute means.'[7]

There is evidence that members of Parliament are aware of the practice of the courts and seek to obtain assurances as to the meaning of provisions which can be used later in their interpretation. This was certainly the case with s 22 of the Education Act 1994. The section concerns the treatment of students who choose to opt out of the students' union of a college or university and provides, rather obscurely, that they should not be 'unfairly disadvantaged, with regard to the provision of services or otherwise'. The minister was expressly invited to give an interpretation of these words 'under the ruling in *Pepper v Hart*'.[8] Commenting on the possibility of such legislative practice, Lord Hailsham saw little value in much of what currently occurs in Parliament:

> 'From the practical point of view, I do not myself see how the collective will of Parliament, as the Bill plods its way through both Houses, can be discerned from the individual speeches from different quarters at different hours of the day, saying different things to a shifting audience of varying size . . . What was said by a Minister or a private member at two o'clock in the morning in the course of a report stage on a hot June night is more likely to mislead than enlighten, and criticism of it by judges, which would not only be legitimate but necessary were it to be admissible, would be constitutionally undesirable.'[9]

Thirdly, Lord Mackay LC was concerned that *Hansard* would be cited in nearly every case of statutory interpretation. It is certainly clear already that *Hansard* is referred to more often than the rule in *Pepper v Hart* would justify. Thus in *A-G v Associated Newspapers Ltd*[10] Lord Lowry referred to the parliamentary history of s 8(1) of the Contempt of Court Act 1981 in support of what he took to be the plain meaning of the provision and commented:

---

7. [1984] Stat LR 76 at 82.
8. Earl Russell, 557 HL Official Report (5th series) col 83; cf the warning of F Bennion, 'Hansard—Help or Hindrance? A Draftsman's View of *Pepper v Hart*' [1993] Stat LR 149.
9. *Hamlyn Revisited: the British Legal System Today* p 69.
10. [1994] 1 All ER 556 at 567.

'having regard to the complicated and controversial parliamentary history of s 8, I deliberately refrain from discussing the question whether it would have been appropriate for your Lordships to apply *Pepper (Inspector of Taxes) v Hart* to the facts of this case'.

Likewise Millett LJ in *Petch v Gurney (Inspector of Taxes)*[11] expressly stated that the meaning of s 56(4) of the Taxes Management Act 1970 was 'too plain for argument' and that reliance on *Pepper v Hart* would be inappropriate. All the same, he went on to note how the parliamentary materials presented in argument by counsel supported his interpretation. The position in practice thus seems to be that judges are only *required* to consider arguments from *Hansard* when the meaning of a statutory provision is ambiguous, obscure or the literal meaning leads to an absurdity. But it seems likely that counsel will frequently undertake researches and present extracts from *Hansard* to the courts in cases well beyond those in which the rule in *Pepper v Hart* applies.[12]

3. Pre-parliamentary materials

The decision in *Pepper v Hart* not only affects the use of parliamentary materials, but also the extent to which account can be taken of Government Green or White Papers and the reports of advisory committees, the Law Commission, Royal Commissions and the like. As with failure to consult *Hansard*, so failure to look at reports such as those of the Law Commission can lead to a divergence between what was proposed and how the courts interpret the resulting statute.[13] In *Black-Clawson International Ltd v Papierwerke Waldhof-Aschaffenburg AG,*[14] a majority of the House of Lords held that a committee report which included a draft Bill, identical in all material respects with the terms of the Act, was admissible as evidence of the *mischief* against which the Foreign Judgments (Reciprocal Enforcement) Act 1933 was directed, but not in order to determine the *meaning* of s 8(1). In *Pepper v Hart*, Lord Browne-Wilkinson argued that:

---

11. [1994] 3 All ER 731; also *R v Secretary of State for Foreign Affairs, ex p Rees-Mogg* [1994] 1 All ER 457 at 466.
12. Counsel are now required to provide the court and other parties in advance with copies of *Hansard* passages to which they intend to refer: *Practice Note (procedures: reference to Hansard)* [1995] 1 All ER 234.
13. See A Ashworth, 'Interpreting Criminal Statutes: A Crisis of Legality?' (1991) 107 LQR 419 at 433-435.
14. [1975] AC 591. The analysis of the law before *Pepper v Hart* in the second edition of this work (pp 158-162) was approved by Lord Lowry in *A-G's Reference (No 1 of 1988)* [1989] 2 All ER 1 at 6.

'Given the purposive approach to construction now adopted by the
courts in order to give effect to the true intentions of the legislature,
the fine distinctions between looking for the mischief and looking
for the intention in using words to provide the remedy are technical
and inappropriate.'[15]

Thus courts are now free to consult pre-parliamentary materials in the same
circumstances as they can consult parliamentary materials, with the caveat
that Parliament does not always follow the views set out in committee
reports or even in Government White Papers. Such documents will, of
course, continue to be useful for identifying the purpose of the enactment.[16]
But the use which is now made of such materials to identify the meaning of
words is illustrated by *R v Jefferson.*[17] Two men were convicted as aiders and
abettors on a charge of violent disorder contrary to s 2(1) of the Public Order
Act 1986 on account of their behaviour after an England victory in a World
Cup match. Section 6(2) of that Act provides that a person commits the
offence under s 2(1) 'only if he intends to use or threaten violence or is aware
that his conduct may be violent or threaten violence'. It was argued that the
offence thus described could only be committed as a principal, since the
words used suggest that the person committing the offence must be using or
threatening the violence. The Court of Appeal rejected the submission. It
took advantage of *Pepper v Hart* to consult both the Law Commission
report[18] which contained the draft Bill on which this part of the Act had been
based, and the Government White Paper[19] which preceded the Bill. Both of
these expressly stated that aiding and abetting would be covered by
the provisions relating to riot (s 1 of the Act) and by implication by other
provisions of Part I of the Act, which included s 2(1).

4. Treaties and international conventions

Treaties and international conventions are a frequent impetus for domestic
legislation. The problems posed by Acts implementing them are different
from those faced in purely domestic legislation, since the courts must strive
not only to carry out the intentions of Parliament, but also to ensure that their
interpretation will not be out of line with that of other signatory states. In
particular, the questions arising are whether the treaty, even if not expressly

---

15. [1993] 1 All ER 42 at 65.
16. Eg *R v Effik* [1994] 3 All ER 458 at 462.
17. [1994] 1 All ER 270.
18. *Offences Relating to Public Order* (Law Com no 123, 1983).
19. Home Office and Scottish Office *Review of Public Order Law* (Cmnd 9510, 1985).

enacted, can be used to interpret the statute, and whether the *travaux préparatoires*[20] of the treaty are also admissible, as is laid down in article 32 of the Vienna Convention on the Law of Treaties and as is the practice in many countries.

On the first question, the Act frequently resolves the problem by including the text of the treaty in a schedule, as in the Carriage by Air Act 1961, which enacts the Warsaw Convention on the subject. In other cases, the Act seeks to give effect to the treaty by a more specific adaptation of English law. Here, there is no doubt, since the decision of the House of Lords in *James Buchanan & Co Ltd v Babco Forwarding and Shipping (UK) Ltd*,[1] that the treaty may be consulted to clarify the meaning of the statute. As Lord Diplock put it in *Quazi v Quazi*:[2]

'Where Parliament passes an Act amending the domestic law of the United Kingdom in order to enable this country to ratify an international treaty and thereby assume towards other states that are parties to the treaty an obligation in international law to observe its terms, it is a legitimate aid to the construction of any provisions of the Act that are ambiguous or vague to have recourse to the terms of the treaty in order to see what was the obligation in international law that Parliament intended that this country should be enabled to assume. The ambiguity or obscurity is to be resolved in favour of that meaning that is consistent with the provisions of the treaty.'

This passage and other dicta make it clear that materials not contained in the Act, be they the unenacted treaty, versions of an enacted treaty in other languages, or the *travaux préparatoires* may only be consulted when the provisions of the Act are themselves ambiguous or vague.[3]

Sometimes the question arises whether the Act or the English text of the treaty is a correct translation of a convention drafted in another language. In such a case, reference to other official versions is permitted and, in the case of conflict, reference may also be made to the *travaux préparatoires*. Such was the case in *Fothergill v Monarch Airlines Ltd*.[4] Article 18(1) of the

---

20. There is no accepted English translation of the term *travaux préparatoires* (literally 'preparatory works') which is used to mean documentary material showing how the text of a treaty or legal instrument came into being.
1. [1978] AC 141. For an example see *R v Secretary of State for the Home Department, ex p Sivakumuran* [1988] AC 958 p 186, below.
2. [1980] AC 744 at 808.
3. Lords Salmon and Edmund-Davies in *Buchanan* [1978] AC at 161 and 167, but cf Lord Wilberforce at 152 (a case involving consulting of the French version of an enacted treaty); also Lord Brandon delivering the unanimous opinion of the House of Lords in *The Antonis P Lemos* [1985] AC 711 at 725-726, 731 (a case involving consulting an unenacted treaty).
4. [1981] AC 251.

Convention on Carriage by Air, enacted by the Carriage by Air Act 1961, made the carrier liable for 'damage sustained in the event of destruction or loss of, or of damage to, any registered baggage', but Article 26(2) required that, in the case of 'damage', the owner had to notify the carrier within seven days. In *Fothergill*, part of the contents of a registered suitcase was found to be missing after transit, but this was not notified to the carrier until four weeks later. It was held that for the partial loss of contents, notification to the carrier was required. Both the English and French texts of the Convention were contained in the Schedule to the Act and s 1(2) provided that, in the event of any inconsistency, the French text was to prevail. It was thus legitimate to compare the scope of the English word 'damage' with that of its French equivalent *avarie*. The House of Lords, like the majority of the Court of Appeal, considered that any doubts could be resolved by looking at French textbooks and judicial opinions on the subject, both as to the meaning of the word and as to the purpose of the Convention. Having consulted such material, the House of Lords did not consider it necessary to refer to the *travaux préparatoires* of the Convention. However, since Lord Denning MR had relied on them in the Court of Appeal, the House took the opportunity to give some guidance on when they might be consulted. Lord Wilberforce thought that they should be admissible only on two conditions: first, that the material involved was public and accessible, and secondly, that it 'clearly and indisputably' pointed to a definite legislative intention.[5] In this case, the minutes of the relevant meetings had been published by HMSO, and this was sufficient to equip bodies such as cargo underwriters, airlines and the like, among whom disputes would typically arise, with the necessary material.[6]

In order to resolve doubts, a statute may expressly permit the use of specified extrinsic material in its interpretation. Thus s 3(3) of the Civil Jurisdiction and Judgments Act 1982 provides that three reports forming part of the *travaux préparatoires* of the enacted Conventions may be used 'to ascertain their meaning and effect', and requires the reports to 'be given such weight as is appropriate in the circumstances'.

5. Conclusion

The decision in *Pepper v Hart* has had a major effect on the use of external aids in the interpretation of statutes. It is appropriate for the editors to

---

5. At 278.
6. See Lord Roskill at 302; *Gatoil International Inc v Arkwright-Boston Manufacturers Mutual Insurance Co* [1985] AC 255.

provide a brief comment on the current state of the law. In one sense, the problems in stating the law highlighted in earlier editions of this work[7] have been removed by the decision of the House of Lords in that case. Although that decision is clear, the way in which its limits have in practice been rapidly overstepped in cases where *Hansard* and such other similar materials have been brought before the courts suggests that the decision will have a more radical effect than was intended. In consequence, we remain concerned about the practical impact of the change. Increased use of pre-parliamentary and parliamentary materials in the interpretation of statutes does create more work for lawyers when preparing cases for litigation (and indeed earlier, when advising clients), even if there are a number of ways of avoiding laborious reading of lengthy reports or parliamentary debates, as noted above on p 158. But these are not a substitute for 'some means of presenting [parliamentary materials] in a short and simple form' called for by Cross in the first edition of this work.[8] The preamble to the EC regulation quoted on pp 126-127 provides one illustration of the sort of statement which could be provided. The Commission set up by the Hansard Society proposed that 'notes on sections' should be published at the same time as the Act.[9] These would provide ministerially approved statements of the purpose and intended effect of each section of the Act and could make the task of interpreting enactments easier. But increased use of external aids to construction is no substitute for the clearest possible drafting of the text of the statute. We shall return to this issue in the section on drafting in Chapter 8.

---

7. See 1st edn p 141, 2nd edn pp 164-165.
8. 1st edn p 141.
9. See p 201 below.

Chapter 7

Presumptions

A. PRESUMPTIONS GENERALLY

Although the word 'presumption' is used with different shades of meaning in different branches of the law, its use always relates in some way to the burden of proof. The implication is that a particular conclusion is likely to be drawn by the court in the absence of good reason for reaching a different one. In the law of statutory interpretation there are two kinds of presumption which merge into each other, and the sovereignty of Parliament gives the clue to the nature of the first kind.

Statutes often go into considerable detail, but even so allowance must be made for the fact that they are not enacted in a vacuum. A great deal inevitably remains unsaid. Legislators and drafters assume that the courts will continue to act in accordance with well-recognised rules:

> 'The mental element of most crimes is marked by one of the words "maliciously", "fraudulently", "negligently" or "knowingly", but it is the general—I might, I think, say, the invariable—practice of the legislature to leave unexpressed some of the mental elements of crime. In all cases whatever, competent age, sanity and some degree of freedom from some kinds of coercion are assumed to be essential to criminality, but I do not believe they are ever introduced into any statute by which any particular crime is defined.'[1]

Long-standing principles of constitutional and administrative law are likewise taken for granted, or assumed by the courts to have been taken for granted, by Parliament. Examples are the principles that discretionary powers conferred in apparently absolute terms must be exercised reasonably, and that administrative tribunals and other such bodies must act in accordance with the principles of natural justice. One function of the word 'presumption' in the

---

1. Stephen J, *R v Tolson* (1889) 23 QBD 168 at 187.

context of statutory interpretation is to state the result of this legislative reliance (real or assumed) on firmly established legal principles. There is a 'presumption' that *mens rea* is required in the case of statutory crimes, and a 'presumption' that statutory powers must be exercised reasonably. These presumptions apply although there is no question of linguistic ambiguity in the statutory wording under construction, and they may be described as 'presumptions of general application'. At the level of interpretation, their function is the promotion of brevity on the part of the drafter. Statutes make dreary enough reading as it is, and it would be ridiculous to insist in each instance upon an enumeration of the general principles taken for granted.

These presumptions of general application not only supplement the text, they also operate at a higher level as expressions of fundamental principles governing both civil liberties and the relations between Parliament, the executive and the courts. They operate here as constitutional principles which are not easily displaced by a statutory text. Although the point lacks clear authority, it is probably true to say that some of them can only be rebutted by express words; nothing in the nature of implication, even necessary implication, will suffice. On the other hand, it is tolerably clear that some presumptions of general application are rebuttable by implication, which need not always be particularly necessary. The requirement of *mens rea* in the sense of guilty knowledge may be excluded by implication from the purpose and background of criminal statutes; more may well be required to exclude defences such as insanity or duress. The principle that no one shall be allowed to gain an advantage from his own wrong is of general application for it undoubtedly applies so as to qualify the effects of statutory words which are wholly unambiguous.[2] But it is somewhat easily rebutted by the statutory context.[3]

To be contrasted with presumptions of general application are 'presumptions for use in doubtful cases'. An example is the presumption that Parliament does not intend to act in breach of international law.[4] This applies where one of the meanings which can reasonably be attributed to the legislation is consonant with treaty obligations and the other is not. This example is on the borderline between the two kinds of presumption, for there are those who would say that the presumption in favour of a construction complying with international law can only be excluded by clear words and is not one which is merely brought into play in cases of ambiguity; but judicial dicta seem to be against this view.[5]

---

2. Eg *R v Chief National Insurance Comr, ex p Connor* [1981] 1 All ER 769 (a woman convicted of the manslaughter of her husband was not entitled to a widow's allowance under s 24(1) of the Social Security Act 1975 notwithstanding its mandatory wording that 'A woman who has been widowed shall be entitled to a widow's allowance . . .').
3. Eg *Hipperson v Electoral Registration Officer for the District of Newbury* pp 77-78 above; *Workington Harbour and Dock Board v Towerfield (Owners)* [1951] AC 112 at 160.
4. See Lord Diplock cited at p 162 above.
5. See p 162 n 3 above.

The rules of language mentioned at the end of Chapter 5 are sometimes stated in the form of presumptions, and other linguistic presumptions, such as that the same word bears the same meaning throughout the same statute, have also been mentioned elsewhere in this book. We have seen how the purpose of a statute, in addition to forming part of its context which may assist the judge to the conclusion that the meaning is clear, may be taken into consideration at a later stage in order to assist in the resolution of an ambiguity. There is then a presumption that if, of two meanings reasonably attributable to the legislature, one would give effect to the purpose more than the other, that meaning is to be preferred. This presumption may conflict with others, notably that in favour of a strict construction of penal statutes. If, after applying rules 1 and 2 of the basic rules set out above on p 49 the judge is still in doubt concerning the interpretation of a statutory provision, rule 2 may come into play again, but this time as a presumption for use in doubtful cases. If, of two meanings which might reasonably be attributed to the legislature, one would and the other would not lead to a result which is contrary to the purpose of the statute, the latter meaning is to be preferred. Here too conflicts with other presumptions are conceivable; but, if we exclude the presumption concerning penal statutes, it is open to question whether the possibility of conflicting presumptions for use in doubtful cases presents great practical difficulties. At any rate it is certain that they could not be arranged in any kind of hierarchy, because their strength is so largely dependent on the particular facts. They are pointers to a certain conclusion, not rules obliging the judge to reach it.

Presumptions are often said to express 'policies of clear statement'. Whether this is the right way to regard presumptions whose operation is limited to particular branches of the law or to doubtful cases is open to question, but it is certainly an excellent way of describing the constitutional principles to be discussed in the next section. They can all be looked upon as warnings to the drafter: 'If you do not express yourself clearly, there is a risk that the courts will hold that your words have not effected the changes in the law intended by those instructing you.' They are all presumptions for use by the courts in cases in which there is an ambiguity in the drafter's words.

B. PRESUMPTIONS AGAINST UNCLEAR CHANGES IN THE LAW

1. The presumption generally

The main presumption against unclear changes in the law goes back to the days when by far the greater proportion of law was common law, and statutes were, for the most part, thought of as minor emendations of that law. In modern times it is possible to make a travesty of the presumption by stating it in some such form as that 'it is to be presumed that a statute alters the common law as little as possible'. So stated the presumption is of course ridiculous when applied to such matters as social welfare legislation concerning subjects on which there is not and never has been any common law. Sensibly stated, the presumption can be of undoubted assistance in resolving ambiguities. To quote Lord Reid in *Black-Clawson International Ltd v Papierwerke Waldhof-Aschaffenburg AG*:[6]

> 'There is a presumption which can be stated in various ways. One is that in the absence of any clear indication to the contrary Parliament can be presumed not to have altered the common law further than was necessary to remedy the "mischief". Of course it may and quite often does go further. But the principle is that if the enactment is ambiguous, that meaning which relates the scope of the Act to the mischief should be taken rather than a different or wider meaning which the contemporary situation did not call for.'

An instance of the presumption against unclear changes in the law in the form stated by Lord Reid is *Leach v R*.[7] Section 4(1) of the Criminal Evidence Act 1898 provides that the spouse of a person charged with an offence under any enactment mentioned in the Schedule *may* be called as a witness either for the prosecution or for the defence. Subject to irrelevant exceptions, a wife could not be called to give evidence against her husband at common law, and it was held by the House of Lords that s 4(1) had only made her a competent witness for the prosecution in the scheduled cases; she was not compellable: 'The principle that a wife is not to be compelled to give evidence against her husband is deep seated in the common law of this country, and I think if it is to be overturned it must be overturned by a clear, definite and positive enactment, not by an ambiguous one such as the section relied upon in this case.'[8] *Francis and Francis (a firm) v Central Criminal Court*[9] offers a more controversial example of the application of the presumption. Section 10(2) of the Police and Criminal Evidence Act 1984 (applied in relation to the Drug Trafficking Offences Act 1986 by s 29(2)) excluded from the protection afforded to items subject to legal privilege 'items held with the intention of furthering a criminal purpose'. The issue arose whether this exclusion was limited to cases in which the solicitor holding the item in question had that

---

6.   [1975] AC 591 at 614.
7.   [1912] AC 305.
8.   At 311.
9.   [1988] 3 All ER 775; Lord Oliver 'A Judicial View of Modern Legislation' [1993] Stat LR 1 at 7; T R S Allan *Law, Liberty, and Justice* (1993) pp 85-87.

intention or could also apply where the relevant intention was that of another person, eg the solicitor's client. Lord Bridge and Lord Oliver considered that the ordinary meaning of the words of s 10(2) covered only the former case. But the majority held that they had the wider meaning. The broader interpretation would maintain the established common law position set out in *R v Cox and Railton*.[10] Since s 10 as a whole corresponded closely to established principles of the common law, it was assumed that it had not been intended to alter the rule in *Cox*. Such an interpretation would also further the purpose of Part II of the 1984 Act, of which s 10 was a part, in enabling the police to have access to evidence of a crime.

No useful purpose would be served by multiplying examples, but it should be pointed out that the presumption applies to changes in statute law. Thus, in *Bennett v Chappell*,[11] it was held that a provision in one of the Schedules to the Local Government Act 1933 under which a poll might be demanded before the conclusion of a parish meeting 'on any question arising thereat' had not altered the law previously laid down in a Schedule to the Local Government Act 1894 which had provided for a poll on any 'resolution'. The 1933 wording was said not to be 'sufficiently plain to indicate an intention to depart entirely from the basic conception of the Act of 1894, that only resolutions were liable to a poll demand'.[12] A change of language on re-enactment will, however, fairly readily be held to indicate a change of law, although this is much less so when the re-enactment is a consolidating statute, for there is a well recognised presumption that consolidating statutes do not change the law.

This last presumption is qualified by the fact that statutes are interpreted first of all in their ordinary meaning and only secondarily in the light of their legislative antecedents. Thus, in *R v West Yorkshire Coroner, ex p Smith*,[13] the majority of the Court of Appeal interpreted s 3(1) of the Coroners Act 1887 (a straight consolidation Act) as requiring a coroner to hold an inquest where 'the dead body of a person is lying within his jurisdiction', even though the death occurred abroad and despite arguments that the subsection merely re-enacted a provision designed originally to resolve conflicts of jurisdiction between coroners of neighbouring counties. On the ordinary meaning of the subsection, a corpse brought from overseas 'is lying' now within the jurisdiction of the coroner and can be subject to an inquest.

Suggestions that Parliament, in re-enacting legislation, must necessarily be taken to have endorsed judicial interpretations of the re-enacted provision

---

10. (1884) 14 QBD 153.
11. [1966] Ch 391.
12. Per Russell LJ at 399.
13. [1982] 3 All ER 1098. See also *A-G (ex rel Yorkshire Derwent Trust Ltd) v Brotherton* [1992] 1 All ER 230.

can no longer be treated as correct since the House of Lords decision in
R v Chard.[14] Section 17(1)(a) of the Criminal Appeal Act 1968 provided that
the Home Secretary could refer 'the whole case' to the Court of Appeal and
that 'the case shall then be treated for all purposes as an appeal to the court
by [the defendant]'. On such a reference, the Court of Appeal (Criminal
Division) refused to entertain matters raised by the defendant which were
unconnected with the reasons for the Home Secretary's reference. In doing
so, it followed decisions of 1956 and 1968 on similar wording in s 19(a) of
the Criminal Appeal Act 1907.[15] The House of Lords held that the words 'for
all purposes' must empower the court to consider all matters relevant to
conviction, whether or not they were connected with the reasons for the
reference. Lord Scarman,[16] with the concurrence of Lords Roskill and
Templeman, took the view that there is no inflexible rule that, where once
words in an Act have received a judicial construction and the legislature has
re-enacted them without alteration, it must be taken to have endorsed the
judicial construction. At best a presumption of endorsement might arise in
circumstances where the judicial interpretation was well settled and well
recognised. Even then, the presumption could not override the grammatical
and ordinary sense of the words. Certainly courts have been prepared to
overrule long-standing interpretations. For instance, in *R v Bow Road
Justices, ex p Adedigba*,[17] the Court of Appeal overruled a decision of 1849
on a statutory provision which was re-enacted in 1872 and again in 1957.

Whether it is correct to talk in terms of a 'presumption' that decisions on
earlier, re-enacted provisions continue to apply is perhaps debatable, but it
is common practice, and the language of presumptions is occasionally used
in relation to cases of statutory interpretation when the fact that Parliament
had the opportunity to reverse the effect of a decision but did not do so is
urged as a reason for following it. No doubt the position is simply that the
re-enactment of a provision which had been judicially interpreted provides
a reason of limited force why the courts should be more than ordinarily
cautious in overruling that interpretation.

2. Special applications

Special examples of the presumption against unclear alteration of the law
are the presumption against ousting the jurisdiction of the courts, the

---

14. [1984] AC 279.
15. *R v Caborn-Waterfield* [1956] 2 All ER 636; *R v Stones (No 2)* (1968) 52 Cr App Rep 624.
16. [1984] AC 279 at 294-295. Lord Diplock's view (at 292) was that a subsequent re-
enactment of a judicially interpreted provision did not affect its meaning. See also *Stubbings
v Webb* [1993] 1 All ER 322.
17. [1968] 2 All ER 89.

presumption in favour of a strict construction of penal statutes, the presumption in favour of individual liberty, the presumption against interference with vested rights, the presumption against interference with property, and the presumption in favour of a strict construction of revenue statutes. They can all be subsumed under the notion of policies of clear statement.

(a) *Ouster of jurisdiction* The presumption against ousting the jurisdiction of the courts is well illustrated by *Anisminic Ltd v Foreign Compensation Commission*.[18] The case concerned a determination made by the Foreign Compensation Commission under the Foreign Compensation Act 1950 of compensation payable for property sequestrated by the Egyptian Government. The Foreign Compensation (Egypt) (Determination and Regulation of Claims) Order 1962[19] required the original owner of property and his successor in title to have been British nationals on 31 October 1956 and on 28 February 1959 if they were to qualify for compensation. In this case the applicant company (the original owner) was a British national on the qualifying dates, but its successor in title was not. The Commission held that, in these circumstances, the applicant's claim must fail. The applicant contended that the nationality of its successor in title was irrelevant to its own claim for compensation, and it sought a declaration that the determination of the Commission was erroneous in law and a nullity. Section 4(4) of the Act provided that a determination of the Commission 'shall not be called into question in any court of law'. By a majority, the House of Lords held that this provision did not prevent a court from investigating whether the Commission had acted outside its jurisdiction. The House concluded that the Commission had wrongly interpreted the Order and had thus committed an error of law taking it outside its jurisdiction. Accordingly, it granted the declaration sought. The subsection was thus limited to preventing the questioning of matters which did not affect the jurisdiction of the Commission. To construe the subsection otherwise would be to permit the Commission uncontrolled power, whereas Parliament must have intended it to restrict itself to the jurisdiction laid down in the Act and in the Order. The interpretation adopted by the House of Lords preserved the jurisdiction of the courts to supervise inferior tribunals. Although the presumption against ouster of this jurisdiction can be displaced by express wording, it is difficult to conceive how Parliament could have been more explicit than it was in s 4(4) of the Foreign Compensation Act 1950, and it gave up the attempt to oust the jurisdiction of the courts in relation to the Commission soon

---

18. [1969] 1 All ER 208.
19. SI 1962/2187.

afterwards.[20] Quite apart from their constitutional position as guardians of the rights of citizens and defenders of the rule of law, the courts take the view that they are the only tribunals really fitted for the task of settling disputes about points of law,[1] and who is to say them nay?

(b) *Strict construction of penal statutes*   The phrase 'penal statute' is used to cover both statutes creating criminal offences and those providing for the recovery of penalties in civil proceedings. In either case the present position is that if, to use the words of Lord Reid in *DPP v Ottewell*,[2] 'after full inquiry and consideration, one is left in real doubt', the accused or person from whom the penalty is claimed must be given the benefit of that doubt. Lord Reid proceeded to stress the point that it is not enough for the provision under construction to be ambiguous in the sense that it is capable of having two meanings, and the same point is embodied in the following frequently quoted passage from one of Lord Esher's judgments:[3]

> 'If there is a reasonable interpretation which will avoid the penalty in any particular case, we must adopt that construction. If there are two reasonable constructions we must give the more lenient one. That is the settled rule for construction of penal sections.'

So understood, the presumption in favour of a strict construction of penal statutes is simply an example of the presumption against unclear changes in the law. For example, in *R v Allen*,[4] the question arose whether a guest who left a hotel without paying his bill committed a criminal offence within s 3(1) of the Theft Act 1978. That subsection created a new offence by providing that:

> 'a person who, knowing that payment on the spot for any goods supplied or service done is required or expected from him, dishonestly makes off without having paid as required or expected and with intent to avoid payment of the amount due shall be guilty of an offence.'

The House of Lords held that these words clearly did not cover the case where a guest left the hotel intending to pay at a subsequent date. Lord Hailsham LC added that, even if the words 'with intent to avoid payment' were equivocal and might possibly be read as including an intention to delay

---

20. Section 3(2) of the Foreign Compensation Act 1969 permitted an appeal on a point of law to the Court of Appeal from a determination of the Foreign Compensation Commission.
1.   See Griffith LJ, *R v Knightsbridge Crown Court, ex p International Sporting Club Ltd* [1982] QB 304 at 312-313.
2.   [1970] AC 642 at 649.
3.   *Tuck & Sons v Priester* (1887) 19 QBD 629 at 638.
4.   [1985] AC 1029.

or defer payment of the amount due, any ambiguity must be resolved in favour of the accused.[5] (He also mentioned that this reading restricted the scope of the subsection to the mischief identified in a report of the Criminal Law Revision Committee which had proposed this amendment to the law, namely that of persons expected to pay on the spot leaving 'without having paid *and intending never to pay*' for goods supplied or services provided.) Allowance must of course be made for the fact that the presumption operates against the Crown, with the result that it requires a liberal interpretation of sections which provide the accused with a defence. This was the ground of the decision of the Court of Criminal Appeal in *R v Chapman*.[6] Section 2 of the Criminal Law Amendment Act 1922 deprived men charged with unlawful intercourse with a girl between the ages of 13 and 16 of the defence of reasonable cause to believe that she was over 16, but there was a proviso that 'in the case of a man of 23 years of age or under, the presence of reasonable cause to believe that the girl was over the age of 16 years shall be a valid defence on the first occasion on which he is charged'.[7] The defence was held to be available to a man over 23 but under 24.

In earlier times the presumption was a good deal more than an example of the presumption against unclear changes in the law. This was especially true in the case of criminal statutes. If they were capable of two meanings, however unreasonable one of those meanings be, it was applied if favourable to the accused. Examples are *R v Harris*,[8] in which case someone who bit off his victim's nose was held not guilty of 'wounding', and the case mentioned by Blackstone[9] in which a statute of Edward VI deprived a man of benefit of clergy if he stole *horses*, but the judges refused to apply this to the case of a man who stole a single horse.[10] Decisions of this sort were amply justified on humanitarian grounds, but they have been rendered unnecessary by the mitigation of the rigours of the criminal law. It is surely correct that under the modern rule it is only necessary that persons liable to a penalty should have the benefit of a genuine doubt about meaning, but not of a spurious one created by excessive literalism.

Undoubtedly some modern cases, such as *Fisher v Bell*,[11] have been inspired by the spirit of the old humane decisions. However, it is clear that the courts nowadays generally adopt a purposive approach even to the

---

5. At 1034.
6. [1931] 2 KB 606.
7. See now Sexual Offences Act 1956, s 6(3).
8. P 12 above.
9. *Commentaries* (1st edn) vol 1, p 88.
10. It was not until 1850 that Lord Brougham's Act (c 21) made statutory words in the singular include the plural, and vice versa, in the absence of provision to the contrary.
11. P 73 above.

construction of penal statutes.[12] For the most part, they seek the interpretation which makes sense of the statute and its purpose, and the presumption of strict construction is merely an ancillary aid for resolving difficult cases. Thus in *R v Bloxham*[13] the House of Lords decided that an innocent purchaser, who subsequently realised that the car he had purchased was stolen and then re-sold it, was not guilty of handling stolen goods contrary to s 22 of the Theft Act 1968. Although citing the presumption in favour of the strict construction of penal statutes, Lord Bridge of Harwich preferred to rely on arguments which showed that to find a criminal offence in this case would be inconsistent with the provisions of the Act and with the report of the Criminal Law Revision Committee which led to its passing.

Although the presumption in favour of strict construction is still frequently cited,[14] the Law Commission has suggested that it has limited application today:[15]

'We are sceptical . . . whether such a principle really exists. It is of course often referred to by the courts, but it is rarely applied in practice. This is because the "principle" cannot sensibly be used as a rule for the resolution of all ambiguities.'

Similar opinions have been expressed by leading academics.[16] Given that, as Professor Ashworth has rightly pointed out, the presumption or 'principle' operates only as a long-stop where doubt persists after all avenues have been exhausted, and not as a rule for resolving all ambiguities,[17] the effect of these opinions is to suggest a reduced importance for the principle. It may be that, as Ashworth also suggests, there are other values at stake in the operation of the criminal law, including the aim of convicting those who culpably cause harm. While citizens must be given fair warning about the likely penal consequences of their actions, 'people who knowingly "sail close to the wind" should not be surprised if the law is interpreted so as to include their conduct'.[18] For similar reasons, Glanville Williams has suggested that the

---

12. See, for example, *A-G's Reference (No 1 of 1988)* [1989] 2 All ER 1, discussed at pp 85-86, above.
13. [1982] 1 All ER 582.
14. See, for example Watkins LJ, *R v Horseferry Road Metropolitan Stipendiary Magistrate, ex p Siadatan* [1991] 1 All ER 324 at 328.
15. *Criminal Law: A Criminal Code for England and Wales* (Law Com no 177, 1989) para 3.17.
16. J C Smith *Codification of the Criminal Law*, The Child & Co Lecture (1986) at p 9; G Williams 'Statutory interpretation, prostitution and the rule of law' in C F H Tapper (ed), *Crime, Proof and Punishment: Essays in Memory of Sir Rupert Cross* (1981) p 72; G Williams *A Textbook of Criminal Law* (2nd edn, 1983) p 12.
17. 'Interpreting Criminal Statutes: A Crisis of Legality?' (1991) 107 LQR 419 at p 432.
18. At p 443.

presumption is not necessarily a disincentive to broad judicial interpretation of statutes intended to criminalise social wrongs:[19]

> 'Nowadays the criminal courts rarely apply the rule of strict construction. They will still apply it if they are in genuine doubt as to the intention of the legislature and if there are no considerations indicating the desirability of a wide interpretation of the statute. But if the statute admits of alternative interpretations and public policy suggests that the wider interpretation should be preferred, the courts will usually apply the wider one.'

He cites *Smith v Hughes*[20] where a woman was convicted of 'soliciting in the street' for the purpose of prostitution, even though she was at a window, making signs to men as they passed in the street. The Divisional Court held that, since the solicitation was projected to and addressed to persons walking in the street, it was made in the street. Similarly the approach of the House of Lords in *A-G's Reference (No 1 of 1988)*[1] to the interpretation of the word 'obtains' in s 1(3) of the Company Securities (Insider Dealing) Act 1985 led them to prefer the wider interpretation which brought the appellant within the scope of a criminal offence. Such cases demonstrate the priority of the (criminalising) purpose of the statute over the presumption in favour of strict construction, and this may indeed lead the courts to overrule a precedent in order to penalise something which the previous decision had determined not to be criminal.[2]

(c) *Individual liberty* The strict construction of penal statutes is closely related to the presumption in favour of individual liberty, especially where custodial sentences are involved. As McCullough J succinctly put it in *R v Hallstrom, ex p W (No 2)*:[3]

> 'There is . . . a canon of construction that Parliament is presumed not to enact legislation which interferes with the liberty of the subject without making it clear that this was its intention.'

In that case, a doctor was held to have no power to detain a patient in hospital overnight and then let her out on leave, nor to renew a patient's detention order, where all the doctor wished to achieve was that the person should continue to come as an out-patient for treatment. The powers under the

---

19. G Williams 'Statutory interpretation, prostitution and the rule of law' in C F H Tapper (ed) *Crime, Proof and Punishment: Essays in Memory of Sir Rupert Cross* (1981) p 72.
20. [1960] 2 All ER 859; see also *Behrendt v Burridge* [1976] 3 All ER 285.
1. Pp 85-86 above.
2. See eg *R v Shivpuri* [1986] 2 All ER 334, overruling *Anderton v Ryan* [1985] AC 560.
3. [1986] QB 1090 at 1104; see also *Bennion* s 273.

Mental Health Act 1983 were limited to detention in hospital for treatment and did not expressly permit compulsion for out-patient treatment, however much this might be in the patient's interests. But the presumption applies only where there is ambiguity in the meaning of statutory words.[4]

This presumption is important in limiting the actions of the police and other officials. They have powers to interfere with a person or to come upon his property only in so far as they are specifically authorised to do so. For example, s 2 of the Street Offences Act 1959 empowers the police to caution prostitutes. However, in *Collins v Wilcock*[5] the Divisional Court held that this did not empower a police officer to detain a suspected prostitute for questioning by taking hold of her arm. There could be no restraint of a person without arrest. In *Morris v Beardmore*,[6] the House of Lords held that the power to administer a breathalyser test under s 8 of the Road Traffic Act 1972 did not enable the police to enter the driver's property in order to administer it. However, cases studied earlier in this book demonstrate an alternative concern among the judges not to circumscribe police powers so as to render them ineffective. Thus the majority in *Wills v Bowley*[7] overrode Lord Lowry's objections based on the liberty of the subject, preferring to give s 28 of the Town Police Clauses Act 1847 an interpretation that would not unduly narrow the police's powers of arrest. In other cases, too, the conditions for the exercise of police powers have been widely interpreted so as not to render them ineffective.[8] The tension between the two approaches is well explained by Lord Wilberforce in *R v IRC, ex p Rossminster Ltd*,[9] which concerned powers of entry conferred on the Revenue:

'The courts have the duty to supervise, I would say critically, even jealously, the legality of any purported exercise of these powers. They are the guardians of the citizen's right to privacy. But they must do this in the context of the times, ie of increasing Parliamentary intervention, and of the modern power of judicial review. . . . While courts may look critically at legislation which impairs the rights of citizens and should resolve any doubt in interpretation in their favour, it is no part of their duty, or power, to restrict or impede the working of legislation, even

---

4. Contrast the approach of the Court of Appeal in *R v Canons Park Mental Health Review Tribunal, ex p A* [1994] 2 All ER 659 with that of the Divisional Court (which did think that there was ambiguity) [1994] 1 All ER 481.
5. [1984] 3 All ER 374.
6. [1980] 2 All ER 753.
7. Pp 86-87 above.
8. Eg *Holgate-Mohammed v Duke* [1984] 1 All ER 1054; *McKee v Chief Constable of Northern Ireland* [1985] 1 All ER 1.
9. [1980] AC 952 at 997-998; see also Lord Diplock at 1008.

of unpopular legislation; to do so would be to weaken rather than to advance the democratic process.'

Once one accepts that state interference must be effective, especially in maintaining public order or other aspects of the public interest, then the presumption in favour of individual liberty is necessarily qualified.

(d) *Vested rights* 'The well established presumption is that the legislature does not intend to limit vested rights further than clearly appears from the enactment.'[10] One striking illustration will suffice. *Allen v Thorn Electrical Industries Ltd*[11] was concerned with the Prices and Incomes Act 1966 under which the Secretary of State was empowered to make orders imposing a 'wages freeze'. Section 29(4) provided that 'an employer shall not pay remuneration to which this section applies for work for any period while the order is in force at a rate which exceeds the *rate of remuneration paid* by him for the same kind of work before July 20 1966'. Did 'paid' mean actually paid or contracted to be paid? The Court of Appeal unanimously came to the latter conclusion with the result that, where immediately effective pay increases had been agreed but not paid before 20 July, the increased rate was the rate of remuneration paid before that date. Lord Denning MR had no doubt but added:[12]

'If I were wrong in this view, I am clear that, at any rate, the requirement in the statute is ambiguous and uncertain, in which case the rights under the contract must prevail. No man's contractual rights are to be taken away on an ambiguity in a statute, nor is an employer to be penalised on an ambiguity.'

Winn LJ used language which, though less common among modern judges, is surely no less significant:[13]

'I must reject as quite untenable any submission . . . that if in any case one finds (a) that a statute is worded ambiguously in any particular respect, and (b) finds also clear indications *aliunde* that Parliament intended that they should have the strictest and most stringent meaning possible, the court is therefore compelled to construe the section in the sense in which Parliament would have desired it to take effect, by giving the words their most stringent possible meaning. On the

---

10. *Re Metropolitan Film Studios Ltd v Twickenham Film Studios Ltd (Intended Action)* [1962] 3 All ER 508 at 517, per Ungoed-Thomas J.
11. [1968] 1 QB 487.
12. At 503. The statute penalised employers who did not comply with it.
13. At 508.

contrary, I think the right view is, and as I understand it always has been, that in such a case of ambiguity, it is resolved in such a way as to make the statute less onerous for the general public and so as to cause less interference, than the more stringent sense would, with such rights and liabilities as existing contractual obligations.'

There is more to interpretation in general than the discovery of the meaning attached by the author to his words. Even if, in a particular case, that meaning is discoverable with a high degree of certitude from external sources, the question whether it has been adequately expressed remains. This question has to be raised in the interests of those who have to act and advise on the words under consideration. In the case of statutory interpretation, there is the further question of the role of the courts when they have doubts about the meaning which the ordinary, or, where appropriate, the specialist, reader would attach to the provision with which they are concerned. When they have notice *aliunde* (from another source) of parliamentary intent, who is to have the benefit of those doubts, Parliament or the holder of the right? The orthodox answer is 'the holder of the right' although, as we shall see, this may require some qualification in the case of certain taxing statutes. The issue is primarily a constitutional one. From the point of view of interpretation pure and simple, it could be argued that, on facts such as those of *Allen v Thorn Electrical Industries Ltd*, those who have to act or even advise on the statute would not be prejudiced if the benefit of the doubt were given to Parliament, for parliamentary intent in such a case is a matter of common knowledge for which all those concerned should make allowance. Against such an argument it could very properly be urged that the descent of the Gadarene slope into confusion would indeed have started if those who are concerned extrajudicially with statutory interpretation had to assess parliamentary intent by criteria other than those which have been dealt with in this book. It only remains to add that, although they undoubtedly represent current legal opinion, the observations of Lord Denning MR and Winn LJ in *Allen v Thorn Electrical Industries Ltd* were technically *obiter* because no member of the Court of Appeal thought there was any ambiguity in the wording of s 29(4) of the Prices and Incomes Act 1966.

(e) *Property rights* There is a general presumption that Parliament does not intend to take away private property rights unless the contrary is clearly indicated. Lord Atkinson stated[14] that there is a canon of interpretation 'that an intention to take away the property of a subject without giving to him a

---

14. *Central Control Board (Liquor Traffic) v Cannon Brewery Co Ltd* [1919] AC 744 at 752; see also Lord Warrington, *Colonial Sugar Refining Co Ltd v Melbourne Harbour Trust Comrs* [1927] AC 343 at 359.

legal right to compensation for the loss of it is not to be imputed to the legislature unless that intention is expressed in unequivocal terms'. After all, the protection of property is generally regarded as one of the fundamental values of a liberal society. However, the modern state has found it necessary to abolish or to qualify property rights in significant ways in order to achieve socially desirable ends, for instance in the field of town planning or in the relationship between landlord and tenant. In consequence, the presumption has a more limited application than in the past. As Lord Scarman put it in *Secretary of State for Defence v Guardian Newspapers Ltd*:[15]

'there certainly remains a place in the law for the principle of construction which the judge applied, namely, that the courts must be slow to impute to Parliament an intention to override property rights in the absence of plain words to that effect. But the principle is not an overriding rule of law: it is an aid, amongst many others, developed by the judges in their never ending task of interpreting statutes in such a way as to give effect to their true purpose.'

That case concerned s 10 of the Contempt of Court Act 1981 which provides generally that no court may require a person to disclose the source of information contained in a publication for which he is responsible, unless the court is satisfied that disclosure is necessary in the interests of justice or national security, or for the prevention of disorder or crime. Unlike Scott J at first instance, the House of Lords held unanimously that the presumption could not be used to create an exception to this press immunity where a person was seeking the return of his own property held by a newspaper. The wording of s 10 was clear enough to grant an immunity where the return of a person's property would lead to the disclosure of the source. (The majority of the House nevertheless ordered disclosure in the interests of national security.)

The courts do not differentiate between statutes which deprive people of property rights and those which merely restrict their exercise, since the two can frequently have the same practical effect.[16] For instance, the Matrimonial Homes Act 1967 created a right of occupation in the matrimonial home for a spouse, even if he or she was not the owner or tenant of the property. In *Tarr v Tarr*[17] the question arose whether the court's power under s 1(2) of the Act to make an order 'regulating the exercise by either spouse of the right to occupy the dwelling-house' included power to order the spouse who was

---

15. [1985] AC 339 at 363. Whether the presumption applies to transfers of property from one public body to another may be doubted: *Sheffield City Council v Yorkshire Water Services Ltd* [1991] 2 All ER 280 at 289-291.
16. *Westminster Bank Ltd v Beverley Borough Council* [1971] AC 508 at 529, per Lord Reid.
17. [1973] AC 254.

the owner or tenant to leave the property. The Court of Appeal ordered a husband, who was the sole tenant of a council house, to leave the property so that his wife and child could live there. The House of Lords unanimously held that the power to 'regulate' the exercise of the right of occupation did not include the power to prohibit its exercise altogether. Lord Pearson said that the Court of Appeal's interpretation would make 'a very drastic inroad into the common law rights of the property-owning spouse'.[18] However, where a sufficient countervailing value is at stake, the courts are prepared to interpret statutes so as to override property rights. Thus in *Davis v Johnson*,[19] the majority of the Court of Appeal and of the House of Lords saw no difficulty in interpreting s 1(1) of the Domestic Violence and Matrimonial Proceedings Act 1976 as permitting the exclusion of an unmarried partner from the 'matrimonial home' of which he was tenant. The subsection specifically permitted such exclusion in the case of married persons, and the Act expressly provided that the subsection applied to a man and woman living together as husband and wife as it applied to the parties to a marriage. In earlier Court of Appeal decisions on the subsection it had been argued that Parliament could not have intended such a result, since it had provided no rules for regulating the property rights of unmarried partners comparable to those which existed for matrimonial breakdown.[20] However, the majorities in *Davis* considered this argument to be of limited consequence where the purpose of the legislation was to prevent violence to the other spouse or to a child of the family.

Even if the presumption has some value, 'in the end', as Lord Pearson said in *Tarr v Tarr*,[1] 'one has to read the enactment in its context and come to a conclusion as to what it means'.

(f) *Revenue statutes*   The presumption applicable to revenue statutes has much in common with the presumptions on penal statutes and against interference with property rights. If clearly worded, revenue statutes must be applied even though they operate against the subject in a manner that may appear to have been unintended by Parliament, but '. . . if the provision is reasonably capable of two alternative meanings, the courts will prefer the meaning more favourable to the subject'.[2] The unwillingness of the courts to tax the subject on unclear wording is illustrated by *Vestey v Inland Revenue Commrs*.[3] Section 412 of the Income Tax Act 1952 provided that

---

18. At 264.
19. [1978] 1 All ER 1132.
20. See *B v B* [1978] Fam 26 and *Cantliff v Jenkins* [1978] Fam 47 at 51, per Stamp LJ.
1. [1973] AC at 264.
2. Lord Thankerton, *IRC v Ross and Coulter* [1948] 1 All ER 616 at 625; also *IRC v Duke of Westminster* [1936] AC 1.
3. [1980] AC 1148.

a person ordinarily resident in the United Kingdom was chargeable to income tax on income resulting from rights to income or capital sums acquired by him 'by means of transfers of assets' to persons overseas. The taxpayers were beneficiaries of overseas discretionary settlements established by members of their families. The Revenue claimed that they were liable to tax on the money over which the various beneficiaries had rights in the hands of the overseas trustees of the settlements. Further, in the absence of statutory provisions apportioning the tax liability among a plurality of beneficiaries, the Revenue claimed the right to determine the tax liability of each of them at its discretion. Overruling a thirty-year-old precedent, the House of Lords held that the section only covered the tax liability of the transferor of the assets and not that of other beneficiaries. To make the latter liable, above all for amounts fixed at the discretion of the Revenue, would be, in Lord Wilberforce's words 'arbitrary, unjust and in my opinion unconstitutional'.[4] Since the wider interpretation proposed by the Revenue was beset by complexities and potential arbitrariness in determining the amounts due, the narrower interpretation in favour of the taxpayers was to be preferred.

There is, however, a complicating factor due to the legitimate state of war which exists between the subject and his advisers on the one hand and the Inland Revenue on the other hand. The former are bent on avoiding payments to the latter so far as they legitimately can, and the latter are bent on procuring statutory provisions which will, so far as possible, be foolproof. Nowadays the courts seek to strike a fair balance between the two sides and do not exclusively favour the taxpayer. In *W T Ramsay Ltd v IRC*[5] Lord Wilberforce restated the old presumption in a qualified form:

> 'A subject is only to be taxed upon clear words, not upon "intendment" or upon the "equity" of an Act. Any taxing Act of Parliament is to be construed in accordance with this principle. What are "clear words" is to be ascertained upon normal principles: these do not confine the courts to literal interpretation. There may, indeed should, be considered the context and scheme of the relevant Act as a whole, and its purpose may, indeed should, be regarded.'

In that and subsequent cases the courts have shown themselves more willing than in the past to examine the substance and not merely the form of tax-avoidance arrangements, and to consider the genuineness or otherwise of the transactions involved, in order to determine whether they are covered by a taxing Act. The courts draw a distinction between legitimate tax mitigation

---

4. At 1174.
5. [1982] AC 300 at 323.

and unacceptable tax avoidance. Lord Goff explained the distinction in
Ensign Tankers (Leasing) Ltd v Stokes (Inspector of Taxes):[6]

> '[Tax mitigation occurs in] cases in which the taxpayer takes advantage
> of the law to plan his affairs so as to minimise the incidence of tax.
> Unacceptable tax avoidance typically involves the creation of complex
> artificial structures by which, as though by the wave of a magic wand,
> the taxpayer conjures out of the air a loss, or a gain, or expenditure, or
> whatever it may be, which otherwise would never have existed. These
> structures are designed to achieve an adventitious tax benefit for the
> taxpayer, and in truth are no more than raids on the public funds at the
> expense of the general body of taxpayers.'

In that case, the taxpayer company was a partner in a limited partnership set
up to finance the production and exploitation of a film. The partnership
engaged in a series of transactions (embodied in no fewer than 17 documents)
in order to take advantage of the first-year allowance under s 41(1) of the
Finance Act 1971 in respect of capital expenditure in acquiring the master
film negative. Under an agreement with the production company, the
partnership was to pay the production company the estimated cost of making
the film and would in return acquire, inter alia, rights of ownership in the
master film negative. The taxpayer claimed the first-year tax allowance in
respect of the payment by the partnership of the costs of making the film, $13
million, and thus of the capital expenditure on acquiring ownership of the
master film negative. But the payment was made as to 25% ($3.25 million)
from the partnership's own money, and as to 75% ($9.75 million) out of a
loan of that amount made to the partnership by the production company. On
the same day, just before the payment of $9.75 million was made, the
partnership received a loan for an identical amount of money ($9.75 million)
from the film production company, which it then paid back to the company
towards the $13 million cost of producing the film. The House of Lords
looked at the series of transactions as a whole and decided that there had
been only real capital expenditure by the partnership in respect of the money
which it had paid out of its own funds ($3.25 million). The payment of the
remaining $9.75 million was cancelled out by the loan received from the
film production company, and no tax allowance could be claimed in respect
of this sum. This illustrates the view of Lord Scarman that, 'the determination
of what does, and what does not constitute unacceptable tax evasion is a
subject suited to development by judicial process'.[7] But while the courts will
thus adopt a realistic approach to the application of tax law and will not

---

6. [1992] 2 All ER 275 at 295.
7. *Furniss v Dawson* [1984] AC 474 at 513.

adopt a narrowly legalistic approach to the interpretation of an enactment, there are often diverging views as to whether a series of transactions is genuine or is merely an artificially pre-ordained set of steps with no other purpose than tax avoidance.[8]

The courts are thus committed primarily to a purposive construction of taxing statutes. While they will not adopt strained interpretations of statutory words in order to bring transactions within an enactment, it is clear that the strict construction of revenue statutes has softened to an important extent in recent years.

C. THE EUROPEAN CONVENTION ON HUMAN RIGHTS AND INTERNATIONAL CONVENTIONS

In Chapter 6 we saw that the courts assume that Parliament intends to comply with the United Kingdom's international obligations and that statutes should as far as possible be construed in a way which is consistent with the provisions of a relevant treaty.[9] In relation to the protection of individual rights, international conventions provide a more sophisticated and contemporary statement of the values which the courts will assume that Parliament intends to uphold than do the traditional presumptions which have been discussed in the preceding section of this chapter. The most important among these international treaties for its impact on domestic law is the European Convention for the Protection of Human Rights and Fundamental Freedoms of 1950. This requires discussion separately from other treaties.

1. The European Convention on Human Rights and Fundamental Freedoms

The United Kingdom was one of the early signatories of this Convention, and since 1965 individuals have been able to bring petitions against the United Kingdom to the European Commission and the European Court of Human Rights in Strasbourg for breaches of the Convention. However, this treaty has not been enacted into our domestic law and so no action lies before the domestic courts for breach of its provisions. The consequence of this

---

8. Contrast *Furniss v Dawson* [1984] AC 474 and *Moodie v IRC* [1993] 2 All ER 49 with *Craven v White* [1989] AC 398 and *Fitzwilliam v IRC* [1993] 3 All ER 185.

9. See p 162, above.

position is that, where there is ambiguity, the courts will as far as possible interpret an enactment consistently with the European Convention, but cannot give effect to the Convention against the express words of a statute.

The current position was clearly stated by the House of Lords in *R v Secretary of State for the Home Department, ex parte Brind*.[10] Section 29(3) of the Broadcasting Act 1981 provided:

'... the Secretary of State may at any time by notice in writing require the [Independent Broadcasting] Authority to refrain from broadcasting any matter or classes of matter specified in the notice; and it shall be the duty of the Authority to comply with the notice.'

In this case, the Home Secretary had exercised this power to require the Authority to refrain from broadcasting the speaking of words by representatives of certain Northern Irish terrorist organisations or by those inviting support for them (repetition of those words by an actor was never banned). It was argued that such a ban was in breach of art 10 of the European Convention which covers freedom of expression. The House of Lords held s 29(3) to be unambiguous and wide enough to authorise the broadcasting ban in this case. Although some of their Lordships sought to demonstrate that there was in fact no conflict with the Convention, it was made clear that s 29 (3) could not be interpreted as subject to a requirement that the Home Secretary exercise his power only so far as it was consistent with the Convention. That would go further than interpretation of an ambiguous provision and would impose an obligation in domestic law to comply with the Convention, a course of action from which Parliament had refrained and which would be 'a judicial usurpation of the legislative function'.[11] As Lord Donaldson MR stated in the Court of Appeal:[12]

'the duty of the English courts is to decide disputes in accordance with English domestic law as it is, and not as it would be if full effect were given to this country's obligations under the [European Convention on Human Rights], assuming that there is any difference between the two. It follows from this that in most cases the English courts will be wholly unconcerned with the terms of the convention. The sole exception is when the terms of primary legislation are fairly capable of bearing two or more meanings and the court, in pursuance of its duty to apply domestic law, is concerned to divine and define its true and only

---

10. [1991] 1 AC 696.
11. At 748, per Lord Bridge.
12. [1990] 1 All ER 469 at 477. For similar views see Lord Denning MR and Geoffrey Lane LJ, *R v Chief Immigration Adjudicator, Heathrow Airport, ex p Salamat Bibi* [1976] 3 All ER 843 at 847, 850.

meaning. In that situation various prima facie rules of construction have to be applied, such as . . . in appropriate cases, a presumption that Parliament has legislated in a manner consistent, rather than inconsistent, with the United Kingdom's treaty obligations.'

The Convention will be of assistance in the interpretation of many statutes affecting fundamental rights. For example, in *Rantzen v Mirror Group Newspapers (1986) Ltd*,[13] the Court of Appeal was concerned with its power under s 8(2) of the Courts and Legal Services Act 1990 to substitute another amount for the sum awarded by a jury in a civil trial, where that sum was, in the words of s 8(1), 'excessive or inadequate'. It considered that, in a defamation case, those words had to be interpreted in the light of art 10(2) of the European Convention, which allowed the exercise of the freedom of expression to be limited by such restrictions as 'are prescribed by law and are necessary in a democratic society . . . for the protection of the reputation or rights of others . . .' The European Court of Human Rights had held that 'necessary' in art 10(2) implies the existence of a 'pressing social need'[14] and that any limitation on the freedom of expression must be 'proportionate to the legitimate aim pursued'. In the light of this case-law and to prevent defamation actions acting as an undue restriction on freedom of expression, the Court of Appeal decided that the English courts' previous reluctance to interfere with jury awards had to be modified and that the courts should make use of s 8(2) to subject jury awards to more searching scrutiny. The Court of Appeal would ask itself not whether the jury's award was divorced from reality, but 'could a reasonable jury have thought this award was necessary to compensate the plaintiff and to re-establish his reputation?'[15] It followed that an award of £250,000 was disproportionate, and a lower figure of £110,000 was substituted. In this case, and in others, the courts have referred to the Convention not only as a treaty obligation, but also as 'an articulation of some of the principles underlying the common law'.[16]

In recent years a number of judges and others have called for the incorporation of the European Convention into UK domestic law.[17] Under EC law, principles of the European Convention have often been applied as

---

13. [1993] 4 All ER 975.
14. *Sunday Times Ltd v UK* (1991) 14 EHRR 229 at 242. The material passage is reproduced in [1993] 4 All ER 975 at 991.
15. Neill LJ at 994.
16. Neill LJ at 993. See also *Derbyshire County Council v Times Newspapers Ltd* [1993] AC 534 at 551, per Lord Keith.
17. See Sir Thomas Bingham MR 'The European Convention on Human Rights: Time to Incorporate' (1993) 109 LQR 390; Lord Browne-Wilkinson 'The Infiltration of a Bill of Rights' [1992] PL 397; Sir John Laws 'Is the High Court the Guardian of Fundamental Rights?' [1993] PL 59; Sir Stephen Sedley 'The Sound of Silence: Constitutional Law without a Constitution' (1994) 110 LQR 270.

among the 'general principles of law which underlie the constitutional traditions of member states' recognised by the European Court of Justice.[18] Under art F 2 of the Treaty of Maastricht, the European Union has bound itself to respect 'as general principles of Community law' fundamental rights as guaranteed by the Convention and as they result from the constitutional traditions common to member states. So, either directly or through EC law, British courts can expect in the future to have to implement the European Convention in a more thoroughgoing way than was stated in *Brind*,[19] and it will become an increasingly important feature of statutory interpretation.

2.　Other treaties affecting human rights

There are a number of other international treaties on human rights which frequently affect the interpretation of domestic legislation. These include the Geneva Convention and Protocol on the Status of Refugees of 1951. For example, under art 1(A)(2) of the Convention, the term 'refugee' was defined as a person unwilling to return to his or her country 'owing to a well-founded fear of persecution'. This was incorporated into the Immigration Rules 1983 and, in interpreting them, the House of Lords in *R v Secretary of State for the Home Department, ex p Sivakumaran*[20] consulted both the Convention and its *travaux préparatoires* to decide that the definition required there to be not just a subjective fear of persecution, but also, objectively, a reasonable degree of likelihood that it was well-founded.

In this context it is important to remember that the terms used in international conventions have to be interpreted not in the context of national law, but in the context of the convention in order to produce uniform interpretation. Thus the term 'custody' can have a wide meaning under an international convention so as to include a father having a right to consent to the removal of a child from the jurisdiction even if he does not have 'custody' under domestic law.[21]

---

18. Eg *Johnston v Chief Constable of the Royal Ulster Constabulary* Case 222/84 [1987] QB 129 (the right to an effective remedy under art 13 of the Convention). More generally, see N Grief 'The Domestic Impact of the European Convention on Human Rights as Mediated through Community Law' [1991] PL 555.
19. Pp 184-185 above.
20. [1988] AC 958.
21. *C v C (minor: abduction: rights of custody abroad)* [1989] 2 All ER 465.

D. PRESUMPTION AGAINST RETROSPECTIVE OPERATION

The presumption against the retrospective operation of statutes concerned with the substantive law could perhaps be treated as a facet of the presumption against interference with vested rights, but it is more convenient to give a separate account of the subject. In order that the presumption should apply, the statute must be genuinely retrospective in its operation. It is not enough that the circumstances on which the operation of the statute depends should have existed before it came into force. The statute must affect some vested right or impose a penalty for past acts which were not penalised when they were committed. This is the principle expressed in art 7(1) of the European Convention on Human Rights:

> 'No one shall be guilty of any criminal offence on account of any act or omission which did not constitute a criminal offence under national or international law at the time when it was committed. Nor shall a heavier penalty be imposed than the one that was applicable at the time the criminal offence was committed.'

A recent statement of the principle is that of Staughton LJ:[1]

> 'In my judgment the true principle is that Parliament is presumed not to have intended to alter the law applicable to past events and transactions in a manner which is unfair to those concerned in them, unless a contrary intention appears. It is not simply a question of classifying an enactment as retrospective or not retrospective. Rather it may well be a matter of degree—the greater the unfairness, the more it is to be expected that Parliament will make it clear if that is intended.'

This statement was approved by Lord Mustill in the House of Lords in *L'Office Cherifien des Phosphates v Yamashita-Shinnihon Steamship Co Ltd*.[2] There the presumption did not prevent a new procedural power of an arbitrator[3] to dismiss a claim for inordinate and inexcusable delay, which came into force on 1 January 1992, from applying to a claim referred to him in 1985 and which was still pending. Lord Mustill stated:[4]

---

1. In *Secretary of State for Social Security v Tunnicliffe* [1991] 2 All ER 712 at 724. The decision in that case was overruled by *Plewa v Chief Adjudication Officer*, p 188 below, but the dictum was approved and applied with a different result there by the House of Lords.
2. [1994] 1 All ER 20.
3. Under Arbitration Act 1950, s 13A (inserted by the Courts and Legal Services Act 1990, s 102).
4. [1994] 1 All ER 20 at 29.

'I must own to reservations about the reliability of generalised presumptions and maxims when engaged in the task of finding out what Parliament intended by a particular form of words, for they too readily confine the courts to a perspective which treats all statutes, and all situations to which they apply, as if they were the same. This is misleading, for the basis of the rule is no more than simple fairness, which ought to be the basis of every legal rule.'

For him, the correct approach was to weigh the various factors, such as the value of the rights, the unfairness of adversely affecting those rights, and the clarity of the statutory language, before answering the question 'whether the consequences of reading the statute with the suggested degree of retrospectivity is so unfair that the words used by Parliament cannot have been intended to mean what they might appear to say'.[5] Here the right to pursue a claim before an arbitrator was weak since the claimant obviously regarded it so poorly that it had not troubled to enforce it from 1986 to the end of 1991 during which period no action had been taken to bring the claim to a resolution. It was therefore not unfair to allow the enactment to apply to claims brought before the coming into force of the new power.

A clearer application of the presumption is to be found in *Plewa v Chief Adjudication Officer*.[6] Section 53 of the Social Security Act 1986 created a new power for the Secretary of State to recover overpayment of means-tested and non-means-tested benefits from recipients or third parties where there had been a misrepresentation or failure to disclose information. The Act came into force on 6 April 1987. The Secretary of State sought to recover overpayment of a retirement pension paid to Mr Plewa from 7 January 1982 to 7 October 1987. Under the previous law,[7] he would not have been able to recover the overpayment if it was shown that Mr Plewa had shown due care and diligence to avoid overpayment, which the tribunal found to be the case. There was no such limitation in s 53. The House of Lords held that it would be unfair to apply s 53 retrospectively and so recovery was limited to the period after the Act came into force.

Lord Bridge in *Arnold v Central Electricity Generating Board*[8] gave a further elaboration of the principle:

'Consistently with the presumption that a statute affecting substantive rights is not to be construed as having retrospective operation unless it clearly appears to have been so intended, it seems to me entirely proper, in a case where some retrospective operation was clearly

---

5. At 30.
6. [1994] 3 All ER 323.
7. Social Security Act 1975, s 119.
8. [1987] 3 All ER 694 at 703-704.

intended, equally to presume that the retrospective operation of the statute extends no further than is necessary to give effect either to its clear language or to its manifest purpose.'

In that case, the Limitation Act 1975 inserted s 2A in the Limitation Act 1939 thereby providing that the limitation period in 'any action for damages' in respect of personal injuries ran from the date of the accrual of the action or from the date of the plaintiff's knowledge, if later. These expressly retrospective provisions,[9] first introduced by the Limitation Act 1963, covered all personal injury actions previously governed by the three-year limitation period of the Limitation Act 1954. But nothing affected the special one-year limitation period from which public bodies benefited until the 1954 Act came into force. Section 2A could not therefore govern a claim against a public body for damages for personal injuries which had become statute-barred in 1944, even though the plaintiff only became aware of the negligence in 1981.

In *Blyth v Blyth*, Lord Denning MR suggested that 'the rule that an Act of Parliament is not to be given retrospective effect only applies to statutes which affect vested rights. It does not apply to statutes which only alter the form of procedure, or the admissibility of evidence, or the effect which the courts give to evidence'.[10] That case turned on s 1 of the Matrimonial Causes Act 1963 under which a husband was for the first time permitted to give evidence in rebuttal of the presumption that adultery was condoned by subsequent matrimonial intercourse. It was held by the Court of Appeal, whose decision on this point was approved by the House of Lords, that s 1 operated retrospectively since it was procedural, not substantive. In the light of the recent statements of the courts discussed above, the distinction between substantive law and procedure, which can be as difficult to draw in this context as elsewhere, is a relevant factor in determining whether it would be unfair to apply a statute retrospectively.

Previous editions of this work have discussed whether the presumption against retrospective operation is one of general application in the sense that it is to be applied unless rebutted by clear words or necessary implication, or is merely a presumption which only comes into play where there is ambiguity.[11] The recent approach of the courts discussed here suggests that the courts operate a two-stage test. First, in the absence of inescapably clear words, they consider whether it would be unfair to apply the provision retrospectively. Second, if they conclude that to apply it would be unfair, this brings the presumption into play in its stronger form as requiring

---

9. See Limitation Act 1975, s 3.
10. [1966] AC 643 at 666.
11. 1st edn, p 155; 2nd edn, p 186.

rebuttal by clear words or necessary implication. As *Plewa* illustrates, once the courts have concluded that it would be unfair to apply a provision retrospectively, they will rarely find themselves constrained to say that Parliament intended to act unfairly in that way. Where the courts conclude that it would not be unfair, then they will give effect to the purpose of the provision which may lead to its retrospective application.

E. CONCLUSION

Now that courts adopt a purposive approach to the interpretation of statutes and admit a wider range of materials from which to ascertain that purpose, the role of presumptions in interpretation is necessarily less important than in the days of more literal interpretation. The use of a presumption might appear to be cutting short unnecessarily the search for the meaning of a provision in the context, above all, of its purpose. The justification for any particular presumption depends on its type. Presumptions of general application encourage a search beyond the ordinary and most readily apparent meaning of a provision in order to find the real legislative purpose. Other presumptions come into play only where a genuine doubt remains after all permissible methods of ascertaining the legislative purpose have been exhausted. In both cases, the purposive approach remains the principal method of interpreting the statute.

In adopting the purposive approach to all statutes, the courts have shown an increased willingness to co-operate in giving effect to legislative policies, in contrast to their earlier tendency to restrict them by appealing to the kinds of constitutional values embodied in the traditional presumptions discussed in section B of this chapter. It may well be that the judicial approach will change, and that the values embodied in the European Convention will be used more frequently to determine constraints within which statutes are presumed to operate. This is a matter to which we return in the next chapter when reviewing current and future developments in the interpretation of statutes.

Chapter 8
Concluding questions

By way of conclusion, it is appropriate to reflect critically on the rules of statutory interpretation as they have emerged from the preceding chapters. These rules have undergone significant change since the Law Commissions reported in 1969.[1] Most of these developments have resulted from judicial pronouncements, although an updated and technically improved Interpretation Act passed in 1978 has made certain common-form provisions unnecessary. Thorough reviews since 1969, notably by the Renton Committee in 1975 and the Hansard Society Commission in 1992, have not recommended any revolutionary or comprehensive changes. Modifications by the courts of particular rules and practices appear to provide an appropriate mechanism for change, with the advantage that the working of any new approach can be kept under review by the courts themselves.

The full impact of *Pepper v Hart* has yet to be seen, and the admissibility of external aids in the interpretation of statutes will be the subject of further judicial elaboration. The role of the courts is thus central to the development of the subject. At the level of general principles, with which this book has been mainly concerned, the subject does not lend itself to legislation. This fact enhances rather than diminishes the role of the academic writer. This chapter will consider how satisfactory are current judicial approaches and academic expositions of principles in producing appropriate rules of statutory interpretation. Finally, it will consider how far changes in drafting techniques could facilitate the interpretation of statutes.

---

1. *The Interpretation of Statutes* (Law Com no 21; Scott Law Com No 11); see pp 17-18 above.

A. THE COURTS

It is appropriate to ask three questions about the current judicial approach to statutory interpretation:
1. Do the courts interpret statutes too narrowly without adequate regard to the purpose of the legislation?
2. Is their approach to the interpretation of statutes designed to effect social change too conservative?
3. Are the courts too timorous when confronted with an obvious mistake or omission in a statute?

In each instance, the answer is 'at times (though increasingly seldom) yes, but not to such an extent as to merit wholesale condemnation, and there have often been important countervailing considerations'.

To begin with the first question, it has been shown in the previous chapters that these days the courts adopt a purposive approach to the interpretation of statutes. This was not always so, and much of the criticism of the approach of the courts to statutory interpretation relates to the excessively literal approach which was sometimes adopted in the past. In their 1969 report, the Law Commissions concluded that:[2]

> 'There is a tendency in our systems, less evident in some recent decisions of the courts but still perceptible, to over-emphasise the literal meaning of a provision (ie the meaning in the light of its immediate and obvious context) at the expense of the meaning to be derived from other possible contexts; the latter include "the mischief", or general legislative purpose, as well as any international obligation of the United Kingdom, which underlie the provision.'

Of course, a literal approach need not be a particularly narrow one. A wide construction of general words may be excessively literal and insufficiently purposive, but the usual charge under this head is one of narrow literalism. The Law Commissions' report refers to cases which have been mentioned in this book: *Fisher v Bell* (flick-knife in a shop window not 'offered for sale'),[3] and *Bourne v Norwich Crematorium Ltd* (cremation not 'subjection of goods or materials to any process').[4] But in 1981 Lord Wilberforce described as ' a tired old myth . . . sedulously propagated by people who do not do their homework' the view that English judges are more literalistic and narrow than

---

2. *The Interpretation of Statutes* para 80(c).
3. [1961] 1 QB 394, p 73 above.
4. [1967] 2 All ER 576, p 71 above.

continental courts.[5] Certainly the examples given in this book support the view that, at least nowadays, judges adopt a purposive approach and seek that purpose in a wide variety of sources, including parliamentary debates. Such an approach avoids the conflicts with the intention of Parliament which were evident in cases where an excessively literal approach was adopted. Naturally, there will always be cases where a statute can be interpreted in more than one way, and where there can be disagreement with the interpretation made by the courts. But there is no longer a general tendency to an over-literal approach. As to the suggestion that judges are too conservative in their approach to statutes designed to effect social change, it is of course possible to cite numerous instances for and against such a hypothesis. The interpretation of the Housing (Homeless Persons) Act 1977 is an illustration. In *R v Hillingdon London Borough Council, ex p Puhlhofer*,[6] the House of Lords decided that it would only interfere with a local authority's interpretation of the term 'accommodation' in s 1 (1) of the Act where the decision amounted to an abuse of power. That approach has been criticised as an interpretation which placed the homeless person too much at the mercy of the interpretations of local authorities.[7] But others reviewing housing law do not see in this and other cases any general antipathy to legislative policy.[8] Furthermore, in adopting a purposive construction, the courts have to recognise that the purpose of social legislation is often to strike a reasonable balance between competing interests. For example, Part VII of the Rent Act 1977 was primarily concerned with giving security of tenure to tenants, but provided an exception in that the owner of a dwelling house could obtain possession of the property at the end of the lease where it was required as a residence for himself or a member of his family.[9] Where the interpretation of this exception is disputed, should a court give effect to the purpose of the Act as a whole by protecting tenants or to the purpose of the exception by protecting the interests of landlords? Could either of these possible interpretations be termed 'conservative' in the sense of unduly resisting the social change which Parliament had legislated to achieve?[10]

---

5.   418 HL Official Report (5th series) col 74 (9 March 1981); see also Lord Diplock, *Carter v Bradbeer* [1975] 3 All ER 158 at 161; Staughton LJ, *BBC Enterprises Ltd v Hi-Tech Xtravision Ltd* [1990] 2 All ER 118 at 123a.
6.   [1986] AC 484, p 80 above.
7.   J Griffith *The Politics of the Judiciary* (4th edn, 1991) pp 140-144.
8.   M Partington and J Hill *Housing Law: Cases, Materials and Commentary* (2nd edn, 1991) p 15.
9.   See Sch 15, Cases 9 and 11.
10.   See *Pocock v Steel* [1985] 1 All ER 434, where the Court of Appeal adopted a literal construction of Case 11 on the ground, among others, that it was an exception to the main policy of Part VII 'which evidently is to give security of tenure to tenants' (at 438). Soon after, Case 11 was amended by the Rent (Amendment) Act 1985 so as to reverse this interpretation. (See also *Hewitt v Lewis* [1986] 1 All ER 927.)

What is often meant when an interpretation of social legislation is criticised as 'conservative' is that it fails to promote the interests of individuals, particularly those who are disadvantaged. It could be argued that the presumptions concerned with protecting the property or money of individuals have not been matched by any presumptions in favour of individuals claiming state benefits. Although the obtaining of grants, benefits and permissions from central or local government plays an important part in the life of the modern citizen, the courts have not considered it necessary to create any new presumptions. Instead, they content themselves with a purposive construction, even if this deprives the citizen of a welfare benefit. For example, in *Presho v Department of Health and Social Security*,[11] the plaintiff was laid off during a dispute between her employer and a union to which she did not belong. Section 19(1) of the Social Security Act 1975 provided that unemployment benefit was not to be paid to a person affected by a stoppage of work at his place of employment unless he could prove that 'he is not participating in . . . or directly interested in the trade dispute which caused the stoppage . . .' The insurance officer refused the plaintiff unemployment benefit on the ground that, if the union in dispute was successful, existing agreements would ensure that there would be a pay rise for all employees at the factory, including the plaintiff. The House of Lords upheld this view on the ground, among others, that—

> 'if the expression "directly interested in the trade dispute" were to be given a narrower and more legalistic interpretation . . . the way would be wide open for deliberate and calculated evasions of the basic provisions of s 19(1) of the Social Security Act 1975 as amended, with the result that the effectiveness of the subsection to achieve its manifest object would be much reduced'.[12]

Although such a judicial approach might be criticised, it is questionable whether it would be right for the courts to engage in promoting the interests of a particular section of society in preference to another without specific direction from the legislature to that effect.

Another allegation of judicial conservatism often made in recent years is that judges fail to take adequate account of the fundamental rights of citizens when they interpret statutes. It is often said that judges have been unwilling to interpret immigration or race relations legislation so as to protect the interests of immigrants or ethnic minorities, and that they have been too

---

11. [1984] AC 310.
12. At 319, per Lord Brightman.

willing to take a limited view of the purpose of such legislation.[13] Such criticism presupposes that the courts should go beyond the immediate purpose of the legislation and should define its purpose more broadly so as to accord with the moral rights of those affected by it. On the whole English judges refrain from such a widely creative role. They do not conceive their function to be that of rescuing individuals from any hardship or injustice which may result from what Parliament clearly intended to enact. Of course, current views on the use of the European Convention on Human Rights as a guide to interpretation may indicate a shift of emphasis towards a more explicitly rights-centred approach to the interpretation of statutes, a shift that would be accentuated if the Convention became part of domestic law.

So far as each of the two questions which have just been discussed is concerned, if the choice is between the ordinary meaning, ascertained with due regard to the purpose of the statute, and something other than the ordinary meaning which appears to give greater effect to the statutory purpose, it is to be hoped that the courts will always opt in favour of the former. The fact that words do not always have an ordinary meaning, even after due allowance has been made for the context, and the fact that ordinary people, as well as lawyers, sometimes take different views about the ordinary meaning of words, does not mean that there is no such thing. Most statutory provisions do have an ordinary meaning when fairly read in their context, and fair-minded readers will usually be in agreement with regard to that meaning.

But what about the case in which there is no ordinary meaning or, if there is one, it produces absurd results? This raises the third question mentioned on p 192: Are the courts too timorous when confronted with an obvious mistake or omission? The answer would be a resounding 'yes' if they really were, in Lord Halsbury's words, 'bound to proceed upon the assumption that the legislature is an ideal person that does not make mistakes'.[14] But we have seen that there are cases decided both before[15] and after[16] those words were spoken in 1891 which show that they do not represent the typical attitude of the courts. It is easy to see why the courts act with greater caution when the apparent legislative error is one of omission, because the reading in of words which are not in a statute, even if it can be said that they are there by necessary implication, looks more like legislating than does the ignoring

---

13. Eg R M Dworkin 'Political Judges and the Rule of Law' (1978) 64 *Proceedings of the British Academy* 259 at 283-285 (reprinted in *A Matter of Principle* pp 9, 28-31); J M Evans *Immigration Law* (2nd edn, 1983) pp 417-425; J A G Griffith *The Politics of the Judiciary* (4th edn, 1991) pp 170-185.
14. See p 103 above.
15. See *Re Wainewright* pp 95-96 above.
16. *R v Vasey and Lalley* , pp 103-104 above, and *Western Bank Ltd v Schindler*, pp 94-95 above.

of statutory words; but the distinction is of doubtful validity. It might be thought to have gained some currency by the reference to the filling in of gaps in a statute as 'a naked usurpation of the legislative function under the thin disguise of interpretation'. These were the words of Lord Simonds in *Magor and St Mellons RDC v Newport Corpn*,[17] and they are certainly not to be numbered among the most helpful of his observations on the subject of statutory interpretation. What was Lord Parker CJ doing but filling in a gap when, in *Adler v George*,[18] he read the words 'in the vicinity of' in s 3 of the Official Secrets Act 1920 as meaning 'in or in the vicinity of'? What was the Court of Appeal doing but filling in a gap when, in *Deria v General Council of British Shipping*, it added the words 'or is to do' to s 8(1) of the Race Relations Act 1976 in order to make good an obvious omission.[19] We saw on p 37 above that Lord Parker could be said to have been merely stating expressly words which were already in the statute by necessary implication, but we also saw how thin is the line between that process and adding words in order to correct an obvious error. The course adopted by the Court of Appeal in *Deria* comes on the latter side of the line.

Surely it would be better for all judges to recognise that they possess a limited power to add to, alter or ignore statutory words in the circumstances mentioned by Lord Reid in his speech in *Federal Steam Navigation Co Ltd v Department of Trade and Industry*.[20] The existence of such a power seems to be established by the authorities, and is frankly recognised in more recent cases. For example, in *Western Bank Ltd v Schindler*, Scarman LJ said:[1]

> '. . . our courts . . . have the duty of giving effect to the intention of Parliament, if it be possible, even though the process requires a strained construction of the language used or the insertion of words in order to do so . . .'

As we have seen, such a view does not consider *all* fillings in of gaps as naked usurpations of the legislative function, but concentrates on developing rules concerning the limits of such a judicial power. All the same, not all judges consider this power acceptable.[2]

The curious reluctance of some judges to recognise what amounts to a power to rectify a statute when construing it, however limited that power may be, is almost as great an obstruction to the development of a jurisprudence of statutory interpretation as the equally curious reluctance of other judges

---

17. [1952] AC 189 at 191.
18. Pp 36-37 above.
19. Pp 37-38 above.
20. P 102 above.
1. P 95 above.
2. Pp 103-104 above.

and some writers to recognise that the ordinary meaning of statutory words must yield to a secondary meaning when the application of the ordinary meaning would lead to a result which 'cannot reasonably be supposed to have been the intention of the legislature'.[3]

B. ACADEMIC LAWYERS

Writing in 1976, Cross asked:

'Why is it that, in the field of the general principles of statutory interpretation, the English academic lawyer does not perform his ordinary function of synthesising and criticising the case-law, and, where appropriate, making proposals for reform?'[4]

This situation no longer exists today. There is now not only a substantial treatise by Bennion systematising the rules on the subject and a journal, the Statute Law Review, founded in 1980; there have also appeared some important monographs and a comparative study of high quality to which reference has already been made in this work.[5] These works have been influenced (and even written) by writers from other jurisdictions, but it is certainly the case that in England statutory interpretation is studied now more closely than when Cross posed his question.

But this does not to mean that Cross's comment about the contribution of academic lawyers has no validity today. Cross identified two features which continue to affect the academic vitality of the subject: the nature of the rules of legal method and the persistent influence of one landmark law review article.

Reference has already been made to the paucity of rules and confusion of principles which justify Lord Wilberforce's description of statutory interpretation as a non-subject, at least so far as law reform is concerned.[6] The point has also been made that a decision on the interpretation of one statute generally cannot constitute a binding precedent with regard to the interpretation of another statute, with the result that a general rule of interpretation, unlike other common law rules, can never be rendered

---

3. Lord Reid, *Pinner v Everett* [1969] 3 All ER 257 at 258, p 40 above.
4. 1st edn p 168.
5. Notably, D R Miers and A C Page *Legislation* (2nd edn, 1990); J Evans *Statutory Interpretation* (Auckland 1988); D N MacCormick and R S Summers, *Interpreting Statutes: A Comparative Study* (1991).
6. See p 39 above.

more specific by the *rationes decidendi* of later cases.[7] The material to be analysed consists mainly of statements of position and of examples of judicial practice, rather than the rules and principles derived from decisions which academics customarily study. Even at the level of the meaning to be attached to particular words:[8]

> 'A question of statutory construction is one in which the strict doctrine of precedent can only be of narrow application. The *ratio decidendi* of a judgment as to the meaning of particular words or combinations of words used in a particular statutory provision can have no more than a persuasive influence on a court which is called on to interpret the same word or combination of words appearing in some other statutory provision.'

Since it is concerned with issues of legal method of this character, the study of statutory interpretation is different from that of ordinary legal subjects. All the same, the subject is amenable to an appreciable degree of systematisation.

For a long time, it was dominated by an article entitled Statutory Interpretation in a Nutshell contributed by Professor J Willis to the Canadian Bar Review for 1938.[9] After warning his readers that it is a mistake to suppose that there is only one rule of statutory interpretation because there are three—the literal, golden and mischief rules—Professor Willis maintained that 'a court invokes whichever of the rules produces a result which satisfies its sense of justice in the case before it'.[10] No doubt the warning had its point in 1938 when practitioners' books tended to state the literal or plain meaning rule without any embellishments referring to the context, including the purpose, of the statute. The Willis thesis was maintained so persuasively that English academic discussions long did little more than treat cases as illustrations of one or more of the three rules. Indeed, although the major specialist works on statutory interpretation concur in the predominance of purposive interpretation within the practice of the English courts, general textbooks designed to introduce students to legal reasoning and to the English legal system persist in using Willis's framework within which to explain current English law.[11] It is perhaps time that those works moved on from the valuable contribution which Willis made in his time to look at the

---

7. See p 41 above.
8. Lord Diplock, *Carter v Bradbeer* [1975] 3 All ER 158 at 161.
9. 16 Can Bar Rev 1.
10. 16 Can Bar Rev 1 at 16.
11. See eg J A Holland and J S Webb *Learning Legal Rules* (2nd edn, 1991) Ch 8; T Ingman *The English Legal System* (4th edn, 1992) pp 216-226; M Zander *Law in the Making* (4th edn, 1994) pp 108-131.

subject in terms of an appropriate contemporary framework, such as is set out in this and similar works.

The recent growth of interest in the subject of statutory interpretation encompasses a number of diverse approaches.[12] Some authors have been concerned with philosophical questions about the nature of interpretation, and some have drawn analogies from literary contexts.[13] Others have looked at the sociology of the production and impact of legislation. Yet others, most notably Bennion,[14] have sought to provide a systematic and rational account of judicial practice in interpreting statutes, an approach that has been enriched by comparative study.[15] This book is situated in the systematic tradition. In a common law system, judicial practice exercises a dominant influence over what is considered correct legal reasoning and thus merits the critical attention of any lawyer. This book represents a limited exposition of the general principles of statutory interpretation as they emerge from current judicial practice. Despite recent developments much remains to be done in this field if a full analysis of this aspect of legal reasoning is to be achieved.

C. LEGISLATIVE DRAFTING

If the difficulties of statutory interpretation have in part been ascribed to inappropriate judicial attitudes and to the failure of academic lawyers to provide a coherent exposition of contemporary judicial practice, the legislative drafter is also a common target for criticism. We saw in Chapter 1 how drafting and interpretation are mutually dependent and how an excessively literal approach to interpretation can lead to excessively detailed drafting. In his evidence to the Renton Committee Lord Denning went so far as to say:[16]

> 'It is because the judges have not felt it right to fill in the gaps and have been giving a literal interpretation for many years that the draftsman has felt that he has to try and think of every conceivable thing and put it in as far as he can so that even the person unwilling to understand will

---

12. For an analysis of different academic approaches to statutory interpretation see D Miers, 'Legal Theory and the Interpretation of Statutes' in W Twining (ed) *Legal Theory and the Common Law* (1986) Ch 7.
13. See J Evans, note 5, p 197 above; R M Dworkin *Law's Empire* (1986) pp 49-62; S Fish *Doing What Comes Naturally* (1989), Chs 4, 5 and 16; S Lee 'Law and Literature: Goodbye Austin, Hello Austen?' (1990) 10 OJLS 252.
14. *Statutory Interpretation* (2nd edn, 1992).
15. Notably MacCormick and Summers, see note 5, p 197 above.
16. *The Preparation of Legislation* para 19.1.

follow it. I think the rules of interpretation which the judges have applied have been one of the primary causes why draftsmen have felt that they must have a system of over-detailed, over-long sentences, and obscurity.'

Yet, seventeen years later, in its evidence to the Hansard Commission, the Law Society stated:[17]

'Another factor in the style of drafting in this country is the Government's inevitable wish to make legislation "judge-proof " to try to ensure that their policy intentions can not be misinterpreted by the courts. This means that the draftsman is required to tie up every last loophole in the Bill, which can make the drafting rather convoluted. This might suggest a lack of trust in the judges.'

If changes in judicial attitudes have not had the desired effect, some have argued that the fault lies in the style of British legislative draftsmanship. Sir William Dale has claimed that other European countries adopt a less detailed and more principled style in their statutes, with less complicated wording and sentence structure.[18] He argues that there should be a change in the current style of legislation:[19]

'We need at least to reduce the verbal impedimenta; to be less fussy over detail, to be more general and concise; and to situate each rule where it belongs, in an orderly and logical development. On this level, the question is largely a matter of style and arrangement. A more profound change is also desirable: a determination to seek the principle, to express it, and to follow up with such detail, illuminating and not obscuring the principle, as the circumstances require.'

Although this is not a book on legislative drafting, a few comments on these suggestions are appropriate.

The Renton Committee considered that the adoption of the 'general principle' approach to the drafting of our statutes would lead to greater

---

17. *Making the Law: The Report of the Hansard Commission on the Legislative Process* (1992) p 278.
18. *Legislative Drafting: A New Approach* (1977) compares the implementation of an international copyright convention in the domestic laws of France, West Germany, Sweden and the UK.
19. *Legislative Drafting* p 335. See also J A C Smith 'Legislative Drafting: English and Continental' [1980] Stat LR 14; T Millett 'A Comparison of British and French Legislative Drafting (with particular reference to their respective Nationality Laws)' [1986] Stat LR 130; Donaldson MR, *R v Northampton Borough Council, ex p Quietlynn Ltd* (1986) 85 LGR 249 at 263.

simplicity and clarity. However, they accepted that this approach to a large extent sacrifices immediate certainty and recognised that this is unlikely to be acceptable at least in certain types of legislation, particularly fiscal and other public law statutes which define the rights and obligations of individuals in relation to the state. They also considered that it would be unreasonable to draft in principles so broad that the effect of the statute could not be assessed without incurring the expense of litigation.[20]

Moreover, the Hansard Commission, after recommending that drafters should always seek for clarity, simplicity and brevity in their drafting, but that certainty should be paramount,[1] went on to say that they did not believe that 'the automatic inclusion of statements of principle or purpose in the body of Acts' would help to achieve that paramount aim of certainty.[2] Instead, they recommended that, for every Act of Parliament, notes on sections, explaining the purpose and intended effect of each section or schedule, should be prepared by Government departments, with the assistance of Parliamentary Counsel, by up-dating the notes on clauses (and notes on amendments) prepared for Ministers during the passage of the Bill through Parliament. They recommended that these notes should be published at the same time as the Act and that courts should be allowed to use them as an aid to understanding an Act, but that the words of the Act should prevail unless they are not sufficient by themselves for determining its effect.[3] This practice, if adopted, would provide the courts with positive guidance as to the purpose underlying a statutory provision and, by doing so in a form closely tailored to the Act itself, would in most cases obviate the lengthy searches through *Hansard* made necessary by the decision in *Pepper v Hart*.[4] It is indeed somewhat curious that, in an era of purposive construction, the purpose underlying the words of a statute still has to be gleaned primarily from the statute itself.

The view that statutes ought, as far as possible, to be drafted in ordinary language was expressed as long ago as 1875 by Thring:[5]

> 'I have a very strong opinion indeed that you ought to use the best popular language, and never use technical language at all unless it be absolutely necessary.'

---

20. *The Preparation of Legislation* para 10.13.

1. *Making the Law* p 56.

2. *Making the Law* pp 60-61.

3. Paras 250-252. For conflicting views on this proposal see the debate on the legislative process: 559 HL Official Report (5th series), cols 1303, 1308, 1309-1310 and 1320-1321 (14 December 1994).

4. See pp 156-160 above.

5. *Report of the Select Committee on Acts of Parliament (1875): Minutes of Evidence* p 121, para 1633. Thring gave evidence as the head of the Parliamentary Counsel Office, established in 1869.

The difficulty of many modern statutes results not from the use of obscure terminology, but from the complexity of the subject matter, coupled with the fact that most changes in the law have to be knitted into the complex fabric of existing statutory provisions; and Members of Parliament are not always receptive to 'the best popular language', sometimes preferring a more 'lawyerly' wording.[6]

The view that British statutes should contain less detail has prompted the suggestion that a larger proportion of the state's rule-making should be located elsewhere than in statutes. On this view, it is for Parliament to enact the general principles, and for the executive or the courts to produce the detailed rules necessary for their implementation, as need arises. Certainly in other European countries such as France, the provisions contained in primary legislation are supplemented by rules contained in subordinate legislation, expressed in judicial decisions, or contained in administrative circulars which guide administrative decisions and on which the citizen is entitled to rely. In practice, this merely has the effect of shifting much of the legislative material from primary legislation into decrees, judicial decisions, codes of practice and ministerial circulars. While the statute becomes easier to read, the citizen concerned to discover the law is sent on a paper-chase and has to collate the material found in all these different sources. This already happens to a significant extent in the British systems of law,[7] but to carry the process much further would be without obvious benefit to the citizen and his advisers. Furthermore, any such shift would have to be assessed in terms of democratic control. At present, statutes are subject to far greater scrutiny in Parliament than the provisions of subordinate legislation, codes of practice and departmental circulars, and, unlike them, can in general only be amended by the passing of another Act. Here again, what is at issue is the constitutional function of Parliament, and it is barking up the wrong tree to suppose that this could be altered by a mere change of drafting practice.

Britain's entry into Europe was expected by some to herald changes in drafting practice and statutory interpretation. In the event, these have not materialised. On closer scrutiny, continental drafting has not proved as flawless as Dale and others believed,[8] a fact recognised in a resolution

---

6. For example, s 1(1)(b) of the Sexual Offences Act 1985 makes it an offence for a man to solicit a woman for the purpose of prostitution 'while in the immediate vicinity of a motor vehicle that *he has just got out of or off*'. Some MPs tried (unsuccessfully) to have the words 'just got out of or off' replaced by 'emerged from or alighted from in the immediate past': see amendment number 24 at the House of Commons Report Stage.

7. See R Baldwin and J Houghton 'Circular Arguments: The Status and Legitimacy of Administrative Rules' [1986] PL 239.

8. See Law Commission *Report on the Proposed EEC Directive on the Law relating to Commercial Agents* (Law Com no 84, 1977) paras 38-41.

adopted by the Council of the European Communities in 1993[9] aimed at making Community legislation 'as clear, simple, concise and understandable as possible'. The guidelines against which Council texts are now expected to be checked include—

> '— the wording of the act[10] should be clear, simple, concise and unambiguous; excessively long sentences should be avoided;
> — the various provisions of the acts should be consistent with each other;
> — the same term should be used throughout to express a given concept;
> — the rights and obligations of those to whom the act is to apply should be clearly defined;
> — the preamble should justify the enacting provisions in simple terms;
> — provisions without legislative character should be avoided (eg wishes, political statements);
> — any amendment, extension or repeal of an act should be clearly set out.'

There is also a guideline to the effect that an act amending an earlier act should do so by textual amendment of the act to be amended. It can fairly be stated that, except as regards the use of preambles, current British practice is in full accord with these guidelines—which is not to say that the first of them is invariably achieved. And it is perhaps significant that *certainty of effect* is nowhere mentioned in the resolution.

It has been noted above on pp 126-127 that Community legislation has elaborate preambles, which both explain the legal basis on which it is made and the purposes of its provisions. Both judges and commentators make the point that these are a significant help in undertaking a teleological interpretation of the provisions.[11] To some extent, the notes on sections recommended by the Hansard Commission would serve the same function, but they would have the advantage of providing a commentary on each specific section. The preamble to EC legislation is essentially general and deals with the Act as a whole, whereas the notes on sections would more specifically explain the purpose of each section.

---

9. Council Resolution of 8 June 1993 on the quality of drafting of Community legislation, OJ 93/C/166/01.
10. The word 'act' here refers to any kind of legislation made by the EC.
11. See T Millett 'Rules of Interpretation in EEC Legislation' [1989] Stat LR 163 at 171; Lord Slynn 'Looking at European Community Texts' [1993] Stat LR 12.

D. CONCLUSION

Although these concluding reflections have been concerned principally to analyse some of the current criticisms of statutes and statutory interpretation and have discovered them to be less well founded than might be supposed, it must not be thought that the current situation is satisfactory. Improvements can undoubtedly be made by way of a more effective purposive interpretation by judges, the provision of explanatory material in aid of a better understanding of the purposes underlying statutory provisions, a more systematic and coherent exposition of the general principles of judicial practice by academics, and the production of more readable statutes by drafters. In addition, many problems with the formulation of Acts of Parliament result not from lack of skill and clarity on the part of the drafter, but from the imperfect state in which, too often, Bills are presented to Parliament and the unsatisfactory way in which they are examined there. The implications of policies have frequently not been adequately thought out, with the result that Bills have to undergo many substantial amendments in the course of their passage through Parliament. Often pressure of time and inadequate attention to detail combine to render parliamentary scrutiny of Bills much less effective than it ought to be. As a result, the Hansard Society Commission is rightly more far-reaching in its recommendations on the pre-parliamentary and parliamentary processes than on the drafting of statutes.[12]

The principal difficulties lie in the implementation of currently accepted ideals for these activities, rather than in the adoption of radically new ideals. We are concerned here with the attitudes and practices of legislators and lawyers and the methods they adopt. These cannot be transformed at a stroke, but can be expected to improve slowly in response to criticisms voiced by Members of Parliament, lawyers and other sections of the community.

---

12. *Making the Law* Chs 3 and 5. The reform of the legislative process received far more attention than improvements in legislative drafting in the debate on the Hansard Society Commission's report, 559 HL Official Report (5th series) cols 1291-1327 (14 December 1994).

Index